# 'WHERE THERE'S A WILL...'

## The Sensational Life of Dr John Bodkin Adams

Rodney Hallworth & Mark Williams

THE CAPSTAN PRESS
JERSEY

Copyright © 1983 Hallworth & Williams

First Published in Great Britain 1983
by
The Capstan Press Ltd
Editorial Offices,
Queen Street Chambers,
Queen Street,
Exeter,
EX4 3RW

British Library          C.I.P.
Hallworth & Williams
'WHERE THERE'S A WILL....'
ISBN 0 946797–00–5

Printed and bound in Great Britain for the Capstan Press Limited by A. Wheaton and Company Limited, Hennock Road, Marsh Barton, Exeter, Devon EX2 8RP.

*"There has been an extraordinary degree
of careless treatment"*

DR A. C. SOMMERVILLE
EAST SUSSEX CORONER

DR JOHN BODKIN ADAMS

*Dedicated to a fine journalist*
*VINCENT MULCHRONE*

ACKNOWLEDGEMENTS

*Photographs by courtesy of Associated Newspapers.*

*Photograph of Charles Hewitt by Mike Alsford.*

**INTRODUCTION**

# Introduction

It was a night Rodney Hallworth will always remember. A night tailor-made for murder talk:

'I met Hannam and Hewitt in a hotel near the top of Beachy Head. It was an awful night. Clouts of wind shook the building, rain spat on the windows and the heaving sea below was a frightening mass of white water. Detective-Superintendent Herbert Hannam, as usual, was immaculately dressed, pale-faced and formal. Detective-Sergeant Charlie Hewitt fidgeting, his nose twitching like a rabbit alert for a nearby fox.

Like me, the policemen drank beer: Hannam pale ale, Hewitt half of bitter. So that's what I ordered. The barmaid knew for damn sure this was no meeting of the East Sussex W.I. She just poured the beer, took the money with a quiet 'Ta', and pointedly stuck her nose into a faded copy of *True Romance*.

Hannam took out a Henry Clay Havana from its case, struck a match and puffed the cigar alight. Blue smoke framed his face and the barmaid absent-mindedly brushed ash from the nipple-end of her sweater. All the time Hewitt was drawing nervous doodles with one finger in a beer pool on the counter. Both men were desperately tired from hundreds of investigative hours. They had the look of cumulative weariness about them.

Hannam suddenly squared his shoulders, glanced around the near-deserted bar and said quietly but deadly: 'I am quite confident Adams is a mass-murderer. He has certainly killed fourteen people. If we had arrived on the scene years ago I think I could have said he killed more.'

Hewitt stopped his doodling and looked up at his boss: 'Don't exaggerate, Guv'nor, he only killed nine. But our job is going to be proving it – too much water has flowed under the bridge.'

Hannam was six years too late on the spot when he spoke and Hewitt six months ahead with his prognosis.'

# Chapter One

*'To shock Eastbourne is unfair: It's like booting an old lady as she sleeps in the armchair of memories.'* DAILY MAIL

At precisely two-thirty each afternoon a black taxi would draw up to a large red-bricked double-fronted house in St John's Road, Eastbourne. The driver would alight and hold open the nearside rear door. At that same moment two slight, elderly women would descend five stone steps from their residential guest-house and enter the taxi, wafting the distinctive smell of lavender-water in their wake, conveying too an unmistakable air of faded gentility in the navy-blue linen coats and coloured straw hats they wore, dotted with imitation cherries and flowers of a bygone fashion.

In life, two inconspicuous almost anonymous sisters: in death, particularly in the manner of their passing, front-page headlines throughout the world.

Every afternoon the Misses Neil-Miller would be occupied in their favourite spring-to-late-summer pastime: a drive down St John's Road into King Edward's Parade, thence along Grand Parade, thronged with visitors in the colourful garb that English south coast resorts attract. Through increasing traffic, passing neat and well-tended public gardens, at times giving way to white-painted double-decker buses that are part of Eastbourne's subtle advertisement as to the cleanliness and purity of this Sussex town: a holiday and retirement centre *par excellence.*

At Eastbourne's famous bandstand overlooking the sea, a huge arena seating 3,500, the spinster sisters would alight to join an appreciative audience listening to selections of overtures and melodies from show and film, as a soporific alternative to the decibel stirrings of Souza, as played by the best of Britain's military bands.

Eastbourne, by its location and apparent unchanging quality, lures the retired community in droves. An attractive, well-spaced town, enjoying eight miles of fascinating coastline, west to east from Beachy Head to Pevensey Bay. A town of flower-decked promenades. Sheltered from inclement northerlies by the rolling hills of the South Downs, and enjoying a winter climate milder than most along the south coast of England. A town of 70,000 people. A watering place, made fashionable in the Victorian and Edwardian decades, and so remaining.

A town rented out for some twelve weeks each year to the summer visitor, when the tangy ozone of salt and seaweed gives way to an all-pervading aroma of suntan oil; when the slap of sea upon shingle and shriek of gulls are replaced by the cacophonous bleatings of Radio One, interspersed with modern, catatonic inducing, so-called music. Fortunately, a fairly ephemeral cyclic happening.

It was to the bandstand each seasonal afternoon from Mondays to Fridays, the Misses Neil-Miller would repair to delight in the music and nostalgia. Often the selections would evoke memories long a topic of conversation to last through their evening meal at Mrs Sharp's before the sisters' customary early retirement.

This was a very simple, uneventful life led by Hilda and Clara Neil-Miller. Lives sheltered from the tempests of circumstance. Both had come to Eastbourne in 1940 from their native Scotland, on the death of their brother and last blood relative. Born within ten months of each other, the sisters were inseparable, quiet-voiced and gentle. Arm in arm when on shopping errands in the town. Hilda Neil-Miller was the eldest, slightly taller than her sister, more authoritative, the organiser, still with traces of Edinburgh in her voice.

Save for a widowed sister-in-law living in Bournemouth, the Neil-Miller's had no family. Their life-style was measured to income sufficient for modest living and guaranteed by investments from their late father's estate and a generous life-time loan of capital from their sister-in-law, the income to be enjoyed, the capital protected, to revert, upon their deaths to the sister-in-law.

Two elderly women, not wealthy but comfortably off, in the evening of their lives, practically without family. Not an unfamiliar situation in Eastbourne, or indeed elsewhere on the south coast. Inconspicuous in life and, like many of their generation, living on the memories of a pre-1939 Britain, almost refusing to accept the tremendous changes, social and political wrought, first, by the war-years and then the austerity-raddled post-war period up to the early 1950s.

With only ten months separating their births perhaps it was not surprising that only thirteen months separated their deaths. Hilda on January 15, 1953, to be followed by Clara, on February 22, a year later.

In this modern society the comment might be made – what wasted, useless lives. But consider the period and generation that governed the sisters' lifetime. Unmarried women of their class did not work. Their time was spent in reading and the arts, perhaps a little sewing and, of course, minor charitable works.

So the times and passing of the Neil-Miller's would hardly cause a ripple on such a placid sea of life. Yet, sadly, it was in their very passing, particularly of Clara, that the two sisters came to the attention of others, including Detective-Superintendent Herbert William Walter Hannam and Detective-Sergeant Charles Hewitt of New Scotland Yard's Murder Squad.

And the reason for their department's particular interest was a bequest. A bequest to the Neil-Miller's doctor, John Bodkin Adams. Surely, one might remark, bequests by patients to their

3

doctors are not uncommon, indeed, quite the reverse. Yet the amount in 1954, of almost £5,000 – perhaps the equivalent of ten times that sum today – was not exactly the norm. And this same Doctor Adams had, it seemed, benefited from many other one-time patients of like will and intent.

Over a period of years the good Doctor had enjoyed cash bequests alone, totalling £45,000, together with gifts of cars (including two Rolls-Royce), jewellery, silver and antiques. John Bodkin Adams had been named as a beneficiary in many wills more than 132, in fact: sometimes in wills of long-standing date but more often of recent compilation. He acted as an executor in other estates.

Doctor Adams was a wealthy man in his own right, senior partner in one of Eastbourne's leading practices, socially prominent throughout south Sussex. An acquaintance and contemporary of many well known and eminent people. At times his patients included the then Duke of Devonshire: the painter Sir Oswald Birley; Admiral Sir Robert and Lady Prendergast: Sir Roland Victor Gwynne, Sheriff of the County; Richard Walker, Chief Constable of Eastbourne: and a number of previous Chief Constables and Magistrates.

Detective-Superintendent Hannam's interest in the Neil-Miller's did not commence with their deaths. Such an enquiry came two years after Clara's passing, as the result of other enquiries into Doctor Adams' late-departed patients. But when Hannam came to check out the Neil-Miller's circumstances, another of Eastbourne's leading doctors made a statement based on information given by a fellow-resident of Mrs Sharp's guest-house at 30 St John's Road, which confirmed in the detective's mind a conviction that all was not well in the peaceful Avenues, Crescents and Parades of elegant Eastbourne.

The fellow guest at Mrs Sharp's, a Miss Welch, gave information in which she claimed:

'Dr Adams was called to Miss Clara Neil-Miller one night in February, 1954. She was suffering from either a severe cold or influenza. He remained in her bedroom for nearly forty-five minutes before leaving. I later became worried as I had heard nothing from the room. I opened the door and was horrified at what I saw. This was a bitterly cold winter's night, the bedclothes on her bed had been pulled back and thrown over the bedrail at the base. Her nightdress had been folded back across her body up to her neck. All the bedroom windows had been flung open. A cold gush of wind was sweeping through the bedroom. That is how the Doctor had left her.'

The statement concluded that Clara Neil-Miller died the following day.

Hannam checked out Clara's bequest to Doctor Adams' of almost £5,000. He also found out that in the few weeks preceding Clara's death she had made out cheques in his favour in amounts of £300 and £500. For what purpose was not clear. Not for medical treatment as, apart from a cold, she was not ill, nor did she receive much in the way of medicines. At the same time Hannam received information from the sister-in-law in Bournemouth, explaining her capital loan to the sisters and who in the course of her statement mentioned she had written some fourteen letters during the last year of Clara's life with no answer. She thought, therefore, that Clara wished to have nothing further to do with her sister-in-law.

In Eastbourne, Hannam confirmed that Clara had not received any of the letters from Bournemouth. The matter was daily becoming more sinister. And then occurred one of those quirks of fate that were to plague Hannam's enquiries. Mrs Elizabeth Sharp, the Neil-Miller's landlady and great friend, a vital witness, was interviewed by Hannam and Hewitt. Both Hannam and Hewitt believed that the evidence of Mrs Sharp would prove vital in the case of the Neil-Miller sisters. Charlie Hewitt has no doubt:

'I always felt the house at 30 St John's was either owned or partially financed by the Doctor. He recommended clients to Mrs Sharp and she recommended victims to him – not perhaps in a calculating or deliberate way but by providing information.'

And Mrs Sharp was the only logical person to intercept letters between Clara Neil-Miller and her sister-in-law in Bournemouth. Adams could not have relied upon a member of Mrs Sharp's staff to do such a thing. Charlie Hewitt continued:

'Mrs Sharp was the key to the whole case. She had been involved with many of the victims. She was ideally placed, running this sort of twilight rest-home for the elderly and she knew so much about their personal and financial backgrounds.'

Twice the Scotland Yard detectives visited Mrs Sharp and interviewed her about her guests over a period of years, about the number that had been patients of Dr Adams, about the interception of letters. Mrs Sharp was scared – very frightened and increasingly so on their second visit.

Hannam turned to Hewitt as they walked down the steps from the house:

'She's cracking, Charlie. We'll have it all next time.'

And Charlie Hewitt agreed.

But there was not to be a third visit. Hannam and Hewitt were called back to London for prosecution conferences. The detectives fumed as they sat tight-lipped and straight-backed on their chairs in the Attorney-General's House of Commons office, listening to Sir Reginald Manningham-Buller and the Director of Public Prosecutions (Sir Edwin Matthews) discuss the cases against Adams.

'When we went up to town for the final meeting with the DPP and the Attorney-General we had intended returning immediately to crack Mrs Sharp.'

Instead the detectives were given extra work in town.

Hannam and Hewitt were engaged running around London, attending conferences and writing up notes for close to a week before they could get back to Eastbourne. Hewitt was convinced after all the months of investigation, they had stayed in Eastbourne two days too few.

Back in Eastbourne matters moved on quickly. Mrs Sharp died. Adams was her doctor. In that same week her body was cremated. Hewitt was particularly frustrated:

'Mrs Sharp hadn't been a well woman, but it was so coincidental that she died when she did – and was cremated so quickly. I always had the feeling and it was never stronger than that – that the good Doctor speeded her on her way. And like so many of the cases left us without a body.'

In subsequent weeks, as Hannam and Hewitt with their assistants interviewed hundreds of witnesses in investigating the deaths of twenty-four men and women, an exhumation order was granted for Home Office Pathologist, Dr Francis Camps, to examine the body of Clara Neil-Miller. The eminent Doctor Camps found Clara's lungs congested. She had died, not of coronary thrombosis as Doctor Adams had signed on her death certificate, but of pneumonia. A fact not altogether surprising to the detectives in light of Miss Welch's description of Clara's last hours.

Yet damning though the facts of Clara's death were, and many the questions that remained to be answered on the money given to Doctor Adams, it was only one of many investigations into curious deaths and bequests. And these investigations were instigated by Richard Walker, Eastbourne's Chief Constable, requesting the help of New Scotland Yard's Murder Squad. Investigations begun as a result of gossip amongst rattling teacups in Eastbourne's hotels and cafés. It was not the first, nor would it be the last time a murder enquiry commenced as the result of gossip.

A gossip requires two basic elements to practise his art, time and an audience. In Eastbourne such requirements abounded and the gossip flourished. Behind curtains of elegant homes in tree-lined squares; the tea lounges of sea-front hotels; at bridge gatherings, cocktail parties and church jumble sales, ugly gossip circulated. It was simply this:
every time a wealthy patient died, he – or more usually she – left Doctor Adams money or chattels in the will.

Such gossip concerning Doctor Adams was not a new phenomenon. It had begun in the pre-war years, was held in moratorium during the war, was revived and intensified after.

As long ago as 1936 Adams had been the beneficiary in the will of a Mrs Alice Whitton, to the extent of £3,000, a substantial amount in those times. A niece, Amy Madge Horton, contested the will, claiming her aunt had not been in a clear state of mind when she changed her will to favour John Bodkin Adams.

The matter ended in the High Court. Adams won the case and kept the money. History might prove it would have been better for him to return that bequest to the family.

So the gossip continued, on and into the mid-1950s. The obese, bespectacled frame of Doctor Adams was a familiar sight in Eastbourne, Savile Row-suited, driving in one of his five motorcars, two being Rolls-Royce limousines, and two MG saloons; the fifth was a Morris Minor.

Such idle talk was well known to the local police. They were also well aware of the poor opinion of Doctor Adams held by others of Eastbourne's medical fraternity. But gossip, and some thought envy, are not necessarily bed-fellows of evidence.

And so the rumours continued unabated because the frequency with which old ladies left money to the Doctor, then swiftly shuffled off this mortal coil became, in certain circles, quite frightening. And then the gossip took an awesome turn, for the afternoon tea groups were not only asking why the old ladies were leaving the Doctor their money but in what circumstances were they dying?

There was ample evidence on the surface to justify such talk. Families in distant parts, away from Eastbourne that is, were learning that Auntie, who seemed quite well on Monday, was dead on Wednesday, having changed her will to benefit the Doctor on Tuesday!

In any retirement town the death rate is inevitably high. Of course it is, people come to Eastbourne and other similar towns, to accomplish that delicate task, albeit in their own good time. Alas, that perhaps is not always possible to arrange. Death has its own sense of timing. As in any retirement town there was nothing particularly sinister in old ladies dying – often quite suddenly, after all, the age was there.

The Chief Constable, Mr Richard Walker, a mild and courteous man, had obviously heard of the Adams rumours, not only on his social rounds but at his office in his official capacity. In his job he was used to rumours. He was able to investigate most and send the gossips scurrying. But the Adams rumours persisted, fastened and fattened, clinging to the mind of public opinion, hard and fast like one of Eastbourne's seashore limpets, not at first sight damaging until one tries to remove, then exceedingly messy.

Richard Walker was proud of his town, conscious of its rather superior image. He revelled in the white summer uniforms of his men, reminiscent of his own service life, some of it spent with the Police Mission in Greece and other sunny climes. He was not about to launch a major murder enquiry without more substantial evidence. Not in his town, and not with the gossips' prime suspect his very own doctor, and medico too of the Sheriff, together with other influential County people.

Inevitably of course it was Doctor John Bodkin Adams himself that tilted police opinion down the road of investigative no-return. Perhaps the deaths of old women in their seventies and eighties brooked too much doubt to make up Richard Walker's mind. But when a vivacious woman, only forty-nine, died after a perplexing four months' widowhood, without being really ill, and more, was the friend not only of the Chief Constable but of an array of glittering social and show business personalities, Richard Walker acted by picking up his phone and asking for New Scotland Yard. The premature death of Mrs 'Bobbie' Hullett was a matter that simply could not be ignored.

Jack Hullet was a retired Lloyd's underwriter who had bought 'Holywell Mount', one of Eastbourne's most handsome houses, which stands where the town ends and Beachy Head begins. He spent thousands of pounds on reconstruction, adding a solarium overlooking the Channel. His gilded initials were incorporated in the wrought-iron gates. Doctor Adams became the family physician.

When Jack Hullett lost his first wife and several years later decided to take an ocean cruise he talked to Adams about his loneliness and how he would like to take a companion with him, Adams suggested a young widow both knew slightly in Eastbourne's social circle. Gertrude Joyce Tomlinson, known as 'Bobbie', a normally gay person, the mother of a teenage daughter, who had felt the loss of her own husband terribly. Without doubt Adams thought the two would be good for each other. And so it proved.

A cruise on the liner *Reina del Pacifico* from Tilbury to the West Indies brought back an engaged couple who were married shortly after their return. At 'Holywell Mount' the Hullett's settled into a mutually happy married life. They were generous hosts and the parties they gave were eagerly anticipated by Eastbourne's select, and even further afield.

Amongst the good friends of Jack and 'Bobbie' Hullett were comedian Leslie Henson and his wife; singers Anne Ziegler and Webster Booth; the actress Marie Lohr; the Bishop of Coventry and of course the Chief Constable, Richard Walker and Doctor Adams. Indeed rarely a day passed without Adams calling, with the odd gramophone record, or when on his rounds, usually in time for tea or a sherry and biscuits.

Late in 1955 Jack Hullett became ill. He told one of his nurses, Sister Mary Wagner: 'Thank God I have a good doctor'. When Hullett was stricken by a heart condition on the night of March 13, 1956, the 'good Doctor' sat on his bed and injected a dose of morphia. Seven hours later Jack Hullett died. Under his will Adams received £500. The residue, after a few bequests, went to his distraught widow.

'Bobbie' Hullett had genuinely felt great affection for her late husband. His death was both a shock and an inconsolable grief. Physically she was a strong person and her friends rallied around to help in every way they could. Doctor Adams also provided help for 'Bobbie' Hullett – to sleep. He prescribed drugs. In four months 'Bobbie' Hullett was dead.

From the day of her husband's death, Adams supplied

'Bobbie' with sleeping drugs. Perhaps in the beginning a wise practice, certainly an action most doctors would follow. But then, most doctors after a week, maybe two, would certainly cut down the level, even stop prescribing drugs altogether. Yet as the weeks passed, the dosage continued. The 'Holywell Mount' staff were to remark later: 'She staggered downstairs most mornings as though she were drunk'.

'Bobbie' Hullett talked of suicide, a common sympton of drug addiction. Still Adams continued to give her dose upon dose. If he failed to realise she was taking too many drugs, her lay friends did not. Said Leslie Henson afterwards:

'Her death shocked me greatly. My wife and I saw her turning into a drug addict. It is a great, great pity as she was such a nice person. We invited her to our home in Harrow to get away from everything but she rushed back after twenty-four hours to get to her pills again. We saw her disintegrating mentally through them. I am certain the pills sent her nearly mad and through them she died.'

Henson was in a show in Dublin when the news came through of 'Bobbie' Hullett's death. He was so shocked, upset and worried, he telephoned Richard Walker of his concern and suspicions and at Walker's request volunteered a statement at Dublin's Central Police Station.

The Chief Constable no longer hesitated, with rumours of other deaths circulating in the town, the sinister aspects of 'Bobbie' Hullett's death became the catalyst for enquiries to be mounted. A few discreet telephone calls were made. It was established that two days before 'Bobbie' Hullett fell into a three day-coma from which she died, she gave Adams a cheque for £1,000. He immediately drove to his bank and asked for special clearance; in hours the amount was credited to his account. At that time Doctor Adams' bank accounts, two current and one deposit, showed credit balances totalling £35,000 and with his investment holdings amounting to a further £125,000, he was not exactly in urgent need of money.

The Chief Constable was a man reluctant to bring sensation to his town, but a man firm in his line of duty. He would say later: 'A number of incidents, backed by very strong rumours, warranted my calling in the Yard.'

The 'Eastbourne Job' as it became known, called on stage a number of notable characters. From New Scotland Yard's Murder Squad came the lugubrious and sartorially elegant Herbert Hannam who had solved the Teddington Towpath Murders in Coronation Year. His assistant was a chipper cockney sparrow, a real 'Jack-the-Lad', Detective-Sergeant Charlie Hewitt.

In Eastbourne co-operation and help with enquiries came from Detective-Inspector Brynwel Pugh, the lilt of Welsh valleys still very much in his speech.

Rumours and action could not be kept altogether quiet. Within hours the press sniffed an outstanding story. In London, Associated Newspapers' *Daily Mail* had information from Eastbourne, whereupon the News Editor decided to send an accomplished investigative crime reporter on his staff to the scene. Thus one of the co-authors of this book arrived in Eastbourne late July of 1956, at the height of the summer season. Hotel rooms were at a premium.

'I'm sorry, Mr Hallworth,' said the manager of the Grand Hotel, 'the only thing I can offer you is the Bridal Suite.'

And from that sumptuous boudoir of silks and brocades, Rodney Hallworth sent his first dispatch of many, in a crime-story that would occupy him for exactly one year and a day, and send him and others, first to Ireland, and then to the Central Criminal Courts of the Old Bailey. The first dispatch line read:

Hallworth, Eastbourne:
To shock Eastbourne is unfair; it's like booting an old lady as she sleeps in the armchair of memories. But fair or not the circus of sensation has hit this queenly resort banging the big drums of suspicion along every street. A drunken news vendor could not have brought more alarm. The gossip started years ago – before the war – and every time a wealthy woman died

12

the tongues in the tea rooms clacked louder and two and two became five. A few weeks ago rumour ran amock and to sift fact from fiction the Chief Constable wisely called in the Yard.

The man chosen was Detective-Superintendent Herbert W. Hannam of the Murder Squad – known to his colleagues as the 'The Count'. His grooming is impeccable, "he has one suit for every day of the week", if he smokes at all it's a cigar and when he speaks every phrase would stand criticism from an Oxford Don. His name first hit the headlines in Coronation Year when he solved the double murder of Teddington Towpath, Surrey. It was his first murder inquiry. He is one of the Yard's intellectuals, regarded as being among their most distinguished lecturers (he toured Holland this year) and has a reputation for thoroughness, patience and if necessary cunning.

He is perfectly suited, therefore, to the Eastbourne job which entails the close interrogation of many people, the sifting of a hundred wills, a thousand documents and a million words. Just one slip, the careless turning over of two pages at once, and the investigation could come to nought.

What then is the 'Eastbourne Job'? It is to establish if a number of women have been tricked of their money over the past twenty years or murdered or both. Already Hannam has confirmed some of the gossip. There are similarities in many of the wills which at a glance certainly look suspicious. More people die per street in Eastbourne than in most British towns. There is nothing odd about that. People come here to die. Many are wealthy and they have to distribute their money somehow, but somehow they seem to have thought along the same lines as they made out their wills.

Eastbourne can be an easy hunting ground for a streamlined confidence man who is prepared to sit in the sun lounges and palm courts sugaring the tea of old ladies. Many of the women are rich but friendless. They have outlived their families, now to limp forgotten through a lonely world of gold.

As Hannam investigates their deaths of long ago he finds that their trinkets and papers, their letters and lavender have gone like the tide of yesterday. Who then can he ask? Their lawyers only know half the story. Yesterday a white haired nurse of 78 was asked about her patients during the last 35 years. She told me:

"My memory fails as I get old – and I'm very old. My files were burned when I was bombed in the war and it's hard to rely on a rusting brain."

Some of the women under investigation were cremated and their ashes cast over the English Channel. Some were buried

13

20 years ago and for them the Yard's forensic skill cannot help. In the police station here detectives try to grab fleeing evidence of their lives as they speak to women in the Registrar's Office, nursing home Matrons, bank managers, doctors, taxi drivers, ailing nephews and nieces, hotel staff, gardeners, cooks, maids, chauffeurs and so on. Daily they consult their colleagues at the Yard who for a week now have spent hours among the files at Somerset House.

Hannam studies every report. Some he checks again personally by visiting an office in the town or driving 10 miles into the countryside. Once he quietly slipped into the ballroom of the famous Grand Hotel as a trio of genteel musicians played Strauss and Chopin. His inquiry began officially 13 days ago. It will not end for another three weeks at least and then there will be conferences at the Yard with legal advisors from the Office of the Director of Public Prosecutions. Circumstantial evidence alone is sometimes enough to convince a jury. Before then gravediggers may be asked to assist in the exhumation of one woman, perhaps two, maybe three. Much depends on any evidence found at the first exhumation. The inquiry will centre around the affairs and deaths of 14 woman one of whom died in 1935. The wills of six of these women, widows and spinsters total more than a hundred thousand pounds. Detectives are curious about bequests they made totalling £45,000. Eight other women are yet to be investigated. Some changed their wills shortly before they died. They were entitled to, but Mr. Hannam would like to know why. In some cases there are people alive who can tell him. In others there are not, so he digs deeper into his huge dossier searching for the answer.

This week the probe extended to Yorkshire, Dorset, Hampshire and Surrey. Whatever the result of the Yard's visit dainty old Eastbourne has already been placed in the crime chapters of the century. It is hard for the Mayor and his citizens who are justly proud of their clean streets, the floral walks, white buses, smart hotels and elegant homes.

If Hannam "pulls it off" it will be regarded as his greatest triumph. If there has been murder here it is murder with a difference. The inquiry has not begun with a finding of a body in a copse and a blood stained knife nearby. It began with talk and a few pieces of paper.

There are some who say it is just a storm in a porcelain teacup. I believe it will end with an arrest but I am forbidden by law to tell you why. And it is too early yet to say how the charge sheet will be phrased.

So began the 'Eastbourne Job'. But what of the central character in this affair? The man at the heart of all the gossip, rumour and now murder investigation, Doctor John Bodkin Adams, M.D.; D.A.; D.Ph., of 'Kent Lodge', Trinity Trees, Eastbourne. What manner of man was he; from where did he come to Eastbourne? Who, in fact, was John Bodkin Adams? The answers begin in County Antrim, Northern Ireland.

# Chapter Two

*'He was a wee bit mean. There was little fun in him'*
PADDY MCCOSHER

The voice of the tall, stooping watchmaker thundered the Word of God through that cluttered Victorian drawing room, the windows of which gazed bleakly over Loch Neagh. His portly wife, who looked like and dressed like Queen Victoria, knelt at his side. By her skirts, eyes closed in fervent prayer, hands firmly clasped together, knelt their first-born son, John Bodkin Adams.

Adams was born on January 21, 1899 in a first floor room above the main street of Randalstown, County Antrim. His father, Samuel Adams, being a watchmaker and a successful one, though a farmer's son from Desertmartin a few miles away in County Tyrone. His mother, Ellen Bodkin, was a kindly soul and a good business woman. Her family owned scutch mills in the same district. She was one of nine sisters renowned for their piety.

In a religious age, in a religious society, the Bodkins were devoutly outstanding among their Methodist brethren. All nine sisters married religious men and men who combined their faith in God with a business acumen which was to spread their name and fortunes all over the world.

For her husband, Ellen chose the farmer's son who was learning his trade as a watchmaker and jeweller in Ballymena.

Soon after they married, Samuel Adams took his first and only shop next door to the hotel in the main street of Randalstown.

His tall, boney figure, all elbows and knees, was soon to be seen cycling a penny-farthing bicycle throughout the country roads around Randalstown, as the determined farmer's son sought the business of farmers and local gentry. Few in Randalstown would now remember him. Although before he died, neighbour Paddy Kane recalled in his strident Ulster accent:

'Samuel had one of the first bicycles ever seen in the district and we used to stand on the pavement in amazement and watch him fly past. He was very popular and was known to be a good man.'

Every Sunday Samuel Adams held a Bible class in the sitting-room above his shop. He was a member of the Plymouth Brethren, kindly yet uncompromising in his faith. Until the day he died he set aside ten per cent of his income for charity. That the figure increased annually was not entirely due to his passion for hard work, for Ellen Bodkin brought her own shrewd mind to bear on the family fortunes. She and her husband bought a plot of land higher up the main street from the grey cement terrace where they had their shop. On it they built workers' cottages. The rents they invested. They bought more parcels of land, built more houses. The Adams family prospered.

By the time John Bodkin was four years old his father, partly because of failing health, thought of retirement. Most of his wealth was invested in sound stocks, with the help of his wife's shrewd advice.

The twentieth century was still new when Samuel Adams moved his family around the shores of great Loch Neagh to Ballinderry Bridge in County Tyrone. It cost him little more than £500 to buy the biggest house in the village, the aptly named 'Fairview'. A solid unpretentious house, with a bow window at each side of the front door, it commanded a wide view of the endless loch and the mountains beyond. A hundred evergreen trees stood in the acre which surrounded the house and an evergreen hedge bordered the road.

There, in 1903 the Adams had their second child, William, a bright fun-loving boy who was to die tragically of pneumonia sixteen years later, after a holiday with his mother and brother at Portstewart. It was in this solid house that John Bodkin Adams grew up. With William he walked hand in hand to the Church School, the little Methodist day school silhouetted on the brow of a hill half a mile from home.

But when William and the other boys romped in the fields at the edge of the loch, John Bodkin Adams went straight home to the severely dressed copy of Queen Victoria. Paddy McCosher, who once lived in the thatched cottage close by 'Fairview', said:

'He never seemed to play with the others. He was a wee bit mean. There was little fun in him.'

There was little fun in 'Fairview' either. Samuel Adams was living mostly on eggs and milk, exerting his failing body only for the sake of his religion. On Sundays the family travelled miles to the nearest Plymouth Brethren meeting place, where Samuel became a notable preacher. The afternoon of each Sabbath was taken up by a Sunday School which the ex-watchmaker ran for adults and children alike. Said one old-timer recalling those days:

'The boys daren't read a book – they hardly dare tie their shoelaces on a Sunday, so strict was their father.'

Yet he was otherwise a kindly man and well liked.

Afraid of his father, little John Bodkin clung fast to his doting mother's skirts. He never let go until the day she died. He became a fat boy, for the most Bunterish of reasons – he loved cream cakes and chocolates. He never smoked or drank – other than a rare glass of sherry – but in his life he never lost the craving for sweetmeats.

When John Bodkin was twelve years old the family moved to Coleraine. The move from Ballinderry Bridge, where the family had been happy, was inevitable, for at Coleraine was the 'Academy' where John must study if he was to reach Queen's University, Belfast, and one of the professions. It was almost certainly to be medicine. One doctor uncle, William Adams, had been Mayor of Chelmsford, Essex, for ten years. In the Far

East grateful Chinese had erected a Bodkin Hospital in memory of another uncle. Two cousins were destined to become doctors, one in Northern Ireland, the second in London.

The family bought a house in Mount Sandel, Coleraine, and called it 'Ebenezer'. Here, while John was proving himself a determined if not a brilliant student, Samuel Adams died and was buried in the local cemetery. In her grief Ellen Bodkin still had charity for others and when one of her sisters died, Ellen took her little daughter Florence into her home – and Florence and John grew up as brother and sister. It was Florence who, in friendly criticism of John's dawn to dusk energy at this time, nicknamed him 'Buzz'. It became his family name. In Coleraine his mother bought him his first motorbike. He rode and tended a succession of them, with a passion he was later to transfer to automobiles.

The family holidayed at Portrush or Portstewart, but while William and the cousins chased the girls, John Bodkin stayed with his mother. Even on holiday he never failed to attend the Children's Special Service Mission run by the Reverend Mr Ovens at Portstewart.

The First World War was raging near its end when the chubby youth from Randalstown enrolled as a medical student at Queen's University, Belfast. His mother and cousin Florence came to the city too, moving into a house in Malone Avenue on Belfast's 'Nob Hill'. Ellen Bodkin had managed her investments well. Her bank balance at that time was the considerable sum of £14,000. She knew the value of money and saw that useful commodity was equally appreciated by her son. John Bodkin grew up to be a careful and acquisitive young man who never spent a penny where a half-penny would do. A relative, himself a prosperous business man, said of John Bodkin:

'He was never mean but he was always careful. We were all brought up with this passion for stability, for having our possessions around us. It is not miserliness but a longing for security. It is so strong in us that I, though worth well over six figures, go in constant fear of bankruptcy, even though I know that such a thing would now be impossible.'

At Medical School young Adams took no part in the high jinks of the other medical students in an age where such letting off of steam was almost mandatory. He was neither brilliant nor dull. He was just a plodder. But one thing about him was remarkable enough to have remained in the recollection of Professor Richard Hunter, the man who taught him anatomy and embryology at Queen's. Professor Hunter said:

'When we used to dissect a body, I would assign three students to one arm, three to another and so on. You usually found that these three students would work together for the rest of the course. But not Adams. He would work first with one group, then with another, wherever he could be fitted in. That is the way he always was – a lone wolf.'

The lone wolf sought hard to keep up with his brainier colleagues. He worked so late in his room in Malone Avenue that he had a breakdown. At first, he thought it was tuberculosis but devoted nursing by his mother and cousin Florence had him on his feet in a few months. He returned to Queen's, crammed two years' work into one and took a reasonably good degree. The year was 1921. One year later his name first appeared on a brass plate in Eastbourne.

In between, the young Dr Adams had served on the wards of a Bristol hospital. When he saw a junior partnership in Eastbourne advertised he applied for it. The first reply said the position was filled but the doctor who filled it withdrew and in so doing led the footsteps of Dr John Bodkin Adams to Eastbourne.

In Eastbourne he first lived in Upperton Road and worked as a junior partner to Dr Emerson and Dr Gurney. His fee was half-a-crown a visit. His aptitude for hard work and his ambition to become established in the resort led him to take all the night calls. He worked to the total exclusion of any social life, making his rounds on his beloved motorcycle with his black bag strapped to the luggage rest. Few people at first took the plump motorcyclist for a doctor, but soon the figure of young Dr Adams on his machine became as familiar in Eastbourne as his watchmaker father had been on his penny-farthing in Randalstown. The Doctor, some older patients later recalled, had a habit of making his visits at mealtimes and never refused the invitation to dine.

His willingness to turn out at night won him many patients who later became friendly towards him. He had been in Eastbourne less than a year when a late-night call took him to Ratton Estate, a seven-bedroomed mansion which was the home of William and Edith Mawhood, a wealthy steel merchant and his wife.

Mr Mawhood had a large staff including a gamekeeper for the pheasant shooting in his own grounds. Mrs Mawhood had broken her leg. The Doctor – 'He was so young I didn't think he was a doctor,' said Mrs. Mawhood – used picture wire to help set it. The operation was not successful and the leg had to be re-set by a London surgeon a year later, yet the Mawhoods took to the earnest charm and lilting accent of the Irishman. He called twice a week, invariably at mealtimes.

Boyhood experience with a gun had made him a fair shot and he joined the Mawhood's pheasant shoots. His enthusiasm for shooting later developed into one of the three of his lifetime hobbies, the other two being automobiles and photography.

The Mawhood's in turn introduced him to some of their rich friends. In good contacts and unremitting energy Adams found the formula for success. He became doctor, advisor and friend to some of the best-known families in south Sussex. He was welcomed into the homes of the 'County' set and those of the City men who had come to the coast to retire. His patients were to include the wealthy patrons of the arts, the landed-gentry, and the hunting, shooting, fishing fraternity of south Sussex. It was a deliberate cultivation. Doctor Adams was sowing seeds that would bear a profitable fruit.

When his partners died he bought out the practice. From William Mawhood he borrowed £3,000 to buy his home, 'Kent

Lodge', a dull square Victorian pile opposite the church in Trinity Trees, Eastbourne. His mother and cousin Florence, who had sold up in Belfast, moved in to keep house for him.

In ten years John Bodkin Adams had become the most fashionable doctor in Eastbourne. His close and lasting friendship with Sir Roland Gwynne, Squire of Folkington Manor and Chairman of Eastbourne magistrates, sealed his social acceptance.

His list of patients grew until three other doctors had joined him in the most prosperous practice in town. His own private and invariably wealthy patients became so numerous that after the Second World War he began to cut down the number of National Health patients and former Panel patients he had once been so glad to have.

Always a fastidious dresser, Adams went to Savile Row for his clothes. In those immediate post-war years he paid as much as £48 for a suit. In that longing for family stability he later had two wardrobes full of suits and boxes of shoes which he had never worn. He bought expensive sporting guns and spent holidays on the grouse moors of Scotland and Ireland.

Returning from one such holiday by train, he met a fellow passenger who was a contemporary from Medical School days in Belfast, to whom Adams let slip the remark:

'The trouble with you fellows in Northern Ireland is that you don't know how to make money.'

Things were going well for Dr Adams. He opened a second and then a third bank account, two current and one deposit. In the early '50s he was making £7,000 a year from his practice and his three accounts totalled £35,000. This was but a part of his wealth. Ellen Bodkin had taught her son well because he drew an annual income of some £5,000 from his investments which now totalled £125,000.

Though his finances were solid, he never lost the family's unreasoning fear of being without money. He always held about £6,000 in cash in his home. His hoarding instinct went further. In his cellar he kept a stock of thirty motorcar tyres, inner tubes and main springs, as he once told a colleague: 'In case there was a war'.

His passion for cars grew so great that at one time he owned five – two Rolls-Royce, two new MG saloons and a Morris Minor. He revelled in the thought that, if a rainy afternoon spoilt the polish on the one car, he could turn out in another dry shiny limousine for a night function or call.

He became cocksure and overbearing. A down-to-earth cousin from Northern Ireland once warned him:
'John, don't lose touch with the ordinary people or one day somebody will find a chink in your armour and slip a knife in it.'

Adams laughed.

But no matter how exaggerated his personality he was never less than an obedient and dutiful son. A maid who once worked at 'Kent Lodge' said:
'He was absolutely devoted to his mother. He fetched and carried for her. Her word to him was law. He was a kind and charitable man and when his mother died he was every bit as attentive to his cousin Florence.'

In 1936 Adams had quietly become engaged to Miss Norah O'Hara, daughter of Eastbourne's wealthiest butcher. Mr O'Hara bought the couple a house but the Doctor's mother quarrelled with the future in-laws over the furnishing of it. Mrs Adams fell out with the O'Hara's and so powerful was her command over her son that he broke the engagement, ever after to remain a bachelor.

Dr Adams never really left the nursery until the day his mother died on March 3, 1943, leaving him her entire estate of £7,043. The grieving son accompanied her body on its last journey over the sea from Stranrear to Larne, to the cemetery in Coleraine where it rests with that of her husband.

Unconfirmed gossip linked Adams with seven woman friends, three of whom swore they would never marry unless it was to him. One lived in Belfast, obviously a passion of his early student days, and the others in Eastbourne and south Sussex. To these women Adams proved a fascination, be it a natural relationship or a desire to mother him. Probably nearer the latter because business men who knew the Doctor quite well never saw him as an ardent bedroom gymnast. Even a quick look at his background shows him to be an over-fat Mummy's boy and it would seem reasonable that the women he knew in later life were only filling the gap left by his mother.

Miss O'Hara always remained his friend. Twice a week he visited her at her home in Pashley Road, Eastbourne, for coffee. He was aware of the attraction he held for women – a magnetism not so easily discerned by his men friends.

But Eastbourne was never in any doubt about his religious upbringing. Like his father before him, Adams conducted Bible classes on Sunday afternoons. He instructed the Young Crusaders. He became Joint Chairman of the YMCA and he worshipped with the Plymouth Brethren. He bought vestments for the priests who visited the Esperance Nursing Home where he had patients.

This was the man at the centre of a mass-murder enquiry. This was Doctor John Bodkin Adams in the mid-1950s. A large man in every way, then in his own fifties, pushing the scales over seventeen stones. A pink fleshy face, in a square head, small-eyed and thin-lipped. Rolling chins sagged over the celluloid collars he wore. His horn-rimmed rounded spectacles appearing too small in that setting. Immaculate well-cut suiting did nothing to ease the bulk of a huge stomach. A brown, green or grey trilby hat would cover his balding head. He was normally grey or blue suited with a pristine white handkerchief emerging from a top pocket.

His was a figure in keeping with the old Victorian image of a 'well-set' man, in that obesity was just a token of a man's social position, able to afford the best of food and drink. For Dr Adams his incurable sweet-tooth resulted in his overweight and yet he still managed to convey an air of healthy wellbeing around him.

If his critics maintained he was arrogant, overbearing and incapable of looking past the bank balance of his patients, they also had to admit he did have plenty of patients. Possibly such patients did all come from a certain social strata but that is not a crime in itself. The medical profession is just that – a profession. The general practitioner functions very much to the dictates of the location in which he chooses to dispense his services. The GP in the North-East of England has a far different practice to the GP on the south coast. And condition of location has often changed a young, dedicated and vocationally industrious medical practitioner into something a little less. This is a fact of life, not confined to the medical profession. It applies equally to the Church, the Law and the Services.

Dr Adams held qualifications not only as a Doctor of Medicine but as a Doctor of Philosophy and with an Anaesthetists Diploma. Was John Bodkin Adams a good doctor? It is believed he had his own doubts and would shy clear of cases he considered complicated, even of common family illnesses any GP would take in his stride. Without doubt Adams' referrals to consultant specialists of cases well within the normal range of a GP's capabilities were high. But as most of Adams' patients were private fee-paying clients, those consultants naturally voiced no objection. The bedside manner of Dr Adams, however, was not lacking in any way and if he suggested a second opinion, the patient was normally far more grateful for the obvious attention than concerned about the additional fees involved.

Adams was patently a pious man. In the 1950s, perhaps more than today, religion played a greater part in the thinking of those in the evening of their lives. Call it conscience or the enlightenment that age brings, whatever, it seems there was a certain amount of reassurance to be tended by such a doctor. And Adams was not loath to openly demonstrate his belief. Rarely would a sentence pass without his invoking the Blessings of the Almighty.

When one elderly woman patient was told by her young maid that Dr Adams always knelt on his knees outside her bedroom for a quick prayer before entering, she instructed her staff to immediately purchase a fitting mat so that the Doctor would not have to kneel on the bare wood.

If the specialists were a little reluctant to criticise Dr Adams, his fellow GP's were not so reticent. 'Oafish bore'; 'inept bungler': 'disgrace to the profession' were but a few direct quotes. If any such comments ultimately reached Adams, as seems most likely in a fairly small community, their effect was not apparently seen on the surface. The broad back of Adams had suffered such criticism for years. The inference being that of professional envy at his highly successful practice.

Yet there were times when the Adams facade of indifference to criticism crumbled, albeit momentarily, to more official rebuke. Particularly when it came from the direction of the Coroner's Office. Comments that were not exactly calculated to stop wagging tongues but by this time representatives of New Scotland Yard's Murder Squad were in town and an investigation was already in full swing.

The life and times of Dr John Bodkin Adams would soon be under intense scrutiny. After many years of rumour, the first sight of fact for the people of Eastbourne came with the inquest on Mrs 'Bobbie' Hullett, held on Tuesday August 21, 1956 – a warm sunny summer afternoon, when the 'Eastbourne Job' really began in earnest.

# Chapter Three

*'There has been an extraordinary degree of careless treatment.'*

DR A. C. SOMMERVILLE EAST SUSSEX CORONER

Fleet Street has every acre of Britain 'covered' by a journalist. If there is a rail crash in Wigan the *Daily Mail*, *The Times*, *Telegraph*, *Express* will have a local reporter to write the story for them or assist their own staff man. From the Orkneys to the Scillies every inch of ground is someone's 'beat'. It is a bit like the Police Force – there is someone on hand day or night. It could be a freelance, the chief reporter of the evening paper or a mature journalist on the local weekly. Eastbourne was well covered by the able Jimmy Donne who looked after the goings-on in the town for the London evenings, BBC and the dailies.

On Thursday August 16, 1956, he sent a letter to those news editors in London for whom he worked:

> I am enclosing for your private information a memorandum of background material for the inquest on Mrs Hullett which opens here at 2.15 p.m. on August 21st.
>
> As my assistant will be on holiday, and in view of the importance of the inquest, I think it would be better if you sent down a staff man.
>
> I could manage myself at a pinch, but copy might be a bit late. And of course it is always on days like that the bodies go over Beachy Head, ships run into difficulties and lifeboats are launched.
>
> So for the first time in five years I am asking every editor of newspapers I represent to send down a staff man and leave me clear for the normal run of news.
>
> With best wishes, Yours sincerely,
> James Donne.

## His confidential memo to news editors ran as follows:

As you may have guessed, I have been quietly collecting information about the mysterious death of Mrs. Gertrude Joyce Hullett here ever since the initial hue and cry died down when the Fleet Street staff men recently returned to London for a short while.

When time has permitted and the chance to talk to a contact has presented itself, I have continued my enquiries and the following information has been checked and re-checked to make dead certain that it is accurate. I cannot obviously disclose the sources of the following information, which I think will be useful to you in assessing the importance of this inquest, but you can take it for granted that it has come from inside sources at top level.

For nearly two months after her husband died in March, Mrs Hullett was very distressed and on the verge of a mental breakdown. During the last fortnight before her death she was much better, and in the last week decidedly cheerful. As your reporter knows, she was suddenly taken ill on Thursday, July 19, and died on Monday at 7.30 a.m., July 23, without regaining consciousness. During all that time the family physician, Dr John Bodkin Adams, was in attendance and should have got Mrs Hullett to hospital, but he did not and only called in a second opinion on Saturday, July 21. On Sunday night, July 22, he telephoned to the East Sussex Coroner, Dr A. C. Sommerville, to say that he "had a very peculiar case on his hands." My information is that the Coroner told him to get in touch with him in the usual way through his officer in Eastbourne. Obviously the Coroner got in touch with Eastbourne's Chief Constable and enquiries were started immediately Mrs Hullett was dead.

The Coroner had in his possession three letters, all in Mrs Hullett's handwriting, dating from April to July, in which she talks of her distress at losing her husband and conveying that life without him was not worth living. She spoke of taking her own life. The first two, one to a sister-in-law and the other to her daughter by a former marriage, Miss Pat Tomlinson, were written in April and June. The last and most important one dated July 17 she wrote to a friend of the family for thirty-five years, Mr Robert Handscomb, who, with a local solicitor, is co-executor of her will. Again she spoke of taking her life.

When she died Mr Handscomb, like the rest of the family, was under the impression that she had died of cerebral haemorrhage and to avoid distress to the family he withheld that letter from the police. Only when police enquiries had been going on for four days and when the cause of death was then believed to be through barbiturate poisoning did he hand the letter over.

My information is that he will be severely censured by the Coroner for withholding that letter and the Doctor will be reprimanded for neglect of his patient. From what I hear in police circles there is going to be "a lot more dirt at the inquest". I can only guess at that. As your reporter was told by me, Dr Adams will inherit Mrs Hullett's Rolls-Royce under her will, which will be through probate in about a month. It is a Silver Dawn, registered in June 1954, and was entered in the July 1954 Midnight Concours d'Elegance of the British Automobile Racing Club at Eastbourne where it was runner-up in its class. The lady passenger to complete the "ensemble" was Mrs Hullett who was known to all her friends as "Bobbie". That much about her will is certain. I am told that the Doctor will also get £1,000 in cash but I cannot check that. What I am certain of is that but for Mrs Hullett's advisers he would have got much more.

Dr F. E. Camps made only a verbal report to a top level conference at Eastbourne Police Station six days after Mrs Hullett's death. His full report has still not been received. I am told that the reason is that at least a month must elapse after the post mortem with this kind of poisoning before he can be certain of it. The twenty-eighth day will be up the day before the inquest.

Such was the information and opinion expressed by a fine journalist. Jimmy Donne was right; the inquest was more than newsworthy. And reports of the proceedings found space not only in U.K. editions but throughout the world.

At the inquest the East Sussex Coroner, Dr A. C. Sommerville, began in sensation by asking Detective-Superintendent Hannam if he would be making a request for an adjournment: 'As you are here to investigate several deaths in the neighbourhood.' Mr Hannam calmly replied: 'I appreciate your inquiry but I have no such application to make.'

A colleague of Hallworth's telephoned the following copy to his paper:

31

This afternoon the jury returned a verdict of 'suicide' on fifty year old Mrs Gertrude Joyce Hullett of Holywell Mount, Eastbourne. She died from an overdose of barbiturate sleeping tablets in the bedroom of her lovely Beachy Head home on July 23. During the five hour hearing the jury heard that her doctor, John Bodkin Adams, had received a cheque for £1,000 from her just before she died and that in her will she left him her Rolls-Royce car. The cheque was presented on July 18, only five days before she died. It was cleared on the 19th through a special bank procedure requested by Dr Adams the bank manager, Mr. John Oliver, told the Coroner. An hour before the inquest opened at the Magistrates' Court in the Town Hall, a queue of middle aged women who lived in the exclusive West Shore district, waited for the public gallery doors to open. Later they were joined by suntanned holiday makers and some patients of Dr Adams. The stout, bald-headed doctor, wearing horn-rimmed bifocal spectacles and a blue serge suit with a blue spotted tie, gave evidence for over an hour. His seat in the court behind his lawyer was only two feet away from the Chief Constable of Eastbourne, Mr Richard Walker, who sat next to Superintendent Hannam and other police officers.

Dr Adams was severely criticised by the Coroner for his diagnosis and treatment during Mrs Hullett's last days when she was unconscious. She was the widow of a Lloyd's underwriter who died in March leaving £94,000.

He was also a patient of Dr Adams. The Coroner asked the doctor: why he didn't tell his co-doctor, called in as a second opinion, of his patient's depressive medical history?

Why he failed to get proper daytime medical attention for her?

Why, after thirty-four years as a doctor, he took the advice of a young house surgeon in administering a new drug?

Why his co-doctor gave antibiotic injections instead of him?

Why he failed to call in a psychiatric consultant about Mrs Hullett's condition before her collapse?

Why he persisted in his diagnosis of a cerebral catastrophe after a pathologist had suggested it might be poisoning?

And why he didn't have Mrs Hullett taken to a hospital or nursing home?

The Doctor summed up in his defence in his broad Ulster brogue when he said: "I honestly did what I thought was best for her."

He sat with his bowed head on his hand while the Coroner addressed the jury on the law of criminal negligence. Said the Coroner:

"There has been an extraordinary degree of careless treatment," but he told the jury that any lesser degree of negligence was not made greater by possible motive, such as by financial matters they had heard about.

Among the fourteen witnesses was Mrs Hullett's daughter by her former marriage Miss Evelyn Patricia Tomlinson, aged twenty, who said her mother once told her: "I have not got anything to live for." As the Doctor left the Court driving his own new sports saloon, fifty women and press photographers surged round him at the side entrance. He said after the inquest:

"The result of the inquest has cleared up all the ugly rumours and innuendos which have been going around. My conscience is clear and I have nothing to hide. I did all I could for Mrs Hullett. I have spoken to Mr Hannam because we were introduced after the inquest."

Many would not have thought the inquest had 'cleared up' all the ugly rumours. Quite the contrary. The Doctor had been severely reprimanded by the Coroner; the man from the Yard had heard it all and such criticism could only inspire him to dig the deeper into his inquiries.

On the same day Hallworth wrote this news story for the *Daily Mail*:

The mass murder of wealthy women during the past twenty years will this week be probed by Scotland Yard's Murder Squad in the most sensational investigation of the country's criminal history. Because the vast extent of murder suspicion is not yet known, the Yard will start in Eastbourne by investigating the wills of dozens of men and women who died in this 'haven of blessed retirement.' It is expected that the names of about twenty-five persons will ultimately be picked out as being the possible victims of a maniac. The probe may extend into the winter months. For the past three days a team of detectives from the Yard's Central Office of Investigation have searched the files of Somerset House.

Their huge dossier will include the names of scores of persons, most of whom are expected to have been wealthy widows and spinsters. They are particularly interested in the wills of persons whose estates were valued in thousands of pounds.

The first check will be to discover who the beneficiaries were in each case and if there are any similarities. Side by side with this aspect will be the investigations into the circumstances of their deaths. Coroners' files on sudden deaths will be handed over to Mr Hannam. Hundreds of people including relatives of the dead persons will be interviewed, not only in Eastbourne but throughout Britain. The Yard particularly wish to interview members of the medical profession, lawyers and hotel employees and staff at convalescent and nursing homes in south Sussex. It is here that some of the richest families in the country have come to spend the twilight of their years and because the bulk of them have been ageing widows, the Yard realise they could be an easy prey for a demon killer.

This investigation began after years of gossip, and last Friday the Chief Constable travelled to London to see the Assistant Commissioner for Crime at the Yard. Since then there have been conferences between the Yard executives, Home Office Pathologist Dr Francis Camps and the East Sussex Coroner, Dr A. C. Sommerville. Detectives began their own investigation some time ago, based chiefly on rumour, but since then startling evidence has reached them which suggests there could be foundation for much of the gossip.

So the 'Eastbourne Job' was well and truly off and running. Its field of characters growing. For the international press now gathered in Eastbourne, the investigations were an editor's joy. Not only was the suspected crime that of murder but possible mass-murder. That doyen of English respectability – the family doctor – was implicated, indeed the obvious prime suspect. Thousands of pounds were involved, bequests of Rolls-Royce cars, jewellery and antiques. The normally responsible English press made up banner headlines – the more sensational continentals had theirs the size of walls.

A sedate elderly woman sunning herself in a deckchair on an Eastbourne beach was startled by the sudden appearance of a photographer. A day later the photograph would grace page one in a German or Italian newspaper with the bold caption 'Is this the one who escaped?' And as a bonus for the editors, the Police Officers assigned to the case were copy in themselves.

For the first time in Easbourne's history its Police Force had asked for the assistance of New Scotland Yard. The very nature of their enquiry was for Fleet Street the biggest crime story since Christie and his murdered women in Notting Hill Gate. More than a hundred newspapermen from London, Europe and North America invaded Eastbourne, which was good for the pub tills and hair raising for the barmaids, though difficult that summer as far as accommodation was concerned. Still, there were the lucky ones. Rodney Hallworth with colleague Harry Longmuir still roughed it in the sumptuous Grand Hotel Bridal Suite. It was in that unlikely setting that profiles of the leading Police Officers involved in the 'Eastbourne Job' were pieced together. Hannam and Hewitt from the Yard and Brynwel Pugh of the Eastbourne CID.

Although Hannam hit the headlines, much silent and difficult work was done by the Head of Eastbourne's CID, Detective-Inspector Brynwel Pugh, Bryn, to a not inconsiderable many.

Bryn first came into contact with the Police Force when he spent a night in a cell at Cardiff Police Station. He was eighteen and had just run away from home. Son of a colliery foreman in Merthyr Vale, Glamorgan, Bryn followed his father into the pits.

On the night he washed off the coal dust for the last time, it was ostensibly to go to a dance with a pal, Wyndham Jones. In his pocket were all his savings – £22. Wyndham had a little more. When the dance ended instead of walking home, the two youngsters tramped over the mountain in search of adventure. They didn't stop until sore feet and aching limbs brought them to a standstill in Cardiff. A friendly policeman, thinking they were just two more lads in search of work, gave them beds in the cells.

Wyndham had a girlfriend in Eastbourne so the two hitchhiked their way there. Wyndham later married the girl and settled in Eastbourne. They had arrived on a Friday night. On Monday morning Bryn Pugh started work as a fitter at Eastbourne Gas Works. Then he was offered a job as a landscape gardener at the Sussex home of Baron Cassells, the Belgian banker. He knew nothing about landscape gardening. In those days unemployment was high so he took the job and stayed there four years.

He was still in his early twenties when he joined Eastbourne Police. After only seven months in uniform, the quietly spoken

Welshman became a detective. He played soccer for Eastbourne Football Club and won medals for track running. He was popular with his colleagues and respected by his 'customers'. Until his death several years after the 'Eastbourne Job' he pushed a handy cue in the local Snooker League.

One irony of the 'Eastbourne Job' was that Dr Adams was Bryn's family doctor. Indeed, had delivered his children.

Of Bryn Pugh, Charlie Hewitt remembers: 'Although Bryn eventually became as convinced as Hannam and I of the Doctor's guilt, it was an uphill struggle initially. After all, to have one's kids delivered by a man thought to be a mass-murderer has a rather chastening effect!'

For Hannam his police career began in circumstances similar to Brynwel Pugh, economic depression, dole and the need for security. At the time of the Adams enquiry he was forty-eight years old. He had been born and brought up in Paddington. His father, a printing works manager, apprenticed him to an icing and pastry cook. Young Hannam liked the job and excelled at it. In his Willesden home he had a silver cup and sufficient diplomas to prove the point. When he was called to Eastbourne he still kept his hand in by baking and icing the family birthday and Christmas cakes.

The Depression threw Hannam out of work. For two months he joined the queues at his local Labour Exchange. Finally, on December 27, 1927, he landed a job – in the Metropolitan Police. He had never wanted to be a policeman but a job was a job and this at least offered a steady living. It was not until five years later that he decided he liked the force well enough to make it his career. He almost didn't make it. In the Entrance Examination he spelt 'obstacle' with a 'k'. 'Just a nervous slip,' he assured the examiners.

He pounded his first beat in Richmond, Surrey. After eighteen months in uniform he married and soon afterwards was promoted to the Detective Branch. He appeared in the Detectives' Room at Peckham Rye Police Station, south of the Thames, wearing spats. He never wore them again. His colleagues fashioned themselves spats of paper and fastened them to their shoes with paper-clips. Hannam took the hint.

But the incident did not discourage his taste for good clothes. Detective Superintendent Hannam, now of Bow Street, wore yellow gloves and carried an umbrella. Later he admitted that the attire caused a stir when he had to interview bumarees at Covent Garden Market. His clothes and his friendly patrician manner won him the nickname of 'The Count'.

When a well-dressed Sergeant, he once had a few off-duty drinks in a Covent Garden pub. After he left, his not so well dressed Superintendent dropped in. The landlord greeted the Superintendent with: 'Hello – you've just missed your Governor.'

A tireless self-educator, Hannam devoured books on law, and accountancy to help him in his job. He became an expert in currency frauds and was made liaison officer between the Yard and the Bank of England. Police training colleagues valued him right up to his retirement as a lecturer. He gave talks on police methods to law and police students in Holland.

A series of successful currency fraud investigations which took him to France and America shortly after the war helped to make his name. He was promoted to the rank of Superintendent in charge of a squad of detectives at Scotland Yard's Central Office of Investigation. He became 'Hannam of the Yard' to the public when he solved the turbulent Teddington Towpath murders on the eve of the Coronation.

On a fine day he would drop off his bus at Hyde Park Corner and walk through St James's Park to his office in the Yard. Bowler tipped forward, cigar going well, he looked like a senior civil servant. The likeness went further. Hannam's speech like his brain was tidy, precise and to the point, though his humour often had a cutting edge. Success sat easily on his well-draped shoulders. He had a suit for each day of the week and wore them in careful rotation. His favourite drink was Scotch and ginger ale, his favourite cigar a Henry Clay Havana.

During his service he was respected, envied and sometimes feared. His superiors occasionally used him for 'rubber heel jobs' which in underworld slang means enquiries into internal discipline. But the men who worked with him always said, 'The Count' was the best governor in the world.

So in the summer of 1956 a black saloon car from the central pool at Scotland Yard drew up outside Eastbourne's Police Station and out stepped 'The Count'. The majesty and serenity of Eastbourne was about to be shattered by one of the strangest murder enquiries of all time. Hannam had the task of finding out if a doctor in the town had wilfully and quietly murdered old and lonely women after becoming a beneficiary in their wills, or whether a kind doctor in the town, who had been so attentive to the old ladies in their last days, had become a victim of jealous tongues and hate.

In this task, Hannam enjoyed the considerable help of Charlie Hewitt. Industrious, with a terrier-like tenacity, Detective-Sergeant Charles Hewitt just had to be policeman. He was the fourth generation of his family in the Force.

Charlie Hewitt was actually born in the same room at Wokingham Police Station as his father. Now his son, the fifth generation Hewitt to join the force, works as a police solicitor.

Charlie Hewitt, the Detective-Sergeant number two to Hannam, eventually retired as a Detective Chief Superintendent himself. Now aged 71, he is the 35th President of the ex-CID Officers Association. A longtime friend and colleague of Metropolitan Police Commissioner, Sir Kenneth Newman, Charlie is proud of his reputation as a painstaking and scrupulously honest copper. In a long and distinguished career he never received a single complaint docket against him.

Dapper and fastidious in his own dress, something that appealed to his 'governor', his smiling friendly manner concealed a determined toughness. That tough streak came in handy in 1948 when Charlie Hewitt was hand-picked for the dangerous job of acting as decoy for the fabulous London Airport bullion raid. Hewitt, then on the Yard's Flying Squad, took the place of a BOAC security officer. He was gagged and bound and pretended to be drugged so as to later identify the raiders. A more than adequate 'number two' for Hannam.

The two detectives were not exactly welcomed with open arms during their Eastbourne enquiries. And Charlie Hewitt remembers it well:

'You must remember the time and the place. Eastbourne not long after the war was a very wealthy, very close-knit community and a very snobby place.'

'Bodkin Adams was connected with everyone of importance in the place and half the county of Sussex as well. The Police Chief was a personal friend – his own doctor was Adams. Everyone had turned a blind eye and closed ranks to look after their own. After all, who could really suspect the town's leading doctor whose patients included anyone who was anyone.'

'The local police were unco-operative, apart from Bryn Pugh, and sometimes obstructive. We were the rotten fish that had been thrown into a smart cocktail party – and no one liked the smell!'

'To be fair to Richard Walker, the Chief Constable, he admitted to Bert Hannam that in delaying calling us in he had made the biggest mistake of his career.'

During the late summer of 1956 and on into autumn the murder enquiry made headlines all over the world, with the exception of the *Daily Express* whose coverage of the event was minimal in comparison. Chief crime reporter for the *Express* at the time was long-serving Percy Hoskins, originally a Dorset lad whose name had been and was to be by-lined on many major crime stories.

But Hoskins did not like Hannam. At the Yard there were two teams playing at the time – those who liked Hannam and those who did not. One can only suppose that Hoskins wanted Hannam to fail, and he was successful in steering the *Express* editorial executives into playing down the enquiry.

Hannam was not a man you could rush to like. Perhaps because he had to be, he was aloof and dispassionate. Whatever was to be the result no newspaperman or reader could deny the immense interest – yes, worldwide – that the 'Eastbourne Job' was providing.

Even if the outcome was debatable, it was still a damn good story which tickled the curiosity of writer and reader alike. So for the *Express* to play it down was ridiculous. It also put their reporter, Arthur Chesworth, in an invidious position. Every hour of the day and most of the night with the rest of the reporters he was running around Eastbourne and south Sussex, picking up new interviews, leads and stories. Like the rest of them he was writing copy. But unlike the others, only a few of his stories were being printed by the *Express* and sometimes those which were printed were so watered down by sub-editors, no doubt on instructions, that they hardly made sense and certainly could not have engendered much interest in the reader.

Among all the upheaval of the first hours and first days of the investigation the Chief Constable kept his head. Since time began, people fed up, worried, mentally ill or tired of life's turmoils have climbed up Beachy Head to end it all. They have fallen off, fainted off, jumped off and even driven off into the blue eternity in their motorcars. The Chief Constable, Mr Walker, gave a press conference and stood up bravely to a barrage of irritating, frustrating, incisive, a few important and sometimes even stupid questions. One reporter happened to mention Beachy Head, at which Mr Walker smiled for the first time and said: 'Keep Beachy Head out of this – it is the backbone of my business.'

By now – the last week in August, 1956 – the Yard's investigation had become intense. Hannam had nominated a number of detectives at the Central Office in London to work for him nationwide and six detectives in Eastbourne had been taken off all other duties to work by his side. Over the weeks, enquiries even spread abroad as police tried to find out how people had died; if Adams was their doctor and if and why they had alarmingly changed their wills in his favour. Like no other enquiry, it was consistently blocked by the ages of the possible victims and the time lag between their deaths and the commencement of investigation. Most of the dead were old and their relatives were either dead themselves or so old that their conversation and evidence could not be relied upon. Hardly one of them would be accepted as a witness in court. Even tracing relatives – and most times they were found to have died – took hundreds of hours of police time.

But Hannam and his superiors in London could see a pattern emerging. There was certainly the fullest possible suspicion and new grounds for the investigation to continue and reach a positive conclusion. Two elderly sisters who had died years ago were exhumed and the graves of other women in the area were photographed with exhumation in mind.

The sisters were the Misses Neil-Miller – 'the inseparable sisters from Scotland'. When Miss Hilda Neil-Miller died she bequeathed her entire estate to her sister Clara who died in February the following year bequeathing the majority of her money to Dr Adams. The sisters were buried together in Langney Cemetery, Eastbourne, in a sandstone grave covered with brown granite stones.

Although post-mortems were held on the bodies of both sisters, forensic scientists could find nothing to assist the police other than the fact Clara had died of pneumonia and not coronary thrombosis, as Adams had stated on the death certificate. But Hannam regarded their deaths as among the most sinister in his fattening portfolio. How was it that in the last year of her life Clara had not received one of fourteen letters sent to her by her sister-in-law from Bournemouth? How was it that in turn the sister-in-law had not received her normal monthly letter from Clara throughout that entire year?

Hannam's dossier on the 'Eastbourne Job' was reaching colossal proportions: the circumstantial evidence, the similarity of demise and bequests, of devastating confirmation in the view of Hannam and Hewitt, that Dr Adams was a murderer. And the motive was for gain.

Towards the end of Hannam's inquiries, and after all his findings had been forwarded to the Director of Public

Prosecutions, Rodney Hallworth had a quiet drink with the Yard detectives in an almost empty Beachy Head hotel on a winter's night that was anything but quiet.

It was a night tailor-made for murder talk. Clouts of wind shook the building, rain spat on the windows and the heaving sea far below was a frightening mass of white water. In the doubtful warmth of the lounge bar Hannam, as usual, was pale and formal. Hewitt fidgeting, his nose twitching like a rabbit alert for a nearby fox.

The barmaid, sensing this was no meeting of the East Sussex WI, poured the beers, took the money and tip with a subdued 'Ta', and pointedly engrossed herself in a faded copy of *True Romance*.

Hannam took out a Henry Clay Havana from its case, struck a match and puffed the cigar alight. Smoke framed his face in a veil of gossamer, the barmaid absently brushed ash from the nipple-end of her sweater, while Hewitt drew a nervous doodle with his finger in a beer pool on the counter. Both men were desperately tired from hundreds of investigative hours. Hannam squared his shoulders, glanced around the near-deserted bar and said quietly and clearly:

'I am quite confident Adams is a mass-murderer. He has certainly killed fourteen people. If we had arrived on the scene years ago, I think I could have said he killed more.'

Hewitt looked up at his boss:

'Don't exaggerate, Guv'nor. He only killed nine but our job is going to be proving it. Too much water has flowed under the bridge.' Hannam was six years too late on the spot when he spoke: Hewitt was six months ahead with his prediction.

Charlie Hewitt remembers that stormy night in the Beachy Head 'pub:

'That night I underestimated the number of murders and so did Bert Hannam. We made those claims mid-way through the investigation. With the benefit of hindsight and a great deal more painstaking investigation I put the figure much higher. Twenty five, in fact.

'Bodkin Adams was the beneficiary in 132 wills. I think he helped many of those people on their way. He eased them out of this life – often for gain – although, again with hindsight, he may have also genuinely given some a welcome release from pain.'

# Chapter Four

*'Mrs Kilgour is dead. You realise, Doctor, that you have killed her.'*                    NURSE OSGOOD

By the time the detectives had finished their enquiries a mass of circumstantial evidence had been unearthed. Statements obtained from local solicitors and bank managers testifying to Dr Adams' insatiable concern with the last wills and testaments of many of his patients: of visits to banks with patients to change details of wills already made: of telephone calls to solicitors insisting on immediate attendance to change, or draw up a new will: of guiding the hand of a comatose patient to sign with an 'X' his last will. All this and more Hannam with his colleagues had dug up.

Hannam believed that Adams altered wills on several occasions so that the deceased were cremated instead of being buried as originally stipulated. Hannam also told Hallworth of evidence obtained that in the last few days of one woman's life Adams forged 32 cheques amounting to £18,000. And of two other women whom Adams influenced to leave their house and live in a flat. Adams then sold their house and for three years kept the money, only being forced to reimburse the women after the service of a writ. Of the time in 1953 when Adams went into one house where a woman had just died and asked to see the will. When told he was not named as a beneficiary, Adams was reported as saying:

'Well, I deserve something for looking after her!'

Thereupon, according to Hannam's witness, Adams rummaged trough the house, picked up a new typewriter and several bric-à-brac, placed these articles in his car and drove off.

And as a picture of Adams as, at the very least, a greedy, avaricious, self-interested man began to emerge, another episode was revealed to further blacken an already tarnished image. And this came from Mrs Mawhood, one of the first people to befriend Adams in his early Eastbourne days, even to the extent of loaning Adams £3,000 to purchase his house in Trinity Trees.

As William Mawhood lay dying, his wife Edith was asked by Adams to leave the bedside a moment. Mrs Mawhood waited outside the bedroom door and heard Adams say:

'Leave your estate to me and I'll look after your wife.'

Mrs Mawhood said of that time:

'I rushed back into the bedroom, grabbed my gold-headed walking stick and struck out at the doctor, and chased him around the bed. He ran out of the room and as he dashed down the stairs I threw my stick at him. Unfortunately, it missed and broke a flower vase. I shouted to him to get out of the house. It was the last I wanted to see of him. I certainly would not tolerate the idea of Adams trying to get into my husband's will.'

William Mawhood died soon after at his house in Prideaux Road, Eastbourne. Said Mrs Mawhood:

'Before my husband died Adams wanted him to sign a cheque for medical fees. I believed the cheque should have been made out to all three doctors of the practice. But Adams said, 'Make it out only to me'. But this was refused and no cheque was issued then. After my husband's death the doctor put in a bill for £500, which in no way matched the treatment or medicines. The trustees of the estate refused to pay that amount and Adams settled for something smaller.'

Thus Adams repaid the Mawhood's kindness.

But such odious machinations performed by Dr Adams were hardly the stuff capital charge legal cases are built upon.

Hannam had listed *nine* cases on which to provide detailed reports for the Director of Public Prosecutions Office to consider. That Hannam had portrayed Adams as a sinister, parsimonious, evil hog of a man, there was no doubt. The East Sussex Coroner had also called into doubt Adams' medical capabilities, but was the Doctor a murderer; indeed, was he guilty of mass-murder? Had Hannam unearthed sufficient evidence for the DPP to agree to a prosecution?

Years had gone by, two at least, twenty in one case, since the demise of patients of Dr Adams under investigation. Many had been cremated in any case and far beyond the Yard's forensic skills. Relatives and one-time witnesses were either dead themselves or so old their testimony from the witness box would be a prosecutor's nightmare.

Did all or any one of Hannam's cases contain the sort of evidence the Crown would consider overwhelming in a court of law? Apart from 'Bobbie' Hullett and Clara Neil-Miller, Hannam's report included:

## The case of Mrs Edith Alice Morrell.

She was the widow of a wealthy Liverpool food importer, Alfred Morrell, who also had considerable interests in shipping. Her son assumed the business mantle after his father's death and Mrs Morrell left her Cheshire home to live in her Eastbourne house, 'Marden Ash', a ten-bedroom mansion in exclusive Beachy Head Road.

Mrs Morrell was crippled with severe arthritis, a condition which made her crotchety and unpredictable. Her passion was growing dahlias. Her greatest ambition was to win the 'Samuel Arno Silver Cup' for dahlias, presented annually by the Eastbourne Horticultural Society. This her gardener, James Carter, achieved for her in 1948 and again in 1949. Two species of dahlia were named after Mrs Morrell, species still grown today, the 'Edith Morrell' and 'Marden Ash'. Large terra cotta blooms, very popular with nurserymen.

Adams became Mrs Morrell's doctor soon after she took up residence in Eastbourne. In the spring of 1949 she went north to visit her son Arthur at his home, 'Thors Hill', Thurstaston, Cheshire. The family business was thriving and with Arthur's frequent trips to the United States, his mother thought it fair to go to Cheshire at times to save Arthur some of the many trips to Eastbourne he made.

In Cheshire, Mrs Morrell suffered a heart attack. She was attended by a Dr Turner and a consultant, Dr Pemberton, at first in a private room in the Cheshire Hospital. For ten days Mrs Morrell remained in hospital before returning to her son's home, and some weeks later travelled to Eastbourne by car to a nursing home in Grassington Road. Dr Adams had her moved to the Esperance nursing home where he sent many of his patients. But Mrs Morrell was not comfortable there and moved into the Cumberland Hotel, into a suite she knew well and where she stayed every year when the staff at 'Marden Ash' were on holiday.

Night nurses attended Mrs Morrell at the Cumberland, for she was still partially paralysed after the heart attack. Early in 1950 she went back to 'Marden Ash'. A team of day and night nurses cared for her and the visits of Dr Adams became more frequent.

Mrs Morrell was a capricious will-maker. In the last five years of her life she made seven. In the first she made in Eastbourne, Adams was to inherit £1,000. In her next three wills he was not even mentioned. Mrs Morrell's bequests to Adams varied according to her humour. In March 1949 she drafted a will leaving to Adams the entire residue of her estate. In a codicil to a later will, dated July 1950, she left him her home and chattels, providing her son had died before her. In her last will, dated August 24th, 1950, she left Adams an oak chest containing silver. Three weeks later, and only eight weeks before she died, she sent for her solicitor, Mr Hubert Sogno, and made a codicil, the only purpose of which was to cut Dr Adams entirely out of her will.

This codicil was effected and under her last will Adams received the oak chest containing silver by favour of her son Arthur, together with her Rolls-Royce and an Elizabethan cupboard he had on a number of occasions expressed a desire to own.

During his years as Mrs Morrell's doctor, Adams took a particular interest in her will-making. On March 8th, 1950, Adams hurried from 'Marden Ash' to her solicitor's office and asked to see him urgently. Adams told Mr Sogno that Mrs Morrell had forgotten to leave him in her last will her Rolls-Royce and box of jewellery which she had earlier promised him. Adams made a point of mentioning that her mind was clear, though he did not mention that he was prescribing drugs for his patient.

The solicitor suggested that Dr Adams should pretend to accept the jewellery box to please the old lady but then hand it back to a nurse in another room. This did not suit Adams. He protested that Mrs Morrell seriously wanted him to enjoy the gifts.

Mr Sogno thought about this. He knew, because the nurses had told him, that it was the wish of Mrs Morrell that they should not be in the room when the Doctor attended her. One result of this was that there were few instances of witnessed conversation between Dr Adams and his patient. Was that enforced confidentiality really Adams' idea?

The solicitor then suggested the matter wait for Arthur Morrell's next visit to Eastbourne that coming weekend. The Doctor disagreed. The solicitor then reminded Adams of some gifts Mrs Morrell had made by cheque some months earlier, gifts that later Mrs Morrell regretted.

Adams pursued the matter and told Mr Sogno to prepare a codicil for the gifts which could be destroyed later if the son did not approve. The solicitor refused and told Adams that was quite impossible. The Doctor thereupon left the solicitor's office.

The Yard's investigations had shown that by this time Mrs Morrell was receiving massive doses of drugs, mainly morphine. It was Hannam's contention that the old lady was already addicted to the drugs that Adams at first supplied in small but continuously increasing quantities for the nine months before her death. These drugs, claimed Hannam, became so massive toward the end that they killed her.

On one occasion Mrs Morrell telephoned the Doctor while he was on a shooting holiday in Scotland and asked him to return immediately. He did.

Why? asked Hannam. Because one of his 1,500 patients was ill? No, the report continued, surely it was because Doctor Adams knew that Mrs Morrell had run out of the drugs he had given her a craving for, and that in a drug-free moment of lucidity might cut him out of her will or dismiss him altogether and engage another doctor.

Hannam also believed that after Mrs Morrell tried to cut Adams out of her will, in the codicil to her seventh will, his impatience overcame him. It may have been, reasoned Hannam, that a better scheme than coaxing himself back into the will, a problem that seemed now insurmountable, would be to kill her, then present her executors with an inflated bill for his services. Such logic seemed confirmed for Hannam, because the fact was disclosed that Adams did present a large bill after his patient's death – for £1,750. A bill that was paid by Mrs Morrell's executors.

Long after Adams presented this bill he told a friend:

'These old women leave me things in their wills instead of fees. They never pay you a penny and if you present a bill they talk about changing their doctor. So, you have to wait and hope that you'll be lucky enough to recoup your fees in the form of a bequest in the will. One can't send one's bills for fees to the executors. It's just not done!'

But Adams did that very thing and had done so on numerous occasions!

## The case of Mrs Julia Bradnum.

In brief, Mrs Bradnum was a strong healthy woman of 82. And on the evening of May 26, 1952 was seen to be well and in good spirits. The following morning she awoke with stomach pains. Adams was called. He remained in the bedroom for five minutes. Ten minutes later she was dead. The Yard exhumed her body also, but it was too decomposed to assist the enquiry, other than to show she did not die of a cerebral haemorrhage as Adams had stated on her death certificate.

Mrs Bradnum lived in a three-bedroomed house at Coppers Hill, Willingdon, on the outskirts of Eastbourne. The house with its neat rose garden has a fine open view of the South Downs. The last day of Mrs Bradnum's life was described by a close friend, Miss Mary Hine:

'With Mrs. Bradnum, some friends had arranged to go on a coach trip that Tuesday. Mrs Bradnum always rose early but was not about so we decided to let her sleep a little more. Later I went up as she was still in bed, she said, "I've got terrible pains in my stomach". She asked for a glass of warm water and bicarbonate of soda.

'I thought she was not looking too well, so I went to a friend's house up the road and telephoned the Doctor's house. He was out but his secretary said he was visiting in the Willingdon area and as she knew where he was she could contact him quickly.

'I tried to get a nurse but couldn't. When I returned to the house I saw Dr Adams coming out of Mrs Bradnum's bedroom. He said she was dead. I was completely shocked. I had only been out of the house for about a half-hour.

'Only a few weeks before Mrs Bradnum died she told me that Dr Adams had brought her a new will. He said something about her other will not being legal. She asked me if I would witness the new one. On the appointed day I went into the living room and Dr Adams pointed to a spot on the paper where I was to sign. I turned over the double piece of paper to see what I was witnessing but Dr Adams put his hand on the writing and turned back the paper. He said, "Would you please sign here, Miss Hine". As soon as I did Dr Adams opened the door and ushered me out.

'Mrs Bradnum was present of course and so was a smartly-dressed woman whom the Doctor introduced as his cousin, Miss Henry. Earlier Mrs Bradnum had told me that the Reverend Mr Ingram and Mr Muddell of Barclays Bank, Willingdon, were to be the executors of her will. But after her death I noticed that Dr Adams was the sole executor.'

A niece of Mrs Bradnum's, Mrs Lily Love, who lived in Bakewell Road, Eastbourne, was similarly shocked at her aunt's sudden death, having seen her well and cheerful on the Saturday, before she died on the Tuesday.

Mr and Mrs Love were so puzzled by events that when rumours were sweeping the town after 'Bobbie' Hullett's death, the Love's wrote a letter to the Chief Constable suggesting that Mrs Bradnum's death, too, was suspicious.

### The case of Mrs Emily Louise Mortimer.

Another widow, Mrs Mortimer died on Christmas Eve, 1946, at Tredegar nursing home, Eastbourne. She was certified dead by her own doctor, Adams, who gave the cause of death as 'cerebral thrombosis'. In her last months, Mrs Mortimer had added a codicil to her will. Shares in the Carron Iron and Steel Company – (worth about £3,000) – believed to have been originally intended for two nieces, were transferred instead, through the codicil, to Adams. This brought the total bequest to Adams to £5,000 having been mentioned earlier in the will to benefit by £2,000.

### The case of Mrs Harriet Maud Hughes.

The final chapter in the life of Mrs Hughes, yet another widow, was told by her domestic help, Mrs Irene Swaine:
'I always thought there was something funny about her death in 1951. It was too sudden. On the Tuesday before she died she seemed quite well. On the Thursday when I called again she was in bed and seemed in a coma. The following day she died. There were times towards the end when she did not seem to be herself or in her right mind.

'She had been taking sleeping tablets. I assume they were prescribed by Dr Adams. There were many bottles of medicine in the room.

Dr Adams started to come to the flat in King Edward Road three months before she died. I am certain that towards the end she was completely under the Doctor's influence. She spoke of changing her will. A few weeks before her death she became ill but then recovered sufficiently to go to her bank in Meads with Dr Adams.

'The Doctor asked the bank manager to make him the executor of her will. Adams explained it was Mrs Hughes' express wish. When Mrs Hughes returned home and after the Doctor had left she told me, "You should have seen the bank manager's face when I told him what I intended. He was most surprised at my choice of executor".'

Mrs Hughes died on November 29th, 1951, aged 66, as a result of cerebral thrombosis according to Adams. The previous July Mrs Hughes had added a codicil to her will that she should be cremated. A month later, in August, another codicil was added, this to leave £1,000 each to a Mr and Mrs Thurston, acquaintances of Dr Adams.

The Yard believed the Thurston codicil was a ruse of Adams. After death Adams was alleged to have received ninety per cent of their bequests – giving the Thurstons ten per cent for the use of their name.

## The case of James Priestly Downs.

Downs was a widower, a wealthy, retired bank manager, who in his last days, tried nine times while in an almost drugged state to sign his will. On the tenth occasion he signed it with an 'X'. Adams guided his hand. In the will Adams was a beneficiary.

The incredible situation was that all Mr Downs had suffered was a fractured ankle when Adams had him taken to a local nursing home. After a fortnight of Adams' treatment Downs was in a coma. A month after he had received his accident James Downs died.

A friend of Mr Downs, Mr Frederick Nash, stated:

'I was surprised to see Mr Downs in such a bad condition when he had only recently entered the nursing home with a fractured ankle. He had hurt himself falling down the stairs at home, rushing to catch the post. I could never understand either why he remained in hospital so long for such a comparatively minor fracture.'

Another close friend, the Reverend Canon F. Hilton Jackson said:

'In April 1955 when I heard that Mr Downs had broken his ankle, I went to visit him. I was completely surprised. He was lying in bed, his mouth wide open, his eyes glazed and he hardly seemed to be breathing. I am certain he didn't recognise me.'

Canon Jackson added:

'Some months before, Mr Downs told me he was annoyed with Dr Adams because while he was ill with a minor complaint the Doctor had sat on the edge of the bed and stroked his hand. He felt it was peculiar conduct for a doctor.'

It seemed to Hannam that Canon Jackson's statement was borne out by evidence that in the previous November, six months before his death, Downs in a fit of temper had burnt a will. He later drafted another will but did not sign it until shortly before he died – with an 'X' and with Adams to guide his hand. Adams benefited to the extent of £1,000 under the terms of the new will.


The case of Mrs Annabella Kilgour.

Mrs Kilgour, a widow, lived in Staveley Road, Eastbourne, and had been ill for several weeks, being looked after by a State Registered Nurse, Miss Osgood. On December 27th, 1950, Adams visited Mrs Kilgour and Nurse Osgood reported she seemed restless.

Adams replied that he would give Mrs Kilgour an injection to help her get a good night's sleep. The Nurse was astounded as she watched the Doctor give an injection which she regarded as being greatly in excess of the normal dose, particularly in view of Mrs Kilgour's age.

'This will keep her quiet,' Adams said.

Mrs Kilgour at once fell into a coma and died the next morning. When Adams arrived Nurse Osgood told him:

'Mrs Kilgour is dead. You realise, Doctor, that you have killed her?'

The Nurse told the Yard:

'I have never seen a man look so frightened in my life.'

Once again Dr Adams gave the cause of death as cerebral haemorrhage. In her will Mrs Kilgour left Dr Adams cash and an antique clock.

During the course of the Yard's enquiries a number of intriguing matters came to their attention. Although bearing a relevance they could not ignore, they were not of legal significance, highly illuminating notwithstanding. One such example was the matter of Mrs Margaret Pilling.

Mrs Pilling, quite simply, was a widow who lived – through the foresight of her family. This member of one of Lancashire's richest cotton families was suffering from nothing more serious than a bout of influenza early in 1951, when her doctor, Adams, was called to her.

Within a fortnight, following heavy drugging, she was 'practically in a coma'. Nurses agreed she should be taken away from Eastbourne. Fourteen days after she left the town and Dr Adams' care, she was sufficiently recovered to attend a London wedding.

The account of Mrs Pilling's treatment at the hands of Dr Adams was told by her daughter, Mrs Irene Richardson, of Cadogan Square in Chelsea:

'My mother was the widow of Walter Pilling, Chairman of Joshua Hoyles, the cotton spinners. She went down with flu. Dr Adams was prescribing pills for her every few hours. After a short while she was practically in a coma and there were times she couldn't recognise me.

'We thought she was dying of cancer and that the Doctor was being kind by not telling us. But we held a family conference and decided we were not satisfied with the treatment. Whatever her illness, she was definitely being drugged. Her condition was deteriorating rapidly.

'There was a showdown with the Doctor, and after taking advice and consulting the nurses we decided to take my mother away. We took a house for her at Ascot near one of her relatives. Within a very short time she was up on her feet, attending Ascot races and a wedding in London.

'Had I not taken her away I am quite satisfied she would have died there. I am perfectly certain that in taking my mother away from Eastbourne I saved her life.'

From such statements, from the spoor-fading evidence of years past, Hannam made his report to the Director of Public Prosecutions.

There was substantial circumstantial evidence. The amount of morphia and heroin injected into Mrs Morrell in the last weeks of her life, for example. But was it enough?

The exhumation of three women was inconclusive. True, the details written by Doctor Adams on those particular death certificates were wrong as to the cause of death but was that in itself completely damning evidence? It was thought doubtful.

Although Hannam, Hewitt, Pugh and the rest had done their best, was it enough? The Yard was convinced that Adams was a murderer, indeed they thought he had killed many times. The study of the Adams character convinced Hannam the Doctor had killed for reward. Although the individual amounts varied between a few hundred and a few thousand, the total was – in the early 1950's – formidable; £45,000 in cash bequests, plus valuable chattels – jewellery, antiques, and of course the two Rolls-Royce limousines.

But the decision lay with the Attorney-General. What charges, other than the capital one of murder, lay available? Hannam and Richard Walker thought, fraud, a forgery charge could hold the Doctor for questioning. With the capital charge hanging over his head, the Doctor might crack and confess. In the event and later, there would be two other charges, those of the wilful attempt to conceal certain drugs and the obstruction of the Police in their enquiries.

It was decided to pursue the capital charge, if at all possible, and it was to this end that Hannam would interview Adams. At first, informally, and later more formally with the legal requirement of the phrase, 'I must warn you anything that you say ...'

In fact, Hannam was to interview Adams four times. On the evening of October 1st, 1956, Hannam was, by chance, passing the Doctor's house in Trinity Trees when Adams drove into his garage. Hannam had a conversation with Adams in which reference was made to the chest of silver left to Adams in Mrs Morrell's will. In that conversation Adams had said:

'Mrs Morrell was a very dear patient. She insisted a long time before she died that I should have it in her memory. I never wanted it. I am a bachelor and I never use it. I know she was going to leave it to me and her Rolls-Royce. She told me she had left it to me in her will. Oh, yes, and another cabinet.'

Hannam reminded Adams that on the Morrell cremation form he had declared that he was not a beneficiary under her will. The Doctor replied:

'Oh, that was not done wickedly. God knows it was not!' Adams went on to explain that he did not want the 'dear relatives upset' and that 'he liked cremations to go off smoothly'.

That informal meeting was, and was so intended, a shake-up for Adams. The next interviews was increasingly nerve-racking for the Eastbourne physician. On November 24th, a warrant was exercised and the Doctor's house searched for dangerous drugs. The third interview was on November 26th, at the Eastbourne Police Station and was at the request of Doctor Adams who said to Hannam: 'You told Mr James, my solicitor, there might be other charges. I am worried. What are they?'

During the course of this interview Hannam told Adams:

'I am still enquiring into the death of some of your patients, Doctor.'

Adams: 'Which?'

Hannam: 'Mrs Morrell is certainly one.'

Adams: 'Easing the passing of a dying person is not all that wicked. She wanted to die – that cannot be murder. It is impossible to accuse a doctor.'

The Attorney-General Sir Reginald Manningham-Buller had made up his mind upon which case to prosecute the Doctor. Again Hannam and Hewitt were summoned to the elegant oak-panelled office within the House of Commons, its blue leather chairs resplendent with the Commons portcullis upon their backs.

Present were the Director of Public Prosecutions, Sir Edwin Matthews, and two doctors. Charlie Hewitt recalls the scene: 'Manningham-Buller asked the doctors two questions. They were about the administration of a heroin dosage, and, what would happen to a patient if no subsequent action was taken by a doctor.

'The Attorney-General listened to their replies and then turned to Bert. "Hannam", he said, "Go down to Eastbourne now and charge Adams with the murder of Mrs Morrell!"

Bert pointed out that he would have to obtain a warrant, so it was agreed we should go in the morning, and then left the Attorney-General's office.

'We were both sick with disbelief, after the announcement that Manningham-Buller was going for Mrs Morrell.'

'It was madness when we had so many better cases and what's more important *with bodies!* Bert and I were shattered. We had gone into the meeting believing that the charge would be manslaughter. We had more than enough to convict on that.'

'But there was nothing we could do but say "Yes, Sir". We were only there out of courtesy. In those days we weren't expected to speak unless spoken to, in that exalted company. There was no way we could have gone up against Manningham-Buller.'

Hewitt continued:

'It was clear to see what happened. The Attorney-General thought it would be an easy charge to prove because of the overwhelming amount of evidence. And so it should have been.'

'But I don't think Manningham-Buller was fully concentrating on the case. He regarded it as an easy vehicle for his personal advancement but he didn't really work at it enough.'

The times may have had a bearing on this lack of concentration. Sir Reginald Manningham-Buller had been Attorney-General (1954–1962) during a period that coincided with the fear that the highest echelons of the British Secret Service had been infiltrated.

Philby, Blunt, Blake, the 1950s had wrought a series of disasters upon the intelligence services. It can be imagined that even the broad shoulders of the Attorney-General of those times would sag under such a weighty burden of knowledge.

It is only fair to record that at this crucial time the prosecution of the Eastbourne Doctor for murder could well not have occupied the forefront of his mind.

The fourth and arrest interview took place on December 19th, 1956, when Hannam with Pugh and accompanied by Hewitt called upon the Doctor by appointment. Hannam wasted no time:

'Doctor, on November 13th, 1950, a patient of yours, a Mrs Morrell, died and you certified the cause of death to be cerebral thrombosis. I am going to arrest you and take you to the local police headquarters where you will be charged with the murder of Mrs Morrell.'

Thereupon Hannam cautioned the Doctor that what he said may and could be used in evidence against him.

Adams looked stunned. There was a pregnant pause as he looked from Hannam to Hewitt and Pugh. At last he said:

'Murder'? then continued, 'I do not think you could prove it was murder – she was dying in any event.'

Adams then went with the detectives. The Doctor, seeing his receptionist in the hall, asked that she should get his overcoat. His voice was that of a severely shaken man. Miss Lawrence herself was distraught but did as she was bid returning with a coat and a few books.

As Adams shrugged into his overcoat she caught hold of his hand, her tears began to flow; Adams said quietly:

'I will see you in heaven.'

And then Doctor Adams was driven to the Eastbourne Police Station, there to be indoctrinated into the degrading ritual of an accused man: the documentation; the formal charge; the fingerprinting; the locking-up. It was a salutory experience. There were to follow another almost a hundred days of remand in various prisons. Eastbourne, Lewes and finally Brixton before his trial at the Old Bailey.

So the Director of Public Prosecutions had made his decision, the charge was to be that of murder – the case, Mrs Edith Alice Morrell. Though to say the DPP had made *his* decision is only partially true. His was the total legal voice of accusation but his office had received plenty of advice. Under the law of England the capital murder charge involving poisoning requires prosecution by the Attorney-General himself, at this time the impressively large and theatrical figure of Sir Reginald Manningham-Buller, QC (the late Lord Dilhorne). He would be assisted by the doughty, abrasive Mr Melford Stevenson, QC, and Mr William Morris.

There were to be numerous meetings, later, when the case was entered upon the calendar. But the balance of Crown opinion lay with Manningham-Buller and the Yard's reports and opinions. Knowing that only details of matters relevant to Mrs Morrell's demise would be allowed in court and that the mass of damaging similarity in questionable circumstances concerning other deaths would remain locked in New Scotland Yard reports, did Manningham-Buller stake his faith in the Adams case on his ability to break down the pious Doctor with known character flaws? To rip him apart in the witness box?

Charlie Hewitt had no doubt:

'The Attorney-General was a political animal who saw this case as a chance to make political capital. He wanted the kudos and the glory. He thought he could get them by breaking Adams in the dock. And perhaps he could have done. The Doctor was a worried man and had come close to breaking down with us already. The pressure was certainly on him and he might well have cracked.'

So the Doctor was charged with murder, subsequently to appear in front of Eastbourne Magistrates to be remanded for committal proceedings and later arraigned to be presented at the Central Criminal Courts of the Old Bailey to appear before Sir Patrick (later Lord) Devlin. There a capital crime trial would make English legal history.

For Dr Adams, Mr Geoffrey Lawrence, QC, would lead the defence. A barrister, tenacious of purpose, meticulous in preparation, more widely known in the divisions of Treasury and Admiralty pleading and mightily successful. As a defence barrister, however, an unknown quantity. Yet the history of leading figures called to the bar sparkles with those who made their reputation and attained public recognition through a murder trial.

The newspapers continued to enjoy a series of field days. Happily it is not often a doctor is accused of murder in the U.K. And it was rare, although perhaps understandable, for so much publicity, to attend upon an accused before he stood in the dock. In fact, the amount of adverse publicity the Doctor was receiving at the hands of the press was of concern to the prosecution, paradoxical though that may seem.

The point being it was not unknown for a trial judge in face of prejudicial publicity to try and tilt the scales of justice back to their point of equilibrium but in thus trying to be fair weigh those scales a trifle in the opposite direction, and without so intending, favour the accused. This was the prosecution's fear. Yet, their fear was alleviated. The judge's summing up was a masterpiece of jurisprudence.

Still, one could hardly blame the press. This case was one almost without precedence in English legal history. True, doctors had been accused of murder before but a mere handful in a proven macabre history that stretched only 134 years at the date of Dr Adams's trial.

It was 1823 in Paris that the first doctor was caught out in murder; through poison being detected in his victim's body. The art of post-mortem began to tell the lurid truth. With the arrest of Dr Edme Castaing, charged with murdering two brothers by administering morphine in order to gain from a known bequest, the centuries of almost fashionable poisonings were at an end. If the authorities could detect a doctor's knowledgeable hand, how could an ordinary nostrum pedlar escape arrest? The old profession of spouse-remover and inheritance-provider belonged to the past – buried along with the Borgias and Brinvilliers. Toxicology and medical jurisprudence stalked the poisoner hand in hand.

The popular arsenic, that powder tasteless, colourles and odourless, indiscernible in both delicate broths or heavy stews, with symptoms not unlike the endemic cholera that had purged Europe for ages, wained in its popularity. Toxicology had advanced its science to detect the cause of death from within the body. Arsenic, an irritant metallic poison, became easy to spot in a buried body, even though most of the body tissue had perished, for on exhumation the arsenic would remain in the immediate soil surround.

Poisoners needed more elusive substances, difficult to detect for years after burial, yet with symptoms that would not arouse premature suspicions. And in the forefront of such knowledge came the medical profession searching for alleviants and cures. And again, as usual with most scientific advances, for every positive advantage found in the treatment of the human body, an abuse of tincture provided an adverse effect. Vegetable drugs, chemical derivatives, the opiates – morphine, heroin; strychnine from 'nux vomica' the seed of an East Indian tree; caffeine from coffee; the coca shrub of the flax order in Bolivia and Peru – *Erythroxylon Coca* – yielded the alkaloid cocaine; quinine, an alkaloid contained in chinchona bark; from the plant genus, *scrophulariaceae*, came digitalin used as digitalis in certain forms of heart disease. New drugs and new technology with which to process them passed into medical and chemical knowledge.

There were many others. Such advantages in drug knowledge led in many cases to a more efficient, wider and safer range of anaesthetics. The medical practitioner now had available a variety of drugs to assist his healing art as never before: a medical practitioner now had available a greater choice of drugs with which to terminate life should that be his intended purpose.

In France, the sinister Dr Edme Castaing used morphine to murder the brothers Hippolyte and Auguste Ballet and, in 1823, became the first doctor sentenced to death for murder as the result of poison being detected in his victims's bodies.

In the 1860s, again in Paris, Dr Couty de la Pommerais, murdered first his wife and then his mistress by using digitalis. Once again 'Madame Guillotine' extracted final justice.

In Stafford, a Dr William Palmer used poison to remove the stygma of horrendous gambling debts that piled up as a result of his bad judgement of horseflesh. An accomplished poisoner who had killed many times before, Palmer grew careless and did not keep up with the growing science of toxicology. His use of arsenic, strychnine, antimony and prussic acid pills was a little too blatant. There was nothing of the finesse poisoner about William Palmer – 'Bill-the-Pill' was always in a hurry. Throughout the county of Staffordshire, Palmer was a much hated man and this hatred led to an Act of Parliament still in force today and known as 'The Palmer Act'. An Act with particular relevance to the 'Eastbourne Job'.

A special Bill was rushed through the House which provided the right for a prisoner to elect for trial in London, if he thought he wouldn't receive a fair hearing in his own district. Thus Dr William Palmer stood trial at the Old Bailey in May 1856, not that it did him much good, for he was found guilty and publicly hanged back in Stafford.

Three years later in July of 1859 another doctor found himself at the Old Bailey accused of murder. His name, Dr Thomas Smethurst. But his trial, admittedly incompetently prosecuted, gave rise to matters of medical jurisprudence that reverberate to the present day.

Dr Smethurst was accused of murdering Miss Isabella Banks, who he had bigamously married for her money. That Smethurst was an out-an-out scoundrel was no doubt and in Victorian England, sufficient to damn him in all eyes. His trial, therefore, became farcical in that, so many were attempting to hang him, the necessary evidence to procure the death sentence was, to say the least, vaguely circumstantial.

It was thought Smethurst killed by arsenic, as traces were found in waste produced by Miss Banks just prior to her death. When Smethurst was arraigned before Magistrates accused of attempting to cause her death, such evidence of poisoning was submitted by a Dr Taylor who performed the autopsy on Dr Palmer's final victim three years previously.

Incredibly the Magistrate allowed bail to permit Smethurst to return to his sick 'wife'. A day later Miss Banks died. Her autopsy was a shock for Dr Taylor. He found no traces of arsenic in her body. Yet his previous tests had found traces in her waste.

At the Old Bailey trial Dr Taylor admitted the first traces of arsenic had not come from Miss Banks at all but from the copper gauze with which he had carried out his tests. A phenomenon colloquially known as 'Paris Green', more correctly copper ethanoato-arsenate... Dr Taylor still maintained, however, that Smethurst had poisoned Miss Banks in some way.

The trial was a sensation. Everybody wanted Smethurst found guilty for he was blatantly such an odious man. The trial judge, Baron Pollack, aware of the shaky evidence, finally summed up over a nine hour period. In which, at one point, he said, 'I do not dwell upon the defence submission that the jury is being asked to decide which medical evidence of the two opposing groups was correct; death by poison or by natural means. While medical evidence was important, the jury in addition must look at all the factors and, in particular, at the conduct of the accused and at any motives he might have had for the crime with which he was charged. You, the jury, I remind, must be guided by the rules of commonsense; the commonsense which operates in the minds of reasonable men. Even if there was no medical evidence before you to evaluate, you would still be called on to decide on the guilt or innocence of the defendant.'

Forty minutes later the jury decided Smethurst was guilty of murder. The judge in sentencing Smethurst exercised a prerogative he enjoyed. And sentenced the Doctor to imprisonment, not to hang. The lack of evidence obviously playing a part in that decision.

The trial verdict caused an uproar. The jury was convinced it was murder proved. The judge had doubts. The public – particularly the intellectuals, were astounded at the findings. Guilty possibly, *but it had not been proved beyond all reasonable doubt!*

The strongest attack upon the verdict came, understandably, from the medical experts. *The Medical Times and Gazette* summed up their concern:

'Is the prisoner guilty? We believe he is. Was he proved guilty? Certainly not!'

The journal found that in their opinion while the balance of *probabilities* was against the doctor, there was a *possibility* that he might be innocent. This raised a point about medical evidence that would rear up in subsequent murder trials concerning members of the medical profession.

Ten medical witnesses had said that Miss Banks had died of poisoning. Seven others gave opinion that death was by natural causes. The journal went on:

'Here, at least, is a division of opinion in the skilled evidence which should make us pause...'

Sixty doctors and barristers, leaders in Victorian society, demanded the release of Smethurst or a retrial. The Government responded by appointing a leading surgeon to evaluate the evidence. He did so, confirming the opinion that Smethurst had not been proved guilty on the evidence available. A warranty of pardon was issued.

Smethurst was released, re-arrested, stood trial for bigamy, was sentenced to a year's imprisonment and upon release disappeared. Strange parallels related to the Smethurst trial would re-surface just over a century later.

Scotland, too, had its infamous doctor poisoner, Edward Pritchard. A religious zealot, who used antimony to bring about the premature demise of his victims. Dr Pritchard met justice at the gallows in the last public execution held in Glasgow, it was in 1865. Throughout his trial, witnesses testified to remarks from one of the doctor's victims: 'Strangely enough I feel well when I'm away from the Doctor – yet ill when near him…'

In England Dr George Lampson used aconitine to murder his brother-in-law, was detected, stood trial at the Old Bailey in 1882, found guilty and hanged.

And if toxicology and forensic science combined to bring the poisoner to justice, technology too began to assist in the detection and conviction of all criminals. The first use of wireless telegraphy to arrest a murderer was in 1910 and the man so arrested, upon the liner S.S. *Montreal* on passage to Canada, was yet another member of the medical profession, Dr Hawley Harvey Crippen, who, for love of a pretty typist, Ethel Le Neve, poisoned his wife Belle, with the narcotic drug lyscine. Crippen was convicted of murder at the Old Bailey and hanged on November 23rd, 1910.

To such cases of legal history was added that of Dr John Bodkin Adams, put up for trial at Court No. 1 of the Central Criminal Courts of the Old Bailey in March of 1957, charged with the murder of Mrs Edith Alice Morrell, six years previously.

# Chapter Five

*'...perhaps it is safe to assume the Doctor was not ignorant of the effects of drugs on human beings...'*
SIR REGINALD MANNINGHAM-BULLER, QC

The Central Criminal Courts of the Old Bailey, that sanctum sanctorum of English law, is not an old building in relation to the law itself, having been completed and first opened for business in 1834. By architecture more Victorian General Post Office than Town Hall but owing a fillial relationship to both. Inside, brick, stone, tile and wood combine to affect a museum-like appearance.

Court No. 1 is nothing more or less than a room. A large room, true. High ceilings under the roof where the main public gallery is set; high latticed windows beneath which the well of court is sunk. A room surprising by the amount of carved oak fitted haphazardly within, as though one early sentence for a misdemeanor constrained a master-carpenter to serve out his punishment by carving out and fitting together as many benches, tables, desks, boxes and steps as he could possibly cram-jam together in the space provided.

As a consequence, stained-oak juts at every conceivable angle to offend both the eye and trip the leg. Yet this apparent juxtaposition seats around two hundred people. Presiding over this area of oaken folly, is the Judicial Bench, and behind a high-backed red leather chair which assumes the focal point of the room. Across the well of court, directly opposite, and raised, but of course below the level of the Judge, sufficient, however, to block a true open view of the court by everyone else, stands square the prisoner's dock. To the side of both Judge and accused, jury benches provide a ringside view.

As the Judge and prisoner face each other across the well of court, between them, in a strange square pit, split by advocates' benches, lecterns and solicitors' tables the main drama of prosecution and defence pleading takes place.

Strangely this gynandrous mix works. Court No. 1 is neither folly nor farce but instead evokes a respectful mystic reverence in which one lowers the voice to a whisper even when no case is being heard. And like the High Priests of Temple, the only loud irreverencies come from barristers when wigless in their arena prior to the commencement of business.

Perhaps it is because of the physical constraint placed upon barristers during trial by jury under English law that the immediate minutes before a case begins see these black-gowned pleaders flapping about the court like vultures or eagles – depending on one's credenda – soaring above a juicy meal. The more important the case, the more flapping, swooping and conferring, for after all – the more important the case, the more there are of the species. In the matter of Regina v. Adams before Sir Patrick Devlin, for the Crown appeared the Attorney-General, Sir Reginald Manningham-Buller, QC, Mr Melford Stevenson, QC, and Mr William Morris.

For the Defence, Mr Geoffrey Lawrence, QC, Mr Edward Clarke, and Mr John Heritage. And these gentlemen were served by a bevy of solicitors and clerks.

A note might be in order here for those not acquainted with English jurisprudence on the role of the Barrister. It is simply this: barristers are members of the upper or advocacy branch of the legal profession in England. Barristers have the exclusive right of audience in all the superior courts to plead a case at the bar (his allotted place in court).

In England the right to call persons to the bar is vested in the four Inns of Court; Middle Temple, Inner Temple, Lincoln's Inn and Gray's Inn. Those intending to become barristers must join one of these Inns, eat dinners there, pass certain examinations. Each Inn exercises discipline over its members, subject to a right of appeal to the Judges. A barrister may not appear in court save on the instruction of a solicitor.

There are two grades of barrister, Juniors and Queen's Counsel (QC or KC depending on the monarch of the time), also known as 'silks' from the better quality of gown material and wig they are allowed to wear.

Situated between the City of London and Westminster, the four Inns of Court can trace their origin to around the end of the 13th century. Inner and Middle Temples are sited close to the Thames below Westminster, on land once occupied by the Knights Templar. Lincoln's Inn and Gray's Inn lie further north within the bounds of the City itself.

These are venerable institutions of legal training as it affects the advocacy branch of the profession. Originally, the clergy were involved in the study and practice of law until prevented by canon law from practising in secular courts. In 1290, Edward I set up commissions of enquiry, the results of which directed that students of law should be accommodated together close to the courts at Westminster.

Thus began a collegiate foundation, known as the Inns of Court and Chancery. And in the beginning embraced other Inns of learning, now long gone, the Chancery Inns of Barnard's, Clement's, Clifford's; the senior barristers' 'club' of Serjeants Inn.

In the constitutional changes during the 17th century, the old system of legal education disappeared. The study of law to be read at a number of universities spread throughout the country. And the modern four Inns of Court set a system of bar-advocacy in which only the 'benchers' of the four Inns may practise as an advocate in the appropriate court.

Barrister students having studied law elsewhere, are obliged by the Council of Legal Education, comprising delegates from the four Inns of Court, to attend lectures and classes as admitted members of one or other of the Inns. Every student is required to attend upon his Inn for a required number of lectures, examinations and dinners in Hall.

The choice or invitation of membership of a particular Inn is an account of a highly individual matter. Family connection perhaps, a college affiliation or one of somewhat more mundane import.

The well-known, not to say, satirically infamous and gloriously talented television producer Ned Sherrin, who was called to the bar as a member of Gray's Inn, made his choice based upon his opinion, 'That Gray's Inn had rather better dinners than the rest'.

Fortunately, Sherrin decided not to practise and entered the arguably less theatrical medium of television.

In 1966 the Inns and the Bar Council set up a senate, which now acts collectively in matters of discipline and legal education although each Inn retains its own constitution and finances.

Judges are appointed to the bench by the Lord Chancellor from a list of senior barristers with a minimum of seven years' experience, and are invariably QC's. Therefore, they are Inns of Court members. In England, at the time of the Adams trial, the total membership of the four Inns of Court comprised a little more than 11,500, including Commonwealth and non-practising members. The number of QC's approximated 350. It is, if not family, a close circle of acquaintanceship, a brethren of sorts: Brothers in Law?

If the Old Bailey could write its own autobiography it would parallel much of the Bible. After all, there would be contained within many names and fables; many dramas and miracles. The decisions of Solomon, the wrongdoings of Cain, the jealousies of Jezebel, the loves of Sheba, have been repeated many times. The human emotion, in all depths and shades of good through evil, paraded in public – a voyeur's paradise.

It was inevitable, following such pre-trial publicity that the public seats were crowded to overflowing. The first day of the Adams trial was suitably treated like the first night of a West

End play. Everyone turned up, and throughout the duration of the Adams trial, Court No. 1 took on the social connotations of an Ascot, a Wimbledon, a Henley occasion. Not only were the world's press present in force but visiting lawyers, law students, off-duty magistrates, doctors, teachers, debutantes, housewives and – on reflection not surprising – Thespians, for the atmosphere they said – the dialogue of the real thing! Yes, the theatre was well represented – but not only in the public galleries.

The suddenness with which Sir Patrick Devlin made his appearance startled all, save the workforce of lawyers, police, ushers. It was an almost stealthy suddenness – a puppet-like figure bewigged and clad in ermine and scarlet of judicial majesty as befitting the upholders of justice – in the name of Her Sovereign Majesty Elizabeth II. The Judge slid across the bench to his chair, paused a moment, his sharp featured intelligent head tilted sideways he acknowledged the formal courtesies accorded his authority with a quickly bobbed bow of his own. An all encompassing bow which fleetingly bespoke an awareness of fiefdom, total wisdom and a Daedalian cunning, all rolled into one.

Patrick Arthur Devlin paraded a career of inevitable progression to the judicial bench. Educated at Stonyhurst College and Christ's, Cambridge. He was President of Cambridge Union 1926 and was called to the bar as a member of Gray's Inn 1929, becoming a KC in 1945. He was appointed a Justice of the High Court, Queen's Bench Division in 1948.

This traditional appearance and greeting of the Judge so took the eye and ear that it was anticlimactic to be aware that the prisoner was in the dock – the accused doctor – red-faced and balding, dressed in a neat blue serge suit. His fingers gripped tightly upon the wood surround, the knuckles clearly white with tension.

Already the clerk, on his feet from below the Judge's bench, is addressing the Doctor:

'John Bodkin Adams, you are charged with the murder of Edith Alice Morrell at her home in Eastbourne, Sussex, in the month of November 1950. Do you plead Guilty or Not Guilty?'

This then is the moment upon which so much supposition had been expounded, both in the public bars of layman opinion and the clubs of legal luminaries. The trial for murder had begun. For Adams a tense and bewildering moment.

'I am Not Guilty, My Lord.'

It was not said loudly, but it was clearly heard. The phrase evoked a feeling of stubborn dignity, with a hint of Ulster in those few words.

The jury was sworn, ten men and two women. Adams watched closely, his large head immobile, eyes gazing intently at his peers-in-judgement. It was swiftly done, a routine gathering-in. And once done the Attorney-General leading the prosecution was upon his feet: Sir Reginald Manningham-Buller, a large man, over six feet tall and built like a rugby front-row forward, black gown swathed around him adding to that already substantial bulk. His job it was to outline the case for the Crown which he proceeded to do, swaying slightly upon his feet holding a sheaf of papers in one hand. In a voice both stentorious and brutal he addressed Judge and jury:

'This is a very unusual case. It is not often that a charge of murder is brought against a doctor... A word about this doctor, you will hear that he is a doctor of medicine and a bachelor of surgery, that he has a diploma in anaesthetics, holds an appointment as anaesthetist to a hospital, had practised anaes-thetics for many years. With his qualifications and experience you may think perhaps it is safe to assume the Doctor was not ignorant of the effect of drugs on human beings...'

A clinical and sardonic delivery. The Attorney-General was florid of face, expansive in manner and a fine orator, as should all barristers be. Yet his oratory took on the cadences of the politician he was. Member of Parliament since 1943, first representing the constituency of Daventry and now, during this trial, the incumbent for South Northamptonshire. Later, in

1962, Sir Reginald would be rewarded for his services, both to the law and the Conservative Party, with his appointment as Lord Chancellor of Great Britain and thus to the peerage as the first Viscount Dilhorne.

At the time of the Adams trial Sir Reginald was 51, having been born on August 1st, 1905. He had been educated at Eton and Magdalen College, Oxford. A member of the Inner Temple, he was called to the bar in 1927 and took silk in 1946.

As with all holding public office, Sir Reginald had his critics. There were those who said he was more politician than barrister; that his attendance upon the House and official duties dulled his perception, blunted his intellect in the courtroom: and, as always in such matters, there was an element of truth in this criticism. Manningham-Buller was noted, not for subtle rapier-like quiet thrust and parry of courtroom argument, but rather for cutting, slashing work as inflicted by a heavy sabre. Particularly in cross-examination did he become a formidable, intimidating figure. Let him get to the heart of the matter and he would charge the opposition down. His well known nickname being 'Bullying Manner'.

The Attorney-General continued to outline the Crown's case, producing for the jury a thumbnail portrait of the dead woman:

'...Mrs Morrell,' he said, 'was an elderly wealthy widow, who left a net estate of £157,000 when she died at her Eastbourne home in November 1950... Two years earlier she had suffered a stroke and became paralysed on her left side... The doctor in the dock was her physician, she was also attended by four nurses, who would later give evidence for the Crown that they never saw Mrs Morrell in any serious pain... A Harley Street authority would be called who would tell the jury that he had formed the opinion that Mrs Morrell was suffering from cerebral arterio-sclerosis, in lay terms, hardening of the arteries, they would be told that for pain to be present in such circumstances would be most unusual...'

In the press benches at the rear of the court, experienced

crime reporters waited for those details of the prosecution's case to emerge that, 'subbed' down, would write the attention-grabbing headline. Squeezed together tightly, with hardly enough room to wield pencil and notepad, comments, *sotto voce,* passed between colleagues and competitors.

'Come on, give us something!'

North American Eastcoast men were eyeing the clock anxiously, a six-hour time difference perilously close to deadline for their evening editions.

At last, what they were waiting for came, as Sir Reginald, forged ahead steadily, his voice not a wit subdued after close to an hour's peroration.

'... you will hear of large quantities of drugs prescribed for her by the Doctor and supplied to her. One of the questions to be considered will be – why were they given? It is one thing to give an old lady something to help her sleep but quite another to prescribe for her large quantities of morphia and heroin... '

And here came the quantities of drugs allegedly given to Mrs Morrell over a period of ten-and-a-half months – this was what the press wanted. And the amounts, even to the layman, sounded formidable indeed...

'Barbiturates: 2,194 grains; Sedomid: 1,400 grains; Morphine and omnopon: 171 grains; Heroin: 145 grains'

The impact such quantities made in court had caused Sir Reginald to pause. He quickly resumed:

'You will hear that these drugs, if administered over a period, result in a serious degree of addiction to them, a craving for them, a dependency on them... The Doctor was the source of supply. Did not Mrs Morrell become dependent on him? Why were these drugs prescribed to an old lady who was suffering from the effects of a stroke but who was not suffering from pain. Perhaps you may think that the answer lies in the changes made in her will.'

Sir Reginald explained that Mrs Morrell's solicitor, Mr Sogno, would tell the jury that she made three wills in 1946, without any mention of the Doctor.

'... In April 1949, after she had been given morphia and heroin for some months, the Doctor telephoned her solicitor saying that she was extremely anxious about her will and wanted to see Mr Sogno that day. So Mr Sogno went to see her and eventually she made another will in which she bequeathed to the Doctor an oak chest containing silver.'

Added Sir Reginald, looking straight at the jury:

'Nearly a year later the Doctor called on Mr Sogno without an appointment and a conversation took place which you may think a very curious one. The Doctor told Mr Sogno that Mrs Morrell had promised him her Rolls-Royce in her will and that she now remembered that she had forgotten this and that she decided to leave him not only the Rolls-Royce but also the contents of a locked box at the bank which, the Doctor said, contained jewellery. The Doctor went on to say that although Mrs Morrell was very ill, her mind was perfectly clear and she was in a fit condition to execute a codicil. Mr Sogno proposed that this might wait until Mrs Morrell's son came at the weekend but the Doctor suggested that Mr Sogno should pre-pare a codicil and that the codicil should be executed and later destroyed if it did not meet with Mrs Morrell's son's approval. Was not that a rather astonishing suggestion?' Sir Reginald raised the tenor of his voice slightly and looked directly at the jury: 'It showed, did it not, a certain keenness?' The heavy, almost Victorian irony, was not lost upon those in court.

The Crown's prosecution continued:

'Mr Sogno went to see Mrs Morrell and Mrs Morrell made another will leaving the Doctor the chest of silver and, if her son pre-deceased her, the Rolls-Royce and an Elizabethan cupboard. Perhaps you might think it significant and sinister that during the period when he was prescribing for her these very substantial quantities of morphia and heroin, the Doctor was concerning himself so much about her will and telephoning her solicitor.

'In September of that year, the Doctor went on holiday and his partner looked after Mrs Morrell. She was annoyed with the

Doctor for leaving her and executed a codicil revoking her bequests to him.'

Then Sir Reginald picked up the first exhibit in the case, a photostat of a graph showing the alleged prescriptions ordered by the Doctor for his patient:

'You will see how the prescriptions increased in quantity. During the last thirteen days of Mrs Morrell's life the rate of morphia was over three times higher than in any of the preceding months and the rate of heroin seven-and-a-half times. Why? What had happened to Mrs Morrell necessitating these tremendous increases? If she had been in acute pain, heavy doses might have been justified, but she was not in acute pain.

'The nurses will tell you that during her last days she was comatose or semi-conscious. That brings us back to the question: Why did the Doctor prescribe such quantities, such fatal quantities for which there is no medical justification? The submission of the Crown is that he did so because he had decided that the time had come for her to die. He knew, did he not, a lot about her will. Whether he knew of the codicil executed while he was on holiday and what happened to it, you may perhaps discover in the course of this trial. The Doctor may have thought that she should have no further opportunity for altering her will.

'On the night of her death, Mrs Morrell was lying unconscious and the night nurse would say she was very weak, except for occasional spasms. She was in a coma. At 10 p.m. the Doctor came and himself filled a 5cc syringe with a preparation.'

The Attorney-General held up a syringe before the jury who seemed suitably impressed at its size, certainly the press were. A barely subdued whistle of surprise echoed and brought a grimace of distaste to the Judge's features. The perpetrator kept his head down, gaze firmly upon his notepad as the prosecutor continued:

'... The Doctor gave this syringe to the night nurse and told her to inject it into the unconscious woman. She did so. The

Doctor took the empty syringe and refilled it with a similar quantity, an unusually large quantity on each occasion, and told the nurse to give the second injection if she did not become quieter. The nurse did not like giving another injection from this large, unusually large, syringe and later in the evening she telephoned the Doctor. She received her instructions and it was her duty to obey them. She gave the second injection. Mrs Morrell gradually became quiet and at 2 a.m. she died.

'Why were these large injections given to an unconscious woman on the Doctor's orders? The prosecution cannot tell you what they were. Mrs Morrell may indeed have been a dying woman when they were given. If she was, then the prosecution submit that she was dying from overdoses of morphia and heroin which the Doctor prescribed and it was murder by him. If, on the other hand, these two injections accelerated her death, it was also murder. The prosecution will submit that the only possible conclusion to which the jury can come is that the Doctor killed her deliberately and intentionally.'

He paused and added:

'The case for the prosecution does not rest here. On the same day, November 13th, 1950, the doctor filled in a form to secure Mrs Morrell's cremation. One question which he had to answer on this form was, 'Have you, as far as you are aware, any pecuniary interest in the death of the deceased?' The Doctor's answer, in his own writing was 'Not as far as I am aware'.

'Authority was given for Mrs Morrell's cremation. Six years later when a Detective-Superintendent from Scotland Yard was making enquiries he asked the Doctor about this cremation certificate, the Doctor said, "Oh, that was not done wickedly. God knows it was not. We always want cremations to go off smoothly for the dear relatives. If I said I was getting money under the will they might get suspicious and I like cremations and burials to go off smoothly. There was nothing suspicious really. It was not deceitful." But for this false answer on the form, there might not have been a cremation and the prosecution might have been in a position to say how much morphia and heroin there was in the body of Mrs Morrell at the time of her death.' Sir Reginald's pause at this point was pregnant with innuendo.

He continued:

'In November 1956 Detective-Superintendent Hannam with two other detectives went to the Doctor's house. They went into the surgery and the Doctor was told they had a warrant for a search of the premises for dangerous drugs. The Superintendent said, "Doctor, look at this list of your prescriptions for Mrs Morrell. There are a lot of dangerous drugs here," and he asked who administered them. The Doctor answered, "I did, nearly all. Perhaps the nurses gave some, but mostly me". The Superintendent asked, "Were there any of them left over when she died?" and the Doctor replied, "No, none. All was given to the patient. Poor soul, she was in terrible agony".'

Again the long pause for effect.

'So there you have the Doctor saying that she was in terrible agony when the nurses will tell you she was comatose and had been comatose for days and had not been suffering real pain. You will hear that the maximum quantity of heroin which should be prescribed in a period of twenty-four hours is a quarter grain, yet no less than eight grains were prescribed by the Doctor on a single day. The maximum dose of morphia is a half grain. There were ten grains prescribed on the 8th November, twelve on the 9th and *eighteen* on the 11th. The prosecution will call medical authorities who will tell you that in their view Mrs Morrell could not possibly have survived the administration of these drugs prescribed in her last five days.'

Again after the now accustomed but now annoying pause, the Attorney-General continued:

'Last November the Doctor went to see Detective Superintendent Hannam at Police Headquarters. The Superintendent said, "I am still enquiring into the death of some of your patients, Doctor". The Doctor said, "Which?" and the Superintendent answered, "Mrs Morrell is certainly one". The Doctor said, "Easing the passing of a dying person is

78

not all that wicked. She wanted to die – that cannot be murder. It is impossible to accuse a doctor".

'In December the Doctor was arrested. He was told he would be taken to the Police Station and charged with the murder of Mrs Morrell. He said, "Murder – can you prove it was murder?" Superintendent Hannam said, "You are now charged with murder," and the Doctor said, "I do not think you could prove it was murder – she was dying in any event". As he left the house he gripped the hand of his receptionist and said to her, "I will see you in heaven".

Sir Reginald repeated, his thunderous voice in crescendo:

'She was dying in any event! I submit to you that the evidence that I and my learned friend will call before you will prove conclusively that this old lady was murdered.'

Then he sat down after a speech lasting one hour and fifty-five minutes.

The press benches had eased their pressure. A number of reporters had quickly left and were at telephones all over the Old Bailey. In the public gallery, too, there was an easing, a clearing of throats, a shuffling of feet, the murmur of conversation.

Every person in that courtroom had his or her thoughts and impressions of the Chief Prosecutor's performance, his revelations and outline of the Crown's case. Some were disappointed at the fabric woven, others impressed at the weight of cloth that wrapped up the Crown's submission. The cynical press was, cynically unmoved. They withheld judgement correctly – what was the evidence?

The first witnesses were chemists giving formal evidence of where the Doctor had received his drugs. A description of the work of pharmacist, the record books. It was here the Judge leant forward and put a question. There was a feeling of relief – he was listening, he was paying attention!

'How many grains would a 5cc syringe hold?'

He was answered:

'Twelve-and-a-half grains, My Lord.'

The fifth witness was one of several nurses who had attended

Mrs Morrell during her final illness. Nurse Stronach was a roundly woman, short and stocky with an obstinate chin, who was going to be asked the impossible – to resurrect minute details which her memory had lost in the deep hole of time. After telling the jury when she was and was not on duty and how and what injections were given, she was asked by the Crown's junior in Mr Melford Stevenson's mellow far-reaching tones:

'Did you see him (the Doctor, who came every night) do anything with a syringe?'

Nurse Stronach: 'He gave her injections.'

'Did you see the Doctor give them?'

The nurse: 'We were not allowed in the room.'

'Who forbade you to be in the room?'

'I think it was Mrs Morrell's wish that we were not in the room'.

'You personally did not see the actual injections given, but you did see the Doctor prepare the syringe?'

'Yes, but I could not tell you what it was.'

'You do not know what the injections which the Doctor gave her were?'

'No, Sir, I have no idea.'

'Did the Doctor ever say anything to you about them?'

'He did not tell us.'

Again the Judge leant forward, half apologetically addressing Counsel:

'Mr Stevenson, is this perhaps a convenient moment to adjourn?'

It was that illustrious authority's courteous way of signalling the end of that first day.

Lord Devlin gathered papers and gloves together, stood, acknowledged the courtesies of his court, and slid along the bench and disappeared. So too did the accused back to his Brixton remand cell. It was 5p.m. on a sunny, crisp March evening that had courtroom observers blinking in the evening sunlight after a day spent indoors.

That region of London in which the Old Bailey is situated has, conveniently, a number of excellent hostelries, wine halls and other premises in which sustenance, together with conversation can be imbibed. Rodney Hallworth et al. succumbed.

'Gin?'

'Christ, no! A bloody great pint – make it bitter.'

'What do you think?'

'... Too early.'

'... Sparse, eh?'

'Why Mrs Morrell?'

'... Cremated after all!'

'Pompous great fart, that Manningham-Buller!'

'... But convincing?'

'Wait 'till 'Lawrence...!'

But such snippits of talk was all public bar surface conversation. Beneath, in the private thoughts of personal reflection, other questions were mutedly asked. Why the emphasis on lack of pain by the Attorney-General? Granted the medical opinion following the stroke would confirm that would be the normal pattern. But some of these reporters had interviewed previous staff of Mrs Morrell's – before her stroke, and hadn't it been established the old lady was suffering from arthritis? Rheumatoid arthritis at that, an extremely debilitating, painful disease, where movement and constriction of movement with the swelling and deformation of joints caused agony. Had the Attorney-General forgotten that? Did not the Crown solicitors research the old lady's medical history? Strange.

'... That was a hell-of-a-syringe, imagine that stuck up your... '

'... Twelve-and-a-half grains, eh?'

'... And twice...'

'... No wonder she croaked... '

'... Ten grains of morphia on the 8th, twelve on the 9th and eighteen on the 11th, bloody hell!'

'. . . What was the normal daily dose?

'Half-a-grain per twenty-four hours, wasn't it?'

There was a flicking sound of notepad pages turning.

'Yes, here it is, "the maximum quantity of morphine which

should be prescribed in a period of twenty-four hours is half-a-grain". There, that's what he said... '

'... Still... '

Experienced court observers relived that first day's proceedings. There were anomalies in the Crown's presentation. It was not forceful enough, damning enough. Strange. And the defence had not yet opened up, had not cross-examined, indeed, had not had the opportunity. They wondered what Geoffrey Lawrence, QC, would make of the Crown's case. The second day left them in no doubt.

# Chapter Six

*'… For this reason – that these books tell the truth,*
*and that we can only get at the truth by looking at*
*these contemporary records!'*

GEOFFREY LAWRENCE, QC

The second day continued where the first left off, with Nurse Stronach in the witness box and counsel continuing by asking her:

'You have told us that the Doctor used to visit Mrs Morrell at about 11p.m. and give her an injection?'

'Yes.'

'That would be after you yourself had given her a quarter grain of morphia at 9p.m.?'

'Yes.'

'And at 11p.m. Mrs Morrell would be fairly dopey and half asleep because of her earlier injection?"

'That is so.'

The nurse described Mrs Morrell's general condition as being very weak and that she was getting duller and duller in every way. On November 2nd, the last day Nurse Stronach was on duty, she said the patient was rambling and semi-conscious.

Counsel: 'Did you ever see any signs that she was suffering pain?'

'She did tell me that she had pains but I considered it neurotic.'

Prosecuting counsel sat down and defence counsel stood up. Rather like riflemen waiting to take pot-shots at stationary targets. Leading for the defence was Mr Geoffrey Lawrence, QC, a slight, somewhat dapper figure with an academician's high brow. Lawrence was 51 at the time of the Adams trial, had been educated at the City of London School and New College, Oxford. He was a member of Middle Temple, called to the bar in 1930 and made silk in 1950. In 1952 he had been a member of the Royal Commission on Marriage and Divorce.

Lawrence was a pragmatist, meticulous in preparation. It was said his fee alone would exceed five figures.

Lawrence: 'Nurse Stronach, how many patients do you think you have attended since Mrs Morrell died?'

'I could not possibly tell you.'

'A great many?'

'Yes, in private nursing we are in and out constantly.'

'You have been constantly nursing other patients during the last six or seven years?'

'Yes.'

'And from what you told My Lord and the members of the jury this morning, you were relying on your memory of events that happened on one case six or seven years ago?'

'Yes.'

'Just tell me a little about Mrs Morrell so far as you were able to know about her case at the time you were there. We have been told she was eighty-one when she died. You knew she was an old lady, did you not?'

'Oh, yes.'

'And she had a great many variations in her condition, sometimes up and sometimes down?'

'That applies to every patient.'

'But all the time she was going downhill – generally deteriorating?'

'Oh, yes.'

'And at the end, as you have said, she was very, very weak?'

'Very weak and frail.'

'And from time to time she had attacks of great irritability?'

The nurse: 'Due to her condition.'

Mr Lawrence: 'Against the nurses, was it?'

'Not only the nurses, other people.'

'It was quite irrational irritability?'

'It was not normal.'

'It was due to the injuries to the areas of her brain?'

'Not only that.'

'That for a start. To what else?'

The nurse: 'I should say a great deal to the amount of drugs she was having.'

Mr Lawrence: 'I thought you were going to say that.'


The questioning and answering continued. Almost flattering, Mr Lawrence got the nurse to reveal that the proper thing to do was to write down all procedures for medication, and in particular injections. As the nurse said: 'We noted down every injection we gave,' adding that all experienced nurses did it, including those who attended upon Mrs Morrell. Mr Lawrence having established that Mrs Morrell died a long time ago and the nurse was relying overmuch on her memory, asked:

'And whatever you wrote in that book would be accurate, because it would have been done right at that very moment?'

The nurse: 'It would.'

Mr Lawrence: 'Everything that happened of significance in the patient's illness would have to go down in the book – everything that was of any importance?'

The nurse: 'We reported everything. A proper report is written day and night.'

Mr Lawrence trying not to look in any way excited jabbed again:

'As distinct from your memory of six years later these reports would, of course, be absolutely accurate?'

The nurse: 'Oh, yes, they would be accurate from each one of us.'

'So that if only we had those reports now we could see the truth of exactly what happened night-by-night and day-by-day when you were there?'

'Yes. But you have our word for it.'

The defending counsel like all barristers will take the word of a witness on oath spoken before a judge but if indisputable material evidence can be presented it is sometimes more sure than a word on oath. Few people in court that moment, and certainly not the jury, were able to interpret the course of Mr Lawrence's questioning.

In just a few seconds it was going to prove one of the bombshells of the hearing. For some time Mr Lawrence had been kind, realising that it all happened a long time ago. In the last minute he had, as if hoping for a miracle, mentioned the nurses' notebooks. Both nurse and barrister had agreed that the contents should be irrefragable

But to innocent bystanders like the public in the back of the court it would surely seem impossible that such little exercise books, probably cast away in a drawer and burned with other no longer wanted trash, should ever be found. Who would have kept such trivia and, perhaps more to the point, why?

Mr Lawrence still on his feet turns to his left and is handed something by a junior. Mr Lawrence faces the nurse and says with controlled excitement:

'I want you to have a look at that book, please.'

The usher takes the book to the nurse who starts to read it. The Judge says:

'Mr Lawrence, is this one of the exhibits in the case?'

Says the defence barrister with inner relish:

'It is not, My Lord, but it will be in due course.'

He turns again to the nurse and asks thrice:

'Is this the night report for June 1950? Is it in your handwriting? And is it signed by you?'

The nurse replies softly: 'It is.'

Mr Lawrence: 'There is no doubt about it? That is the very book of the daily and nightly records kept by the nurses attending Mrs Morrell and it is your own record?'

The nurse as if needing a quick pick-me-up herself said quietly:

'It is.'

The bombshell had burst. The press benches and emergency chairs were half emptied. The Attorney-General appeared to be flabbergasted. What were these schoolgirl books to show and why were the defence so willing to bring them out of retirement? Mr Lawrence still in command extended his control and said firmly:

'I have not finished with it yet.'

The Judge pointed out that if the book were going to be evidence the Attorney-General had a right to see it. But to add a splash of further colour to an already colourful moment Mr Lawrence says:

'At this stage, My Lord, I desire to say that we have the whole of the nurses' reports on this case from June 1949 to November 13th, 1950 when Mrs Morrell died.'

His statement put his opposition into further tremors. Quickly the Crown prosecutors are shown the books.

The defence, only just on stage, had caused a major upset. Mr Lawrence's disclosures had a noticeable effect upon the Crown prosecutors. They were staggered, quite obviously taken by surprise. Their reaction was not lost upon the jury. Indeed, to experienced criminal courtroom gamblers, Lawrence had trumped an ace and the prosecution's hand no longer appeared so impregnable. And Lawrence was still dealing.

Mr Lawrence smugly trying to put his victory into the background, carried on with his questioning as though he was asking an errant boy why he was cycling without lights. He asks the nurse:

'Let us look at your first day. When did you go on?'

Nurse Stronach: 'I cannot remember the exact day.'

Mr Lawrence: 'Of course not. I am not suggesting that you can. You cannot remember after some years,' then adding icily, 'But we can see what you wrote there in the report.'

He went on: 'Am I right in thinking that the nurses made their entries one after the other, the night report following the day report and so on, as each nurse relieved the other?'

'That is how it was done.'

Mr Lawrence: 'Now let us go through your entries.' He reads: 'June 14th – had milk and brandy (three drachms). 11p.m. one sedormid tablet given, milk and brandy repeated, complains of pain and says she has not slept well. 3 a.m. patient awoke perspiring freely, refused to be turned over. Said that it hurt her to turn. 6.15a.m. Patient awoke in a temper. Said she had rung the bell and I had not answered it. Said I had left the bed all untidy and that I am a nasty common woman.'

He added: 'We have now read your entire entry for that night and two things are clear – first, you did not give an injection and, second, the Doctor did not visit.'

Nurse Stronach's reply was not more than a mumble. But Lawrence could make something even of that indistinct half-comment: 'Well, it is what you wrote down. Let us look at your entry for June 8th. Again there is no record of any injection and again no record of a doctor's visit, is there?'

The nurse: 'It doesn't say he did not call. It is not proof that he did not call that night.'

Mr Lawrence, standing erect: 'Nurse Stronach! You realise that this is a serious case?'

'Indeed I do.'

'Before you saw this book you told me that everything of importance would have been put down in your record made at that time, didn't you?'

'Yes.'

'And that was the truth?'

'Yes.'

'It is quite clear then that in the first spell of night duty you never recorded yourself as having given any injection at all of any kind and you never recorded a visit from the Doctor in the evening?'

'Not that I have recorded.'

'Are you saying that you, a trained nurse who recorded every drachm of brandy, would not have recorded an injection of a quarter grain of morphia if it had been given, or put down a visit from the Doctor if it had occurred?'

The nurse's reply was not easily audible.

Mr Lawrence remonstrated: 'Do not mutter. We cannot hear you. Are you saying that you would not have put these down in the book?'

At last her reply: 'No.'

Mr Lawrence continues: 'We will now look at your second period at Mrs Morrell's. When you went back on duty in October, there was a big difference in her condition from what it was in June. She had deteriorated very much. Let us see what you put down for the day only one month before she died. The entry for 4p.m. says, "Patient became restless and picking at bedclothes", and in your writing, "Hypo injection omnopon two-thirds given 4.40p.m.". You gave it?'

The nurse: 'Yes.'

Mr Lawrence: 'Do not think I am blaming you or criticising you but you told me earlier this morning that you had never given Mrs Morrell any injection except morphia.'

The nurse: 'I believed that was true.'

'What this entry shows is that your memory was playing you a trick, does it not?'

The nurse: 'Apparently so.'

Defence barrister: 'Obviously so.'

The nurse: 'It must have done. I cannot remember. It is a long time to remember these things.'

'That is exactly what I suggested to you. It was a long time ago and mistakes of memory can be made. This was one of them.'

For a long while the barrister reads the entries in the books:

'Patient very thirsty. Brandy and water taken. 7.30p.m. Visited by the Doctor. Hypodermic injection morphia grains one-quarter, heroin grains one-third, omnopon grains one-third. Brain very fuddled, does not know where she is.

October 16th – patient very excited, hypo injection morphia grains one-quarter, heroin – omnopon – slept.

October 20th – patient was stripping bedclothes. Complained of pain across the forehead. General condition very low. No injection, no visit from the Doctor. October 22nd – patient had a good night... seems brighter. Breakfast boiled egg, bread and butter, bramble jelly, two cups of tea. No injection and no doctor's visit. October 23rd – very restless... her speech indistinct. Water 6oz taken during night, cried at intervals. Asked for fruit jelly. 5.30 a.m. Asked for drink and was given some milk and soda. 7 a.m. Persuaded to take a sedormid tablet with Malvern water but tried to push the nurse away. A good night but patient in a confused state of mind. Has a very quiet morning. Special injection given by the Doctor. Lunch at 1 p.m.

Became very restless, talking at random. Seen by the Doctor in the morning. Special injection given. Patient depressed and sullen. Cried. Supper at 6.30 p.m., tomato soup, croutons, Malvern water, jelly taken. October 31st – Doctor's instructions omit morphia and omnopon. Instead give at night half heroin and one-third during the day.'

Mr Lawrence placed the book on the table and said:

'We have now been through the whole of your records for that time, we have not found one single instance where you gave that injection of one-quarter grain of morphia by itself you were talking about. And you recorded only one or two visits by the Doctor, and then we find you knew exactly what injection was given. You told my learned friend this morning that on your very last day with Mrs Morrell she was rambling and semi-conscious. Do you remember saying that?'

The nurse: 'I do.'

'We have your own record of that day. Let me read it to you. You wrote down what this semi-conscious woman consumed for lunch, a small quantity of partridge, a small quantity of celery, a small quantity of pudding and a small quantity of brandy and soda. That is not the picture of a semi-conscious woman, is it?'

The nurse: 'She would not have been having much. These would have been quite small quantities.'

Mr Lawrence, exuding a weary patience, spoke with deliberate clarity:

'I did not say that she had an enormous meal. I said she had a small quantity of partridge, a small quantity of celery, a small quantity of pudding and a small quantity of brandy and soda. Let us face this, Nurse Stronach, it is another complete trick of your memory to say that the day you left, Mrs Morrell was either rambling or semi-conscious?'

'I have nothing to say.'

'You have nothing to say?'

'No.'

Mr Lawrence: 'You also told my learned friend that Mrs Morrell was always very dopey and half asleep. That the Doctor gave her that night's injection because you had already given her one. That turns out to be quite inaccurate too?'

'Well, since the day nurse had already given her an injection...'

Mr Lawrence: 'Your evidence was that you did it.'

'So I understood but I did not do so.'

Mr. Lawrence sat down. What had he done? From the confused memory of the now upset nurse and from the jottings of a notebook, had Mrs Morrell attended a Lord Mayor's banquet? Or to keep her from an earlier death from starvation had the nurses tried to ease a few morsels of food into her unfeeling lips?

The Attorney-General who has been known to bully witnesses in his time is now very gentle with the nurse. He would like to find out something more about the special injections given by the Doctor and mentioned in the nurses' reports. He asked her if she knew what this injection was.

The nurse said she could not remember. She felt she did know at one time but now she could not remember.

The Attorney-General: 'I want you to be absolutely frank about this and if you have any doubt about it, do say so, for this is a very serious matter. To the best of your recollection now, were you at any time informed by the Doctor what this special injection was?'

'No, not by the Doctor.'

The Crown had finished with her and clearly, Manningham-Buller was out-of-sorts. It was now the Judge who intervened. If the Crown wanted to leave Nurse Stronach alone the Judge felt a certain elucidation was necessary by asking her if the Doctor ever wrote prescriptions in her presence. She said he often did.

The Judge: 'Was that because someone had told him that the supply was running out, or because he found out himself?'

'He would probably ask and we would tell him how the drugs were going.'

The Judge: 'He would write out a fresh prescription and would give it to the nurses?'

'Yes, and we would give it to the chauffeur, Price, who took it to the chemist. When he brought them, they would be taken in by the cook; she would bring them to the dining room to the nurse on duty who would put them away. The nurses had charge of the locked cupboard in the dining room where the drugs were kept. If the Doctor wanted drugs from the cupboard, he would ask for them and we would produce the key. But he usually had his own drugs from his bag.'

The nurse was thanked by the Judge and allowed to step down.


The second nurse to enter from the lonely, marble-floored waiting area outside the courtroom was Sister Mason-Ellis who had attended Mrs Morrell earlier and also up to the time of her death. Sir Reginald asked her simply:

'When the Doctor visited Mrs Morrell, were you present in the room?'

Sister Mason-Ellis replied just as simply:

'I was not.'

In an assuming voice, the Attorney-General asked: 'The Doctor was alone with Mrs Morrell?'

'Yes, we were asked to leave the room.'

'That happened every time the Doctor was there?'

'I think so.'

'Did you yourself see the Doctor give an injection to Mrs Morrell?'

'I could not answer that.'

Once again time, and too much of it, inhibited her answer. She added softly:

'It is so long ago.'

Surely that phrase – 'so long ago' – will sooner or later act as a barricade to simple thinking and direct conclusions by any member of the jury. To make matters worse, the witness could hardly be heard.

After asking the nurse to speak up the Attorney-General enquired as to the condition of her patient in November. The nurse, a married woman, slightly built and fragile-looking, seemed to be searching for answers which on oath she could not honestly find.

The burly prosecutor, whose very presence added fear to the frightful atmosphere of the court, had asked her to remember something, perhaps quite suddenly, which had happened a long time ago. Fumbling for her words the nurse replied:

'That was six years ago... I could not honestly and truthfully answer about her then...'

'Could you tell us something about her general condition?' asked the prosecutor almost despairingly, peering down a long black tunnel. The nurse again looked around the court as if seeking help for a faulty memory and said with meek irritation:

'It was so long ago. Honestly – it was six years ago.'

The Attorney-General abruptly sat down and spectators in court wondered why he had bothered to stand up in the first place.

For the amount of information he had gleaned to convince any juryman that the Doctor had killed was precisely nil. And yet this was a prosecution witness. The jury looked puzzled. The press certainly were in no doubt. They *were* puzzled!

In his cross-examination the subtle Mr Lawrence established that this nurse commenced her attendance upon the patient because the nurses at her home were always changing owing to

Mrs Morrell's bad temper. He also established that she was a difficult patient and, because she had suffered a stroke, she had to be lifted into her wheelchair and that, in addition to her physical disabilities, she showed signs of cerebral irritation.

He established that, as early as August 1949, Mrs Morrell was under routine sedation and that every night Nurse Mason-Ellis, during her time in attendance, had given Mrs Morrell a hypodermic injection of a quarter grain of morphia and one-third grain of heroin. Mr Lawrence again tied the nurse down not so much to what she remembered but what was written in the books. He also established from the witness that, where a patient has had a stroke involving brain irritation, it was good medication to ensure that such a patient should sleep at night. It was good courtroom medical background, if a trifle soporific.

But there was nothing soporific about the headlines of the next morning's newspapers. The headlines were to become even bigger by the next sensation which broke only seconds after Mr Lawrence stood on his feet the following day.

Pertinent and almost aggressive the defence counsel whips out the words as he faces the frail sister:

'Last night after you left the witness box you were talking to Nurse Stronach and Nurse Randall, weren't you?'

'That is right, yes.'

'The three of you were talking in the hall of this building, weren't you?'

'Yes, we were.'

'The three of you travelled together from Victoria to the coast?'

'Yes, we did.'

'With the evening papers in front of you, reading together the report of this case?'

'That's right.'

Each successive positive answer added to the witness's discomfort.

'And discussing it together.'

Suddenly the reporters who had been listening to what happened six years ago found themselves making notes of something which happened last night. They sensed that another Lawrence bombshell was about to burst.

His voice stinging Lawrence says:

'All three of you travelled back to London this morning by the 8.04 train – again in the same train, this time with the morning papers in front of you and discussing this case together?'

'Yes.'

'Did one or the other of you say something to this effect – "Don't you say that or you will get me into trouble"?'

The nurse even paler of face than before:

'I cannot answer that.'

Disbelieving the lawyer almost repeats her answer and says:

'You cannot answer it?'

'No.'

Lawrence frowns and draws out the silence. The papers in the lawyer's hands are rustled by his impatient fingers. Speaking now slowly, intently, he says:

'Perhaps I did not make my question clear. Let me try again. In the course of your discussion in the train this morning, did one or other of you – it may have been you, it may have been Nurse Stronach or Nurse Randall – say words like this: "Now listen, don't you say that or you will get me into trouble"!'

Reeling just a little the nurse said quietly:

'Yes I think one of them did say that but which one I am afraid I cannot say.'

'Was it you?'

Denying the charge as though she was in a police station facing a uniformed sergeant, she said: 'Oh, no.'

'Then it was either Nurse Stronach who had already given evidence, or Nurse Randall who has not yet been called. Which of these two was it?'

Bewildered the nurse muttered: 'Must I answer that?'

95

Suddenly the Judge intervened and answered her question unequivocally: "Yes."

As though revealing the end of a thriller book the nurse relented and said:

'Then it was Nurse Randall.'

And to whom did she say it?' lunged the barrister, the rapier in this courtroom duel, foil tip held high ready for the *coup d'essai*.

'She spoke to both of us.'

'Surely to you?'

'Yes.'

'You, as you know, are not only in the middle of giving your evidence, but in the middle of being cross-examined by myself on behalf of the Doctor.'

Feeling and looking as though he were ten feet tall Mr Lawrence's raised arm points to the witness box, his question flicked out like Toledo steel:

'What was it she told you not to say?'

The court sat as a silent block of human suspense. After many seconds the nurse said almost with abandon:

'I cannot really remember. I was not terribly interested if I may say so.'

Mr Lawrence began to feint again, opening up his target:

'I am not asking you, Sister Mason-Ellis, about something that happened six years ago. What were you talking about this morning when Nurse Randall said, "Don't you say that or you will get me into trouble"?'

Replied the nurse: 'About the drugs.'

Doggedly Lawrence sustained his attack lunge riposte: 'And what was it you were not to say?'

Suddenly a little enlightenment:

'There has been a little confusion.'

Pause.

'You see, the drugs were kept in a drawer, not in a cupboard, and there was no key.'

Mr Lawrence: 'Did you know that Nurse Stronach told My Lord yesterday that those drugs were kept in a locked cupboard of which the nurses kept the key and produced the key when the Doctor wanted to go to the cupboard. Did she tell you that?'

'I believe I saw it in the paper. We did not have any key at the time that I know of.'

'You saw it in the paper and so far as your recollection goes it was untrue. If there was no cupboard there was no locking and the whole of it was untrue?'

"Yes, that is why we were discussing it."

'That is why you, in the middle of your evidence, with the Doctor on a charge of murder, were discussing the case with a witness you knew was giving wrong evidence.'

Mr Lawrence stood back. 'Is that right?'

'I did not give the evidence.'

'You knew Nurse Stronach had given these answers?'

'Not until I saw it in the paper.'

'You knew it then because you read it.'

'Yes.'

'When you were sitting in the hall of this building last night before you left to catch your train home, were you not told by Superintendent Hannam you were not to talk to each other?'

'Yes.'

'And notwithstanding that, you all go down in the train together and come up again this morning and talk it over among yourselves?'

'From the newspaper.'

'Did you talk to her about the notebooks?'

'Not the contents. I just said I was glad they had been found.'

'Did she agree with you?'

'She did not really answer me.'

'You are glad they have been found?'

'I am.'

'For this reason – that these books tell the truth, and that we can only get at the truth by looking at these contemporary records.'

'Exactly.'

Lawrence's *coup d'essai*.

97

For the second time in the early stages of the trial the defence had made the vital point – that the records told a more truthful story than the memories of the witnesses. What still has to be determined though: did the records tell the truth?

The drama of the train journeys was over. Mr Lawrence, the ubiquitous, had proved that his contacts, agents, spies, or whatever you can call informants to the legal profession, had overheard Hannam and had travelled between Victoria and the coast in both directions. He had proved that the nurses had broken a police command by chatting. He had established that something or other was kept in a drawer and not in a locked cupboard. It seemed a dramatic victory at the time but on later analysis it did not match the impact of the moment, other than the confusion of memory which may well prove to be the all important highlight of the case. At its most voluble, that very confusion was sowing seeds of doubt within the jury.

More quotes followed from the nursing books establishing that Mrs Morrell was bad tempered and weepy – even suggesting that the nurse in the witness box had refused to do her duty properly and that the patient herself wished she was dead and that she knew a doctor who would put her to sleep forever.

On May 30th the evidence suggests Mrs Morrell had a bright and happy morning looking at television and Dr Adams gave her a cytamen injection which is a vitamin preparation.

The defence could now be certain that these morning injections were vitamin preparations because as the nurse said:

'Yes, when they were written down.'

Mr Lawrence: 'As a trained nurse, you would not have put anything down that was not correct?'

'That would have been shocking!'

On June 18th, it seems Mrs Morrell had an outburst and called her nurse a slum woman and a brute. The elderly patient with little time to live became so argumentative that she threw off the bedclothes and bit the bed in anger. Mr Lawrence managed to get agreement that this type of behaviour had occurred without any increase at all in the drugs she had been having over the previous months. Mr Lawrence continues, and looking down at his copy of the nurses' reports, says: 'Let us look at September 24th – "Breathing rapid, at times 34" – which means 34 breaths a minute?'

The nurse: 'Yes, that was very fast.'

Mr Lawrence: 'When people are under the influence of morphia and heroin, their breathing tends to get slow, does it not?'?

'Yes, slow.'

'And this was just the opposite? And quite typical of the closing stages of cerebral irritation?'

'Yes.'

Mr Lawrence moving towards the end of the entries and the death of the patient says:

'On November 3rd the Doctor ordered one sedormid tablet only to be given on waking and nothing more until after the visit of her son that afternoon, as he wanted her to be clear mentally. "Patient very lachrymose and sullen. Did not want to see her son and cried most of the visit. Later patient became hysterical, said I was trying to kill her. Supper at 6.30, soup, brandy and water, jelly taken".'

Again reading, the barrister said:

' "On November 8th, sat in a chair for eight minutes then returned to bed. November 9th, asked for chicken soup and had a cupful, also queen's pudding and ice-cream. Asked for sherry in her soup and ate half a baked apple.

November 12th," – What is the first word you have written there?' He looks towards the nurse.

Reading from her copy she says: 'Awake.'

Mr Lawrence: ' "Awake but quiet. Half a glass of milk and brandy three drachms taken".'

He makes the point that although death is only a short while away she was not in a coma.

Sister Mason-Ellis: 'Well, not according to my report.'

Mr Lawrence: 'More than once you have agreed with me that these reports are the best way the truth is to be found. You do not want to go back on that now, do you?'

'Not at all.'

'So when you wrote "Awake" on the last afternoon before she died, she must have been awake?

The nurse: 'She must have been.'

The barrister: 'Therefore she could not possibly be in a coma.'

He didn't ask for an answer. The nurse, after enlightening the jury where the drugs were kept, added that Mrs Morrell's son wrote and thanked her for her work after his mother died and sent her a present, a cheque for £50 which was not in her will but was a gift Mrs Morrell wished her to have.

The Attorney-General asked the nurse further questions in re-examination. He dwells for a moment on the nurses' books and asks:

'Would you ever wittingly leave anything important out of the nursing reports?'

'Of course not.'

'There is no entry by you recording Mrs Morrell as suffering severe pain?'

Answer: 'She did not appear to have any pain at all, as far as I am concerned.'

'If she had appeared to be suffering from any severe pain, would you have entered that in your notes or not?'

'Most certainly.'

The Attorney-General jabbed: 'Are morphia and heroin painkillers?'

'They are.'

'Throughout the whole of the period you were attending Mrs Morrell she was having at first morphia and heroin, and later morphia, heroin and omnopon?'

'She was.'

'Have you ever before, for any other doctor, given morphia and heroin mixed?'

'I cannot remember that. Heroin is not often used.'

Everyone in the court seemed to look at the Attorney-General as he asked measuredly:

'Have you, in your experience as a nurse, ever administered them as a routine injection given every evening?'

The nurse replied very firmly: 'No.'

The Attorney-General sat down and the Judge started to question the witness trying to clarify how the number of injections were given, if some of them were administered by the Doctor alone. After some preliminary questions, Sister Mason-Ellis said that the nurses kept a record of all dangerous drugs and noted the amounts used in the books in case at some later stage they were asked to account for them. She said:

'We wrote down on bits of paper the number of tablets we took out of the tubes.'

The Judge, querying her reply, said:

'Bits of paper?'

The nurse: 'Strips of paper, anything we could find to write on.'

The nurse explained that the injections were often tablets dissolved in distilled water.

The Judge: 'Now if you had been out of the room and then come back, and the doctor told you the wrong figure of tablets, you would have discovered it sooner or later?'

Reply: 'We would have – but usually the Doctor had his own drugs from his own bag and his own syringe.'

'And on those occasions you just relied on what he told you?'

'Yes.'

The next witness was Dr Walker, a medical referee at Brighton Crematorium, who was on duty at the time Mrs Morrell's cremation form arrived. He gave technical details of the cause of death and who was with her at the time and that he for certain had no pecuniary interest in the dead woman and that the form showed that death was not due to violence, poison, privation or neglect. It appeared from his evidence that the accused had filled in the forms correctly. The rather deaf physician who seemed to have spent many morbid years checking cremation forms, left the box and most of the court wondering why he had been called. The only obvious relevance of his evidence was that Dr Adams had not stated on form BCDF, or whatever, that he had murdered the deceased.

The next witness was the now almost infamous Nurse Randall whom few people in the court had ever seen before in their lives but who had been pre-judged by most of them as a chatterbox.

The Attorney-General using almost a replica of his previous questions asked Nurse Randall if she had ever injected a mixture of morphia, heroin and omnopon on the instructions of any doctor other than the tubby, little man in the dock. She said she could not recall having done so. The prosecutor pressed on:

'Have you ever on the instructions of any other doctor given a routine injection of morphia and heroin?'

The nurse replied sternly: 'No'

'At any time while you were nursing Mrs Morrell, did you see any sign that she was suffering from severe pain?'

'Not suffering pain. There was stiffness because she was unable to walk.'

She added that when the Doctor saw the patient alone he always asked for a glass of hot water which was established earlier as an aid to giving her injections.

Nurse Randall recorded in one night report that Mrs Morrell was breathless and in a collapsed condition which the nurse felt was due to heroin not suiting her. She told Dr Adams this but he replied that in his opinion heroin had nothing to do with the patient's condition. Nurse Randall certainly gave the impression that she disagreed with some of the Doctor's treatment. Not long before Mrs Morrell died she said she gave her half a grain of heroin at one o'clock in the morning and another shortly before 2 a.m. then another at 7.40 a.m. She emphasised in her report that this was done "on the Doctor's orders". When the prosecutor asked her why did she do that, the nurse replied:

'I think it was because the 1.55a.m. injection followed so closely on the other one.'

The Attorney-General continued:

'All this time she was going downhill quickly. Larger quantities were given. By November 8th she had half a grain of heroin, half a grain of morphia and millesimal of atropine at night and an hour later she was still awake and given an identical injection. She had no sound sleep and by early morning she was getting irritable and aggressive and a third injection of the same drugs was given.

'The next night we have the same pattern. She slept until 1 a.m., then became wide awake and was given half a grain each of morphia and heroin with atropine. At 4.30 a.m. she was fidgety and talkative and the same injection was repeated.

'On the 10th she had an injection of hyperduric morphia by the Doctor at about 10 p.m. and the Doctor leaves instructions to have heroin, one grain, hourly if necessary."

The Attorney-General paused and,looking at the nurse, said:

'That was a new development?'

But before Nurse Randall could reply, Mr Lawrence jumped to his feet and said reprimandingly:

'I must ask the Attorney-General not to lead in that form.'

Sir Reginald, hardly looking at the defence lawyer, continued unperturbed.

'I will put the question in another way. Had you any similar instructions before to give one grain of heroin hourly if necessary?'

The nurse looking almost pleased at being really positive said firmly: 'No.'

Sir Reginald continued: 'And at 4 a.m. that night you gave the one grain of heroin?'

Looking at the nurses' report he reads on:

"Gives a sharp cry at every touch, twitching more pronounced. Later she dozed off but soon became fidgety again and was given another whole grain of heroin."

He reads: "7.30 a.m. Awoke very restless and confused. 8 a.m. Visited by the Doctor – injection of hyperduric morphia given".'

Placing the book down in front of him Sir Reginald asks:

'Can you say whether or not during these last nights of her life she was receiving more injections than in any previous period you had been nursing her?'

Nurse Randall: 'I should say she was having more.'

'Did the Doctor tell you why to give heroin one grain hourly if necessary?'

Replied the nurse: 'No.'

The prosecutor continued:

'On the night of the 11th we see that the Doctor went back to giving her half a grain each of morphia and heroin. At 1 a.m. she was again fidgety and talkative and this time the injection was half a grain of hyperduric morphia and a half grain of heroin. At 3 a.m. she was still awake and at 3.40 a.m. she was given another grain of heroin. "Patient has not had a very good night – no sleep until 7 a.m. – talkative and very jerky – taken no nourishment – becomes violently agitated".'

The Attorney-General continues:

'And the report of November 12th – her last night – goes, "Patient very weak and restless. 9.30 p.m. Paraldehyde 5cc given intravenously by the Doctor. 11.30 p.m. Very restless – no sleep – 12.30 a.m. Seems a little quieter – appears asleep. 2 a.m. Passed away quietly".'

The Attorney-General asks the nurse:

'Did you perceive any jerks?'

Reply: 'Yes, they were very bad.'

'How bad? – Could you give any indication?'

'They were so bad I could not leave her and they almost jerked her out of bed.'

The prosecutor as if pinning his question to the overcoat of the nurse said:

'Have you ever seen jerks as bad as that in any other patient?'
The nurse replied strongly: 'Never.'

'When this 5cc injection was given, what was her condition?'
'She was not conscious. She might have been semi-conscious.'
'I want you to tell the court how this injection came to be made. The Doctor came? What happened when he came?'
'She was very jerky.'
'What did the Doctor do?'
'I think he was trying to do something to make her quiet for the night, as I was alone.'
'Where was the injection prepared?'
'In the dining room.'
'Whose syringe was it?'
'It must have been the Doctor's – it was the first time a 5cc syringe had been into the house.'
'Who prepared it?'
'The Doctor.'
'Who injected it?'
'I think the Doctor did.'
'And when it was given, what did the Doctor do then?'
'He refilled the syringe and gave it to me in case she was restless in the night. He just said if she was restless to give it to her. He didn't say any time.'
The courtroom was still and quiet, filled though it was with several hundred people. But they were hearing of the last sad hours of an old lady. And the man accused of her murder was amongst their number. So there was a deathly silence save for Nurse Randall's replies to the prosecution's questions.
'She was quiet for about an hour, then the spasms became much worse and you had to stay with her? You tried to get in touch with the Doctor by telephone but he was out?'
'I did not want to give her another injection.'
'Why not?'
'It was too soon after the previous.'

'But you did give that other injection?'

'I did'

'At 1 a.m.?'

'Yes.'

The Attorney-General asked: 'What was the effect?'

The nurse replied: 'She became quieter and I awoke the other nurse because I could see that the patient was passing out.'

'Did she pass out?'

'At about 2 a.m.'

At that point the third day in court ended.

The court rose but not before the Judge told the nurse not to discuss the case with anyone.

As though in respect for what they had just been privy to, the public filed out slowly and quietly. Even the press took their thoughtful expressions silently to the 'pub.

# Chapter Seven

*'The only conclusion I can come to is that the intention on November 8th was to terminate her life.'*
DR DOUTHWAITE

The following day – day four of the trial the Attorney-General began business by asking Nurse Randall:

'When you recorded paraldehyde 5cc as given by the Doctor on the night of Mrs Morrell's death how did you know it was paraldehyde?'

'I must have been told.'

'By whom?'

'By the Doctor.'

'Where did this paraldehyde come from?'

'I think the Doctor must have brought it.'

'Had you got any paraldehyde in that dining room?'

'No, not then.'

'Where did you keep the nursing notebooks?'

'In the drawer in the dining room.'

'What usually happens to the books on the death of a patient?'

'I usually take them and keep them for a while and destroy them. We don't show them to the relatives, it is rather distressing for them.'

'What happened,' asked the Attorney-General, 'to these nursing books?'

Said the nurse: 'I don't know.'

She was then asked if on the morning of Mrs Morrell's death the Doctor had arrived before she went off duty. She said he didn't. Said the Attorney-General:

'Did the Doctor ever look at these books?'

'Sometimes, yes.'

The Attorney-General sat down. And Nurse Randall prepared to face the defence.

Mr Lawrence establishes from the nurse that she first went to attend Mrs Morrell in February 1949, and that although Mrs Morrell was a largeish, well-made woman, she was an invalid. She thought the patient was only having morphia at that time. The nurse agreed that the patient was very restless and she agreed with Mr Lawrence that the object of the Doctor's treatment was to give her rest at night. She also agreed that the regular treatment of morphia and heroin injections hardly varied up to around September 1950.

Having established that Nurse Randall was on duty at the time in September when Dr Adams was on holiday in Scotland, Mr Lawrence invited the nurse to look at the books and see what happened. Morphia grains and heroin grains were given at 8 p.m. and omnopon when necessary. In the absence of Adams his partner, Dr Harris, was in charge and, added Mr Lawrence, 'We have not seen any reference to omnopon before. Now it appears here with Dr Harris. It is also quite plain, isn't it, that on that night the usual injection was stepped up?'

'Yes,' replied the nurse.

'Later that night Dr Harris was telephoned. Mrs Morrell was wide awake, very restless and complaining of feeling queer. Dr Harris came and one tablet of omnopon was given, with two tablets to be repeated s.o.s. (if necessary).'

The nurse agreed that was correct.

'Omnopon contains fifty per cent morphia?'

'Yes.'

Mr Lawrence then invited her to assess the result of the treatment. In the notebook the remark is made, "Seems very much brighter 6 a.m. and not so heavy".

Mr Lawrence again invited her to assess the situation. The patient had been in a bad state of restlessness and Dr Harris had to deal with it because his partner, the accused was away. Says Mr Lawrence:

'He does so by increasing the morphia and heroin and introducing omnopon at night?'

'Yes.'

'When later on her condition got worse, that was exactly the way the Doctor tried to deal with it?'

'Yes.'

'Everybody's endeavours were directed towards getting her some sleep?'

'Yes.'

'And from your notes it is quite clear, is it not, that Dr Harris continued to use the same drugs the Doctor had been using?

'Yes.'

'It looks, doesn't it, as if the doctors, the Doctor and Dr Harris, coupled no doubt with good nursing, were coping with the case very well?'

'Yes.'


Nurse Randall agreed that Mrs Morrell did not like nurses staying in her room, even at night, but they managed to do their job by looking in at the door from time to time.

Mr Lawrence stressed: 'And it was her wish that you were not in the room when the Doctor was there?'

'Yes.'

He then asked the nurse when she was specifically asked to recall Mrs Morrell's case and she thought it was in August the year before, when she made a written statement to Superintendent Hannam. After Mr Lawrence made the point yet again that memories are not always as reliable as the written word, Nurse Randall agreed that she gave Mrs Morrell an injection of morphia and heroin on the instructions of Dr Harris.

Before the nurse can be released from the witness box and allowed to return to her seaside home, even though just for a night, the Judge wants to know from her what is the normal dose of paraldehyde, to which she replies:

'It depends how you give it, but I think 4cc or 5cc is a very large dose'

The Judge: '2cc would be the normal dose?'

'It would.'

'Is it a dangerous dug?'

'It helps to make you sleepy.'

But the defence counsel had done his homework well, as would be demonstrated time and time again throughout this trial. For Mr Lawrence faced the nurse:

'I must challenge what you said. Do you know what the British Pharmacopoeia dose is of paraldehyde? I must put it to you formally that the British Pharmacopoeia full dose is 120 minims or 8cc. Do you know that?'

Nurse Randall: 'I did not know that.'

Mr Lawrence was magnanimous to a degree, totally understanding:

'Of course not, you cannot be expected to know all these things.'

His apparent knowledge is not lost upon the jury.

At the opening of the fifth day of the trial Mr Lawrence is concerned about entries made in the nurses' log on the night Mrs Morrell died. With Nurse Randall in the witness box, he reads out the last five separate entries.

"10.30 p.m. paraldehyde 5cc given by the Doctor. 11.30 very restless. No sleep. 12.30 a.m. restless and talkative and very shaky." The words 'very shaky' were underlined twice. "12.45 a.m. seems a little quieter – appears sleepy. Respiration 50. 2 a.m. passed away quietly."

Lawrence asks: 'There is no mention here on this night from start to finish of any twitchings or jerkings at all?'

The nurse: 'No, not there.'

'I want to ask you about the evidence you gave to my learned friend, the Attorney-General, about this jerkiness. Do you see that in the entry for 4 a.m., the night before, you have written "Twitchings more pronounced".'?

'Yes'

'That was the word you used to describe the condition?'

'At that time'

'What you told my learned friend was in substance this, that the words "very shaky" on the last night were meant to include the jerkings?'

'Yes.'

'Do you still say that?'

'Yes.'

'After all the answers you gave the other day about how accurate you were in your notes and how important it was to be accurate?'

'This was written after the patient had died.'

Mr Lawrence raising his voice just a little asked: 'Are you standing there, in the face of this record made by you on the patient's last night, and saying as a trained nurse of twenty-five years or more that when you wrote these words "very shaky" and underlined them, they were intended to mean something quite different from what they had meant when you had used those very words in earlier reports?'

'Yes, I do. They were more intense.'

'What was more intense?'

'The shakiness and the jerkiness.'

'Why, if you were recording something quite different, did you use the same words?'

'I just don't know. I suppose I wrote it down quickly.'

'Let me suggest to you the reason why you used the same words. The reason was that you were describing the same shakiness that you had often described in the past months – it was greater in degree – that is why you underlined – but still the same kind. That is it, isn't it?'

'I can only remember how very dreadful they were, the jerks.'

Mr Lawrence: 'That is what you say now, but at the time you only put down "very shaky", didn't you?'

Before Nurse Randall, who now looked distraught, could say anything else, the Judge asked her:

'Have you got now – as apart from what was written down – a clear recollection in your mind of her being jerky an hour before she died?'

Suddenly Nurse Randall's memory need not fight the years. She stood in the witness box as if she had just walked in from the death room. Answering the Judge, she didn't whisper as she had done in earlier evidence, but shouted:

'I have! And I never want to see anything like it again!'

Although she never said it, and would not have been allowed to do so, she seemed to be agreeing with the prosecution charge that treatment by the Doctor had ended the life of one of her patients in a distressing manner and one she had never seen before.

Mr Lawrence seemingly unconcerned by her exclamation, said coolly:

'It is quite obvious, is it not, that she was not in a coma?'

Nurse Randall: 'She would be in a coma or heavy sleep for a time after the injections.'

'A heavy sleep and a coma are not the same, are they?'

'No.'

'Nurse Randall, are you trying to be as accurate as you can be?'

'I am, Sir.'

'If a patient is described as "awake", she is plainly not in a coma?'

'No.'

'If a patient is described as "talkative", she is plainly not in a coma?'

The nurse: 'She would be rambling or not knowing what she was talking about.'

Mr Lawrence: 'Are you listening to what I am putting to you or not?'

'I am, yes.'

'You told the Attorney-General that she was in and out of a heavy coma, didn't you?'

'I don't remember.'

'Well, you can take it from me now that this is what you said. Do you want to withdraw that now?'

'I probably meant heavy sleep.'

'Do you want to withdraw or alter these answers?'

'I must have meant heavy sleep – she wouldn't respond to light or have her mouth cleaned, whereas if she was not in a coma she would have sucked a swab.'

Mr Lawrence: 'That is exactly what you recorded here as having done on the last night but one. In your report you say she had sucked a swab on forceps. Can you point out to me any entries of yours in the last three nights that indicate that this woman was in a coma?'

'No.'

'You have one record of paraldehyde 5cc given by the Doctor, but there is no record anywhere of any subsequent injection. This was the last night of her life, wasn't it, and if the second injection, which is not recorded, was given by you...    ?'

Here the nurse interjected and raising her voice, said: 'I did give it.'

Mr Lawrence, quickly: 'Allow me to finish the question. If this second injection was given by you, it was the last injection before her death?'

'Yes.'

'And it was given by you on your own responsibility as a nurse, having failed, from your own evidence, to get in touch with the Doctor?'

'Yes.'

'And within an hour of being given that injection the patient was dead?'

'Passed away, yes.'

'Nurse Randall, it is just not conceivable, is it, that you would have left that injection out of the record if you had in fact given it?'

The nurse persists: 'I did give it.'

'You cannot have it both ways. If it was a matter of some importance it would have gone into the book.'

'I may have left it out because it was the last one and I had other things to see to.'

'You have no recollection seven years later why it was not in the book?'

'No, I haven't.'

'Your memory isn't trustworthy.'

'It appears not to be.'

She agreed, not that it mattered any more, that if her memory was right about that injection there was a serious breach of duty that night.

Going back a little, Mr Lawrence asked:

'When the Doctor went away on his holiday in September 1950, Mrs Morrell was very upset?'

The nurse agreed.

'He came back all the way from Scotland for a day or two to see her? Did she tell you that she was going to alter her will and cut the Doctor out of it?'

'Yes, she did. She was very angry at the time.'

Nurse Randall ended her tussle with the defence barrister by telling him that in the dead woman's will she received £300.


The cross examination by the defence of Nurse Randall had at times been sharp. To what avail? To establish that memory can be faulty after a passage of six years? We all know this. To try and cast doubt on the second massive injection, massive as defined by the prosecution? Here Lawrence had been less than convincing. Whatever the state of her memory, Nurse Randall had stated she had given a second injection of 5cc paraldehyde and that a bare hour later the old lady passed away. Now that injection, recorded or not in those little exercise books, was something no one would forget. Few in that courtroom doubted Nurse Randall. She *had* given that last injection.

The Attorney-General stands, and after asking the nurse about what injections she has given patients and on whose instructions, he has to sit down again because the Judge has spoken, which is all judges have to do to keep everyone else quiet. Addressing Sir Reginald, now back on his feet for the Judge's question, he says:

'We all now know a great deal more about the medication in this case than when you opened it. Are you going to invite the jury to say that these two, or one, whatever it was, injections in 5cc's were given by the Doctor with the intention of causing the death of Mrs Morrell?'

The Attorney-General replies:

'I do submit that they were given deliberately and that they accelerated the death of the patient, but I will not elaborate, My Lord, I adhere to that and I have medical evidence which leads me to say that.'

The Judge quietly: 'I am very much obliged to you – that is what I wanted to know.'

The Judge then asked Nurse Randall about paraldehyde's distinctive smell, and if she could smell it when in a syringe, and if its smell would be more intense when given by the mouth. Her answers seemed to satisfy both the Judge and the defence, and after eight hours on the witness stand she was allowed to step down and, for all anybody knew, take the train home and never go near a court ever again.

It was now Friday afternoon and the evidence of a young nurse, who for a short while had attended Mrs Morrell, ended the first week of the trial. For the lawyers it was a working weekend, for the rest a holiday, but for the Doctor another weekend in prison.

It was the turn of the Sunday papers to summarise that first week. Carefully respecting, as they must in England, that the accused is most certainly innocent until proved guilty. So most of the copy revolved around the sub-characters and personalities.

This was not the case with Continental editions of papers and magazines, rather more noted for their lurid style than a strict adherence to the truth.

The following Monday a number of minor witnesses were called who, helpful as they were, contributed little to either

115

side. Mrs Morrell's chauffeur agreed that she was a generous woman and after only three years in her service she had left him £1,000.

The next relevant witness was Mr Hubert Sogno, Mrs Morrell's solicitor, who had been practising in Eastbourne since 1930. It was in 1948 that Mrs Morrell became his client. He immediately informed the jury that she was a prolific will-maker. Mr Sogno hinted quite clearly that Dr Adams was also interested in her wills. The Attorney-General asked the solicitor:

'In April 1949, did you have a telephone conversation with the Doctor?'

He did.

'Will you describe the conversation?'

Mr Sogno: 'The Doctor said he was telephoning on behalf of Mrs Morrell who was extremely anxious about the contents of her will, and she desired to see me urgently that day.'

'Did you go to see her?'

'I did.'

'And was a further will made?'

'It was.'

'Did that will leave anything to the Doctor?'

At this point Mr Lawrence intervened by saying: 'My Lord, I object. I do not think that the contents of the earlier wills can be evidence unless they are properly proved.'

The Attorney-General acceded, and went on:

'Did the Doctor call at your office at any subsequent time?'

Mr Sogno: 'He called about a year later in March 1950, and told me that Mrs Morrell had promised him many months before that she wanted him to have her Rolls-Royce in her will, and she had remembered that she had forgotten to do this. The Doctor said she now wanted to leave the car to him and also a locked box at the bank which she said contained jewellery. The Doctor said that although Mrs Morrell was very ill, her mind was perfectly clear and he had no doubt that she was in a fit condition to make a codicil. I reminded the Doctor of some gifts

Mrs Morrell had made by cheque some months ago and which she after regretted. I suggested the matter should wait until Mrs Morrell's son came who was expected at the end of the week, but the Doctor said she was very uneasy and wished to get the matter off her mind. I suggested that he might ease her mind by pretending to receive the box and then handing it back to the nurses in their room. The Doctor said no. Mrs Morrell seriously wished him to enjoy her gift. He told me I should prepare a codicil and that it could be destroyed later if it did not meet with the approval of her son. I told him that was quite impossible.'

The Attorney-General: 'And on August 24th there was yet another will?'

The solicitor agreed; it was the last will and in it the Doctor received what he had requested – the chest of silver and the Rolls-Royce. The Attorney-General had finished for the moment.

Mr Lawrence asks: 'When the Doctor talked to you on Mrs Morrell's behalf, had he made a point to you that he wanted, as a Doctor, that you should go without delay and deal with the matter, so that her mind was at rest?'

'He certainly asked me to go and see her without delay. I am quite willing to assume that was his reason.'

Mr Lawrence: 'All in all, she made six wills?'

The solicitor agreed, and when he was asked if she sent for him again he said she did at the time the Doctor went on holiday to Scotland in September 1950. Mr Sogno agreed that Mrs Morrell was angry with the Doctor and asked the solicitor to prepare a codicil to her last will in order to deny the Doctor any bequests.

Mr Lawrence: 'Was this codicil legally executed?'

'It was.'

'What happened to it?'

Mr Sogno: 'The codicil I would say is all in small pieces. It was torn up by Mrs Morrell.'

Mr Lawrence: 'Did her tearing it up put the Doctor back into the will?'

'Oh no. Tearing up a document is not an effective way of reviving gifts. The codicil cutting him out was never validly revoked before her death.'

Mr Lawrence summed it up by saying:

'So that when she died in November the Doctor was not in any way a beneficiary under her will?'

'That is correct.'

'For anything at all?'

'For nothing at all.'

The defence lawyer: 'So in short it comes to this, that when afterwards the Doctor did receive the chest of silver it was really only by favour of Mrs Morrell's son, the residuary legatee?'

Mr Sogno: 'He said, by all means the Doctor should have the chest, because it was his mother's wish.'

Mr Lawrence: 'So the Doctor did not get the chest of silver under the will at all? And if he got the Rolls-Royce it was also not under the will?'

The solicitor agreed.

The finer legal points about will-making fell upon marginally interested ears, yet they were important. The Doctor had received a box of silver, a Rolls-Royce limousine: by whatever way he received them, he benefited from Mrs Morrell's death.

A slight argument in the press benches reinforced that discussion. There could be no doubt, it was fact. Once again the Doctor benefited. But wait! Not once again. Adams was on trial for the murder of Mrs Morrell and no one else. Other gifts, other matters, not concerning the Morrell trial, were not evidence here.

Detective-Inspector Pugh, head of Eastbourne CID, went into the witness box to say he was present at the time of arrest. He was followed into the box by Superintendent Hannam, who had a word war with Mr Lawrence who was attempting to belittle the policeman by asking a lot of slick but unnecessary questions.

On the eighth day of the trial the prosecution introduced their big gun, or rather, the very tall Dr Douthwaite, a Harley

Street specialist and Senior Physician at Guy's Hospital. Having established with the Attorney-General the various types of strokes and blood clots that a human being can suffer, the doctor was asked by the prosecutor:

'How long can life last after a cerebral thrombosis? (The type of illness Mrs Morrell suffered)'

Dr Douthwaite said a person could live for many years. The Attorney-General asked what was the proper treatment for a patient suffering from such an illness.

The doctor: 'Within a few days, as soon as one is able to obtain co-operation of the patient, one should at once try to mobilise the patient and encourage movement of the body ... massages, exercises and so forth.'

The Attorney-General: 'Is there, in your opinion, any justification for injecting morphia and heroin immediately after a stroke?'

The doctor: 'No justification whatsoever.'

'Is it right or wrong to do so?'

'Wrong. In all circumstances, wrong.'

The press bench came to life, notebooks flapped and pencils scurried across pages. This witness, this expert medical witness, was supplying positive evidence, clearly and emphatically. He was writing their copy with his answers.

The Attorney-General: 'What about morphia alone?'

'Morphia alone should not be given to someone who has had a stroke – unless there is an episode of acute mania and then only a single injection.'

'What would be the effect of morphia and heroin on an old lady who has had a stroke? Would it have an effect on her prospects of resuming a normal life?'

'It would greatly interfere with her rehabilitation.

'Is it necessary to use sedation immediately upon someone who has suffered a stroke?'

'It is not necessary.'

'Is it desirable?'

'Not in general. I am not referring to something given to ensure sleep – sedation there is quite reasonable.'

The Attorney-General: 'When you talk of that, does it include morphia and heroin?'

'Completely excludes.'

'With someone of this age who has suffered a stroke, is it necessary to keep the patient as quiet as possible in the daytime?'

'No, not in the daytime.'

'Is there a risk of another stroke if the patient is not kept as quiet as possible?'

'On the contrary – there is more risk of another stroke from thrombosis, for clotting is more likely to occur if the patient is kept quiet.'

'Would you expect a patient suffering from a stroke to exhibit signs of irritability?'

'I would expect a woman of her age to suffer to some extent from arterial sclerosis and this would lead to a degree of irritability.'

The Attorney-General: 'And would that be a justification for administering morphia and heroin?'

Dr Douthwaite: 'Oh no, completely contrary. It would give rise to addiction and certainly those drugs as such are not nearly so effective as much safer drugs for that purpose.'

'Were those drugs available in 1950?'

'Oh yes.'

'Is morphia liable to produce addiction?'

'Very liable. The individual is liable to become addicted in a fortnight, certainly within three weeks.'

'What would be the addicted patient's attitude towards the doctor who is supplying the drug?'

'Dependence on the doctor.'

'For what legitimate purpose can morphia and heroin be daily administered over a long period?'

'Only for severe pain that can only be quelled by no other means.'

'Can you tell us something about the normal dosage of morphia?'

'A quarter grain. The British Pharmacopoeia gives the maximum dose as one-third grain.'

The Judge intervenes to ask the Attorney-General: 'The normal dose – in what time?'

The Attorney-General facing the doctor: 'At what intervals is this maximum dose supposed to be given?'

The doctor: 'To people in pain it could be given perhaps over four hours. If there were really agonising pain it might be given every hour.'

He then asks the doctor about heroin and gets the reply:

'Heroin is a stronger drug than morphia. It is more dangerous. Its action is similar to that of morphia, but it differs in important respects – it powerfully depresses respiration.'

'Can you give an idea of how it compares with morphia in that respect?'

'About three or four times as powerful.'

'What is the maximum dose?'

'According to the BP, one-sixth grain. Heroin is seldom given more than once every six hours except in cases of terrible pain. It has very little sedative effect.'

'What then is the effect of a routine dose of heroin?'

'The effect, very simply, is a craving for more. It supplies pleasurable excitement.'

'In your opinion, should heroin be given to old people?'

'No.'

'In any circumstances?'

'It is axiomatic that people over seventy should not have heroin unless they are suffering from some incurable disease.'

These are strong unequivocal answers. Those journalists used to court proceedings and who had past experience of medical evidence listened in rapt attention. Their very experience had led them to observe on more than one occasion that medical evidence could normally be summed up with the word 'ambiguity'. Dr Douthwaite appeared the exception.

The doctor, at the invitation of the Attorney-General, talks about drug addiction, which means that once a tolerance has been reached the drug has less effect, lasts a shorter time, and larger doses have to be given to reach the same effect. As the drug effect wears off, the patient suffers from a craving and excitability. In order to overcome the acquired tolerance you could either stop the drug and the tolerance would disappear, or increase the drug, overcoming the tolerance and satisfying the craving.

Asked about the results of stopping the drug, Dr Douthwaite explained:

'The patient will be terribly ill and have acute pains in the limbs and collapse. This is the state of withdrawal.'

'We have heard from other witnesses about the twitchings suffered by Mrs Morrell. Could they be produced by administration of heroin?'

'Oh, yes, they could!'

The Attorney-General, switching now to paraldehyde, which he established has a revolting smell, asks the doctor:

'Is it a sedative?'

'Yes.'

'Could it be used to endeavour to stop the twitchings?'

'Yes.'

The Attorney-General: 'What would be the effect if it were superimposed on a heavy administration of morphia and heroin?'

Dr Douthwaite replied firmly : 'It would be likely to produce death.'

The Judge then asked if paraldehyde was a dangerous drug by itself and was told it was not.

The Attorney-General asked: 'The immediate cause of Mrs Morrell's death was certified by the Doctor as cerebral thrombosis – are there any signs in the nursing reports to justify that conclusion?'

'None.'

'We know that another practitioner, Dr Fox, endorsed this. Can you tell whether a person died of cerebral thrombosis by external examination?'

'You cannot.'

'Is there any justification or legitimate ground, in your view, for administering heroin and morphia together?'

'No.'

'What can be the medical object of giving a routine injection of morphia and heroin?'

'There is not one.'

Referring to the nursing books the Attorney-General quotes an entry for June 1950, one-third grain heroin and five-twelfths morphia and asks the doctor:

'How would you describe that dosage?'

The doctor: 'A very heavy dosage.'

The Attorney-General asking about November 10th, reads: '"May have heroin one grain hourly if necessary"', to which Dr Douthwaite replied almost aggressively:

'A high dosage and an astonishing instruction!'

The Attorney-General refers to November 12th, when three half-grains of heroin and two grains of morphia had been given in twenty-four hours. He asks:

'Dr Douthwaite, I want you to express your considered opinion as to the effect on the same paralysed lady of eighty-one of the dosage given in these last days, allowing for the tolerance acquired by previous routine injections.'

Says Dr Douthwaite: 'I believe it would have produced jerky convulsions and ultimate death.'

The Attorney-General perhaps trying to build up on atmosphere of importance for the jury, did not look at the doctor, but asked him in a slow, low voice:

'What conclusion do you draw from the dosage administered in the last few days – what conclusions do you draw as to the intentions with which that dosage must have been prescribed?'

Dr Douthwaite looking directly at the prosecutor replied softly:

'The only conclusion I can come to is that the intention on November 8th was to terminate her life.'

Assuming the jury heard all that, the Attorney-General asks one more question, so there can be no doubt:

'If it was true that she was given those two 5cc injections on the night before she died, what would be the effect of this paraldehyde on top of the heroin?'

Dr Douthwaite: 'To make the heroin more lethal.'


The last two replies stunned the court. Here was one doctor almost looking at another doctor and saying: 'You murdered the old girl'.

Sitting next to Rodney Hallworth in the press box was colleague Harry Longmuir and, behind, colleague Percy Hoskins, the man who months earlier had advised the *Daily Express* to play down the Hannam investigation into Adams – the crime reporter who had tried to assume the investigation would fail and that there really wasn't any murder.

But as Dr Douthwaite gave his final reply to the Crown prosecutor, Percy Hoskins whispered to Longmuir and Hallworth, referring to the Doctor whom months ago he really didn't want to know, and said: 'This guy is a dead duck.'

In the way of national newspapers, a view, a slant, a policy, toward a given situation is reflected in the paper's copy. In matters of news and crime, unrelated to politics, the news editor would set the paper's policy. As far as Hallworth's paper was concerned the policy decision of his news editor had a distinctly personal note.

During the summer of 1956 Donald Todhunter, then news editor of the *Daily Mail* was on holiday in Yugoslavia and had an unexpected encounter that was to reflect itself in the paper's attitude to the Adams case.

On the terrace of the Argentina Hotel, Dubrovnik, he was introduced over pre-lunch drinks to Lord Goddard, the Lord Chief Justice of England, who was attending an international jurists' conference at the neighbouring Excelsior Hotel. From this chance meeting grew a friendship that extended over many years taking in reciprocal entertaining at Lord Goddard's London home and at Rules and the White Tower restaurants.

To this day Todhunter refuses to break the confidence imposed on him by Lord Goddard concerning the lengthy conversations both apparently enjoyed in Dubrovnik as they exchanged views and anecdotes on the law, politics, wine and Fleet Street.

But when he flew back to London, Todhunter saw no reason to change his plans for the coverage of the Adams trial and for the publication of the voluminous background material prepared by crime reporter Rodney Hallworth for publication in the event of a conviction of the Doctor.

Of that friendship with Lord Goddard, Todhunter will only say:

'He was a great judge and a warm man for whom I felt sincere affection. He was acutely aware of the bench's responsibility to the public during the years of violence that followed the war. He weighed each summing up and sentence with a mind that was needle-sharp yet compassionate and humorous. Lenient when he saw fit, he regarded his duty the need to impose punishment to match the crime and I suggest there would be fewer victims of mindless brutality today if the spirit of Lord Goddard lived on.'

Thus the *Daily Mail's* policy remained unchanged. Unlike the *Daily Express*, Todhunter was convinced there had been a wrongdoing. Unlike Percy Hoskins, and many others, who suffered a complete change of heart and conviction on day four of the Adams trial, Todhunter would never vacillate over his opinion of Adams.

On the next day Dr Douthwaite who, until this point only experienced cosy conferences with Crown experts wanting the head of Adams, now had to meet the brilliant, acid-tongued defence lawyer who wanted to offer the jury a different story.

Above the Old Bailey stands the statue of a blindfolded goddess ..: holding up in one hand an unsheathed sword, in the other a pair of scales. The blindfold symbolises impartiality; the scales the weighing of justice; the sword the awful power of a just law.

During a trial those same scales would tilt as the weight of prosecution or defence evidence finally emerged. But no one in Court No. 1 of the Old Bailey could remember those scales see-sawing as much as they did during the Adams trial.

Mr Lawrence seeming as if he only wished to help looked at Dr Douthwaite and said:

'I want you to be quite clear what your opinion to My Lord and the jury is in relation to the charge of murder. Have I understood it correctly in this way, that as a doctor and a specialist yourself you are saying the Doctor formed the intention to terminate life on November 8th and carried that intention into effect over the next five days?'

Dr Douthwaite: 'Yes.'

'I think it follows from what you said yesterday that the murderous intent, in your view, was present in his mind from November 8th onwards to the end?'

'Yes.'

'I hardly suppose you have often expressed a graver or more fateful opinion on a matter than that?'

'No.'

'Before going into the witness box and expressing that opinion had you satisfied yourself that you had every piece of relevant evidence before you on which to judge?'

'Yes.'

'You gave evidence in this case before the magistrates?'

'I did.'

'When you gave evidence at that stage you were entirely in ignorance of what her treatment by the Doctor had been before January 1950?'

'Yes.'

'And you gave your evidence broadly on the hypothesis that for the last three or four days of her life this lady had been in a continuous coma?'

'Yes.'

Said Mr Lawrence: 'This turned out on the facts to be quite wrong?'

'Yes – not a continuous coma.'

'Do you know where she had her stroke in July 1948?'

'In Cheshire I understand, during a visit to her son.'

'Had you made any enquiries before giving evidence against the Doctor yesterday – had you made any enquiries yourself or asked anybody about the symptoms of her stroke – the circumstances – the treatment she had in Cheshire?'

Dr Douthwaite: 'I have said in conferences it would be very interesting to know what treatment she had before she came into the care of the Doctor.'

Mr Lawrence: 'Interesting, in the sense, that it would be relevant and material to the medical picture? And did you ask for this relevant material information to be found . . . before you reached your final conclusion?'

'I did not regard it as my duty to find out facts of that sort. The facts on which I am expressing an opinion are the facts which have been presented to this court – I was told that the information was not available.'

'Who told you it was not available?'

'I am not certain. It was at one of the conferences by counsel for the Crown.'

'It would be most important to know before condemning the Doctor's treatment from the start, as you did yesterday, what happened in Cheshire?'

And the ubiquitous Mr Lawrence whose agents follow nurses to the end of the line and rummage in old drawers for nursing documents, this time produces medical data from Cheshire. And from it he shows that Mrs Morrell was first of all put on light drugs, but did not respond very well, so the Cheshire doctors started her on a quarter-grain morphia after which the old lady slept. And the doctors kept her on morphia whilst in their care.

Once again Lawrence had scored vital points. And no one in that court missed the fact that morphia was first prescribed for the patient by doctors in Cheshire – not by the accused Doctor!

And those in court experienced in matters of prosecution and defence pleading summed up the Attorney-General's efforts thus far as inept.

Once again their own witness was forced to unravel the prosecution's previous bindings and all because the leader in the prosecution's team had made the lazy or stupid decision that the Cheshire medication was of no importance.

No importance! Yet Dr Douthwaite at prosecution conferences had requested that simply available evidence. A lazy or stupid decision indeed, for now the prosecution team were held up in public court as bumbling incompetents. And Lawrence would not miss such defence opportunities.

Having demonstrated his ability to find nursing records in almost any quarter of the globe Mr Lawrence asked Dr Douthwaite: 'From these records certain things at least are clear, are they not? That she was a very ill woman – complained of severe pain – and after two nights of attempting to give her sleep by barbiturates, the doctors at the hospital resorted to morphia?'

What else could Dr Douthwaite reply but: 'Yes.'

Mr Lawrence: 'And every night for the rest of her stay in that hospital and under those doctors, she had morphia?'

Again: 'Yes.'

And after these injections there is some record of her having slept?'

'Yes.'

'What you were saying yesterday was this – no doctor should give morphia to a patient with a stroke except in one instance only, that is if the patient had acute mania and then in one isolated injection. Does the field of condemnation that you are spreading from the witness box include Dr Turner of Cheshire for having given the patient morphia after a stroke?'

'If that was the treatment for the stroke, yes!'

Mr Lawrence: 'It does? – gracious me!' – spreading out his hands in a theatrical gesture of disbelief. Then he adds:

'We are left with this – that three doctors – two of whom are not on a charge of murder – deliberately gave this particular patient injections of morphia night after night. If I understand, you are condemning as a matter of medical practice each of these doctors' use of morphia in this case?'

Dr Douthwaite: 'If it was used simply on account of the stroke.'

'The pain was a consequence of the stroke? You cannot have it both ways.'

'We do not know where the pain was.'

'Do you think that is an answer to my question – it does not matter in what part of the body the pain was, does it? – the pain was a consequence of the stroke?'

'It is probable.'

'Are you saying that this woman who has had what you admitted to be a pretty severe stroke goes into a hospital and is then very distressed and complains of pain – are you really saying that that pain had nothing to do with the stroke?'

'It is possible, though not probable.'

Mr Lawrence established that all the other doctors had seen Mrs Morrell but Dr Douthwaite had not, and that only the man on the spot knows best. He then asked:

'Could six or twelve months have been a reasonable prognosis in terms of expectation of life after her stroke?'

Dr Douthwaite agreed.

'Now the reasonable object of a general practitioner's treatment for what he could reasonably expect to be the remaining months of that woman's life would be to make her life as tolerable as it could be to her and as it could be to those who had to look after her?'

Dr Douthwaite: 'The first object would be to restore her health.'

Mr Lawrence: 'That of course is the highest level, but no doctor in his senses would think that short of a miracle he could restore a woman of 79 or 80 to her pre-stroke health?'

Dr Douthwaite agreed. Dr Douthwaite further agreed that

the local doctor has to do his best for what is left of a life, and whatever anyone may opine about the use of various drugs the patient was reasonably active during the daytime. The rather nasty relationship between a probing barrister and a doctor who felt he knew his stuff but could not say so continued. In fact the able and highly qualified Dr Douthwaite was squirming at the end of Lawrence's foil, pinned in a corner by the prosecution's omissions and his own strong convictions. Convictions unuttered because of the constraints placed upon him by the wording of the charge against Dr Adams. It was a dilemma for Dr Douthwaite from which the prosecution could not recover.

Mr Lawrence: 'Now if you are dealing with a case where you are giving morphia either to deal with pain or some physically degenerated condition the time will come when you won't be able to deal with what you are trying to deal with by means of a level dosage?'

Dr Douthwaite agreed.

'And you are at the point where you find that you have to adopt one of two courses? One is to stop the drug, which in the case of an old woman verging on eighty might very well cause collapse, with risk of death?'

Dr Douthwaite agreed. He also agreed that the other course was to continue and give her more, which is what Dr Harris did with comparative success.

After more deliberations between the two contestants in the ring about the dilemma of increasing drugs or risking collapse Dr Douthwaite succeeded in getting a word in and saying:

'This is a problem which often confronts us and my practice in teaching has always been that if a patient is dying it is ridiculous to worry about addiction. If the strong probability is that the patient will not live for more than a month or two you cannot worry about addiction. If the prognosis is very doubtful about time, addiction should be carried in mind.'

For the next ten minutes the couple warmly discussed, agreeing and disagreeing, the merits of morphia and heroin and how other doctors regarded them.

Then they discussed the dead woman's final days, chiefly from the nurses' notes. Mrs Morrell was now getting restless and aggressive and was not sleeping. Doctor and barrister agreed that that was the situation which confronted Adams on the morning of November 8th – the diary date on which Dr Douthwaite said the final journey to murder was conceived.

Mr Lawrence then centred on November 9th – "The second day of the murderous period," – and added:

'Let us see what this murderous doctor did. It is clear from this record . . . that the only sleep she had during the whole of that day and the following day was fifteen minutes at eight in the morning and twenty after lunch.'

Dr Douthwaite further agreed that if this lack of sleep had been permitted to continue the old lady would have collapsed. He also agreed with the barrister that because of the previous treatment Adams could not cut her off from what she had been having because that would have meant death.

Invites Mr Lawrence: 'Now look at the next report. The patient was confused and talkative. The Doctor was there at 10 p.m. He gave her an injection of hyperduric morphia and she slept for six hours. Do you notice the selection of that type of morphia?'

'I do.'

'It is a slow-action drug?'

'It is.'

'On the eve of murder – a slow acting drug? A strange choice for a murderer?'

Dr Douthwaite lifts his shoulders, pouts his lips and doesn't seem bothered.

Mr Lawrence then states that Adams gave Mrs Morrell some atropine which is classed as an antidote to morphia and is sometimes given in conjunction with morphia to offset some of the effects, such as vomiting and constipation.

'So on the second day on which you are saying the Doctor carried out his murderous intention she was given an injection which contained an ingredient which is an antidote to morphia?'

Still seemingly uninterested Dr Douthwaite agrees. And Mr Lawrence asks him:

'Do you realise that fact?'

Dr Douthwaite: 'Yes. The purpose for which atropine is usually given with morphia is to reduce the dryness in the throat. It was a very weak solution.'

Mr Lawrence: 'Here is the man who was murdering her, giving her, however weak it might be, an antidote?'

Dr Douthwaite, had he been at a cocktail party, might have fallen asleep but he replied, 'Yes,' in such a way that the court felt it just didn't matter.

Mr Lawrence: 'It was the Doctor's duty to produce sleep but sleep was no longer produced. Those drugs were no longer working. In other words, their hypnotic value had gone?'

'Yes.'

'And then he tried one more variation. On the last night he tried paraldehyde which clearly was one of the safest remedies for insomnia.'

Agreement.

'And 5cc is quite a common dose, and even if another 5cc was given it would still be within permissible limits?'

Agreement.

'Could anything else have been given in this last stage?'

'He might have given hyoscine.'

'Anything else?'

'There are several others that could have been given with safety.'

'Including paraldehyde?'

'Yes, including paraldehyde.'

To those listening in court Dr Douthwaite seemed to be attempting a double-act, or was being pushed into one. He was adamant earlier when discussing the last injection of paraldehyde with the Crown lawyer that this made the heroin injection more lethal and helped tip the old lady into her coffin. Yet just now he gave the impression, rightly or wrongly, that the dear Doctor had used one of the safest remedies for insomnia. If it made sense to the judge, it did not make sense to some of the lesser beings in the gallery.

The scales of justice were taking on the ludicrous oscillations of a child's mindless see-saw. During day four of the trial even Adams' own supporters had written him off, including the redoubtable cynic but vastly experienced chief crime reporter, Percy Hoskins, of the *Daily Express*.

Then came day five and the Attorney-General was held up to such ridicule by the defence, their prime medical evidence held in so much doubt, that the prosecution's cause would have been better served had Dr Douthwaite not been called upon at all!

After five days of trial the farcical performance of the prosecution had scarcely made a solid hit point. Whilst the defence were points to the good. Those journalists, like Hallworth, who had dug deep into Adams' murky past, looked on incredulously. How could the prosecution lay themselves open to so many of Lawrence's telling sallies. The shaking heads upon the press bench took on the ague of a St Vitus. But who could blame them.

The Attorney-General, for he led the Crown's case, was poorly prepared and was suffering as a result from a more efficient defence.

Mr Melford Stevenson, junior to Sir Reginald Manningham-Buller was doing his valiant best. It was obvious when Stevenson was upon his feet the prosecution case benefited. Alas, for that same prosecution, Melford Stevenson was not leading.

# Chapter Eight

*'I should not think of giving as little as 5cc in a
case like this – I never give less than 6cc.'*

DR HARMAN

By day ten, when most legal observers would have thought the
trial would have reached somewhere around the judge's
summing up, it was barely half-way through. But when fellow
beings are dealing with the most serious charge on earth
everyone's patience is summoned to deal with every jot and
tittle of the evidence. Even irrelevancies are acceptable. If time
is wasted by throwing everything in that is infinitely better than
that something should be left out.

On the tenth day Dr Douthwaite was still in the witness box
and the morning opened with Mr Lawrence saying to him and of
course to the jury:

'I am not inviting a Harley Street opinion about the skill
of a general practitioner, I know what your view has been
over these last days. But at least it is a possible alternative
that this GP was following a consistent course with these
drugs to produce the result which it was his duty to produce.
Dr Douthwaite, there is no necessity to postulate a murderous
intent.'

Whatever Dr Douthwaite had done over the weekend, which
was an interval in the trial, he was certainly not standing in a
witness box. A game of golf perhaps. So he was refreshed, and
replied vigorously to counsel:

'In the first place, with great respect, where I live has nothing to do with my knowledge or opinions. I have given evidence of intent to terminate life.'

Mr Lawrence: 'What I put to you is this – that on the factual history there is no need to postulate an intent to murder?'

The doctor: 'I am forced to postulate that on the drugs given in the last days of November.'

Mr Lawrence: 'If you will not come the whole way with me, at any rate you will come some of the way in agreeing to a possible alternative view. You would conceive it is quite possible, would you not, that another doctor might not find himself forced to the same conclusion?'

Dr Douthwaite: 'Yes, we all have different opinions.'

That modest statement may later appear to be the whole crux of the case. If doctors disagree, what layman can form a judgement? And twelve of them who would have to do so in seven days' time listened to those six words: 'Yes, we all have different opinions.'

The Attorney-General then rises to re-examine and after dealing with the Cheshire days and the fact that back in Eastbourne Mrs Morrell had plenty of sleep, Sir Reginald asked:

'What about this so-called drugs dilemma?'

Dr Douthwaite: 'There are drugs which can be used to get a patient gradually off heroin and morphia.'

'Would there have been a risk?'

'No risk if it had been attempted early enough'.

The Attorney-General: 'When her first expectation of life had been fulfilled to the maximum and even exceeded, was there not now a new lease, a high expectation of life to be prognosticated?'

'Oh, yes'.

'How would you qualify the doses prescribed?'

Dr Douthwaite stilled the court even more by saying: 'Colossal.'

The Attorney-General keeps up the tension:

*Dr John Bodkin Adams leaves the coroner's court after the inquest on Mrs Bobbie Hullett.*

*Adams, his mother and cousin, Florence Henry.*

*Late 1930's at a Y.M.C.A. sale of work, Adams is third from left.*

*Social occasion at Holywell Mount. The Hulletts House.*

*Dr Adams arrested: Det. Superintendent Hannam (left) and Det. Sergeant Hewitt escort the Doctor from Kent Lodge, passing a woman patient on the way.*

*Three Prosecution Witnesses: Nurses, Randall, Stronach and Mason-Ellis.*

*Mrs Bobbie Hullett: her death be-gan the investigation.*

*Mrs Edith Morrell: Dr Adams charged and acquitted of her mur-der.*

*Mrs Julia Bradnum: her niece, Mrs Lily Love also called in the police.*

*James Priestly-Downs: Only a fractured ankle, yet dead in a month.*

*Dr A. C. Sommerville: the East-Sussex Coronerwho criticised Adams' treatment of Mrs Bobbie Hullett.*

*James Walker: Chief Constable of Eastbourne, who called in New Scotland Yard's murder squad.*

*Mrs Margaret Pilling: her family 'rescued' her from the doctor and she lived.*

*Miss Mary Hine: asked to witness Mrs Bradnum's new will, naming Dr Adams as a beneficiary.*

*Dr Douthwaite: Witness for the prosecution.*

*Dr Harman: Witness for the defence.*

*Dr Ashby: Witness for the prosecution.*

*Miss Dorothy Lawrence, Adams' Receptionist.*

Det. Insp. Pugh, Head of Eastbourne's C.I.D. and witness, Bank
Manager, John Oliver.

The Rt Hon: Judge Melford
Stevenson: Junior to the Attorney-
General in the Adams murder trial.

Sir Geoffrey Lawrence: his brilliant
defence gained Dr Adams' acquittal.

Mr Justice Devlin signs autographs
in Holborn Viaduct during the Adams' murder trial.

*The Lagney Cemetery Gravestone of the Neil-Miller sisters.*

*The Exhumation of the Neil-Miller sisters.*

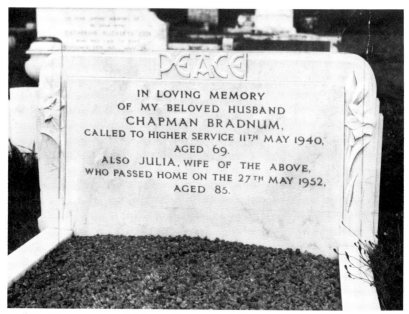

IN LOVING MEMORY
OF MY BELOVED HUSBAND
CHAPMAN BRADNUM,
CALLED TO HIGHER SERVICE 11TH MAY 1940,
AGED 69.
ALSO JULIA, WIFE OF THE ABOVE,
WHO PASSED HOME ON THE 27TH MAY 1952,
AGED 85.

*The Gravestone at Ochlynge Cemetery of Chapman and Julia Bradnum.*

*The Exhumation of Julia Bradnum.*

Dear Miss Room.

I am sorry I had not an opportunity of saying "Au Revoir" to you before leaving. I hope all goes well with you & your relations.

I am very well and not worrying. I also sleep well which is very good. We get plenty of food & alas without my usual active round. I am afraid I will put on weight ++

All good wishes for 1957

Yrs sincerely
JB Adams.

*Letter from Dr John Bodkin Adams to his housekeeper, Annie Room.*

*The hunter: Ex Det Chief Supt Charlie Hewitt.*

*The Hunted: Dr John Bodkin Adams about to face a first interview with New Scotland Yard Detectives.*

*Mrs Julia Bradnum and husband Chapman.*

*Left: Det. Sergeant Sellers and Det. Inspector Pugh, head of Eastbourne's C.I.D.*

*Sir Reginald Manningham-Buller, Attorney General at the time of the Adams murder trial.*

'Has anything said in this court affected your opinion as to the death of Mrs Morrell?'

'No.'

'To what do you attribute her death?'

'Drugs, probably assisted by paraldehyde.

In the absense of paraldehyde, in my opinion, the morphia and heroin administered on the last few days would have killed her.'

The Attorney-General sat down and Dr Douthwaite who had reiterated his grave verdict on the behaviour of a fellow in medicine sitting in the dock below him, then faced the Judge who said he would like to question him.

The Judge, speaking slowly and meticulously said:

'Before the jury can convict they must be satisfied that there is an act of murder. In the circumstances of this case it means that the Doctor either administered the drugs himself with intent to kill, or gave directions to the nurses that he hoped and intended would, if carried out, kill the patient. Now I think I am right in saying that the Doctor paid seventeen visits to Mrs Morrell in the period between November 8th and 12th and on all or most of these occasions he either administered drugs himself or left directions for the nurses as to what they were to do.

'If the case of the Crown is right, then one or more of these acts was attempted murder and I should like to be able to assist the jury by pointing out to them precisely what in relation to each act it is that forces you to postulate murder was being committed or attempted.'

Dr Douthwaite: 'I may have to postulate it in relation to the doses that had gone before, or more exactly, in relation to the doses that were not given. She was given no morphia from November 1st to 5th, the days when only heroin was given. By withdrawing morphia from her for five days he would certainly reduce the acquired tolerance to it. I wondered what was the possible reason, and that is why I did not make up my mind on the probable desire to terminate life until I saw that the return to morphia on November 6th was followed by a rapid increase together with large doses of heroin. Clearly this was not an attempt to wean her from addiction, a late realisation of what was happening. If it had been so, why should not the heroin be reduced first rather than the morphia? My conclusions after that were based on the rapidly mounting doses, and very large doses, of the last five days.'

The Judge: 'Are you saying that morphia was deliberately withheld in order that it might be re-introduced fatally?'

Dr Douthwaite: 'That is what it appears to me, because I can see no other reason for it. There was no attempt at any substitution.'

The Judge: 'When you consider a doctor's method of treatment, would the very last thing you would think of be murder?'

'Quite true, My Lord.'

'You would explore every other hypothesis before?'

'Yes.'

'Let me invite you to consider this. You criticise the Doctor's treatment. He embarked upon the wrong line from the beginning?'

'In my opinion he did.'

'But murder is not suggested as an explanation of that?'

'No.'

'The alternative explanation would seem to be that he did not understand the right use of dangerous drugs.'

It seemed an alternative that Dr Douthwaite could not swallow and he said:

'That could be concluded. I cannot believe that a medical man of his experience and qualifications is not aware of the action of those two drugs.'

The Judge: 'He may have the wrong ideas – he may have old-fashioned ideas – is this a possibility?'

'Yes, it is possible. I do not think he would not know the dangers of morphia and heroin.'

'Is it possible that he might have thought, however wrongly in your view and in spite of the dangers, that it was the right treatment to give?'

Dr Douthwaite, still more than doubtful: 'He might have thought so, I suppose, in the early stages.'

'Therefore, you start with a man who is taking a wrong line of treatment, not for sinister reasons, but because he is not taking the right line?'

'Yes.'

'Are you prepared to postulate that when he re-introduced the morphia on November 6th he must have intended to kill?'

'I am.'

'He did not kill as a result of that so the next day the injection is increased to a half grain?'

'Yes.'

'And he also left instructions that the same doses might be repeated during the night?'

The Judge, leaning forward slightly and folding his hands in front of him, added:

'Can I take it that in giving those instructions he was making sure, as it were, that if the first doses did not work doses would be given during the night until it did work?'

'Yes.'

'And the next morning he finds the patient is not dead, so he gives a special injection? But I think you said you disregarded the special injections?'

'I had to, because I do not know what they were.'

The Judge continues:

'Well, he finds that she is not dead and he leaves instructions that she might have a half grain of morphia and a half grain heroin if necessary. He is carrying on with what you say can only be a lethal dose?'

'Yes.'

'Then he makes his third visit in the evening. He finds she has not had any dose during the day, it had not turned out to be necessary. So he gives an injection of heroin and hyperduric morphia and directs that it should be repeated if necessary. Do you attach any appreciable importance to the change to hyperduric morphia?'

The doctor does not.

'So he is trying again a lethal dose, in your view, and leaving instructions for the lethal dose to be repeated?'

The doctor agrees.

'Then he visits her again on the next day, November 9th – she is still alive – and gives her one grain of morphia. Would that be a dose intended to kill?'

The doctor agrees.

'And he leaves behind him instructions to give a grain of heroin s.o.s., and you would say that this grain of heroin might well have been fatal?'

The doctor agrees.

'Then he visits her again the next morning. This is the eighth visit. He gives her a half grain morphia and she falls asleep. That half grain – the only conclusion you can draw with regard to that is that he intended to kill?'

'That is my view.'

Asks the Judge: '...Instructions left to change the dose to a half grain of both morphia and heroin...Doctor, do you regard this combination as any more or less lethal?'

Dr Douthwaite: 'Oh, yes, indeed – the combination is more lethal.'

'Then the Doctor comes again in the evening and finds that the lethal dose has not worked, so he doubles it to one whole grain each of morphia and heroin which is the largest injection so far?'

The reply is, 'Yes.'

'How soon might he have expected that dose to work and bring about death?'

'It would add to the accumulation so one would expect death within two or three days.'

'The medical picture appears to show that he was giving rather more doses than were really necessary?'

The answer was, 'Yes.'

'Might he not reasonably have waited a few days to see the result without giving more?'

'He might well have.'

The Judge: 'Now we come to the last day and the fourteenth visit when she had an injection of paraldehyde. You said at one time that it made death certain, if death were not certain already. In your view it was certain?'

'Yes'.

'In a matter of days?'

'Yes'.

'The Doctor gave the paraldehyde because he was tired of waiting for the other drugs to work?'

'Yes – a small injection of paraldehyde could have been given for an innocent purpose but 5cc was meant to kill.'

The Judge: 'Does it really matter then whether the second injection of paraldehyde, about which there has been a great deal of dispute, was given or not?'

'No'.

The Judge: 'I think I have the picture quite clear now in my mind. Your view, if I may summarise it for the jury, is really this – that the first time that the design for murder emerges from the medical pattern is when the Doctor drops the morphia and concentrates on the heroin, the only medical explanation for that being that he intends to re-introduce morphia with lethal effects, and then and thereafter all the subsequent injections, any one of them could have been lethal and can only be explained on the basis that they were intended to be so. And that goes on until he takes to paraldehyde to bring about her death more quickly?'

And Dr Douthwaite agrees with his Lordship.

And Dr Douthwaite, all his medical reasonings convincing him of Adams' guilt, although in the matter of the alleged murder of Mrs Morrell the patina of prosecution is thin in places, exerts his witnessing to the maximum and in so doing inadvertently presents the defence with another opportunity to nullify any positive evidence for the Crown.

Some defence lawyers would have left it at that, but not Mr Lawrence. He felt that by circumnavigating the issue once more he could compound doubt with more doubt. He decided not to let Dr Douthwaite go, but to cross-examine him again. With the clarity and precision, if not the volume, of a toastmaster, he uttered:

'I want first of all to understand the theory of murder which you were explaining to My Lord. Am I right in thinking that it is really made up of two limbs? The first limb being that the Doctor withdraws morphia for some days in order to reduce tolerance? The second being that he re-introduced morphia and thereafter gave increasing doses in conjunction with heroin too bring about a fatal result?'

Dr Douthwaite: 'Yes.'

'You know quite well that the dosage during the last five days was well within the experience of general practitioners in terminal stages of illness without producing fatality?'

Dr Douthwaite pauses to look at previous papers, then says:

'There were five grains of heroin on November 11th and that is thirty-five times the normal maximum dose.'

Mr Lawrence: 'It is no use taking one day in isolation without looking at what has gone before to see what the tolerance might be – what I am putting to you is this – if this had been a case of a patient suffering from a spinal carcinoma, for example, the picture of that dosage complete over those days would have been well within the experience of the profession?'

Dr Douthwaite: 'It would have been a dosage suggesting a desire to terminate life.'

Mr Lawrence: 'You would be driven in the witness box to say that the GP who followed that course was a murderer?'

'I would say he was giving large doses of drugs and those drugs would have caused death.'

Mr Lawrence: 'Would you mind facing the question...? You would not say in those circumstances that the general practitioner was a murderer?'

'No.'

The Judge asks: 'Do you say you would be forced to the conclusion that he intended to kill?'

142

Dr Douthwaite: 'Yes, My Lord. When I was asked earlier I deliberately said the drugs were given to terminate life. I do not know whether that is synonymous with murder. I did not introduce the word myself.'

Mr Lawrence added sternly: 'Murder, Dr Douthwaite, is killing with the intention of killing.'

The Judge intervenes: 'I am anxious there should not be introduced into this, questions that may be partly questions of law. It may be a matter of law, I don't know, and it may be a matter of medical practice, that if a doctor gives drugs knowing that they will shorten life but gives them because they were necessary to relieve pain, he is not committing murder.'

Mr Lawrence: 'This was a case of senile deterioration and in the last days the patient was suffering acute distress and lack of sleep. Would a doctor dealing with this case not be in the same position as the doctor who was dealing with acute pain in the final stages of an inoperable disease?'

Dr Douthwaite: 'I disagree. I think I have made it clear that this distress, especially these terrible twitchings the nurse told us about, were largely the result of drugs. Your example of someone in terrible pain is quite another matter. There is a profound difference between the acute pain in the terminal stages of inoperable disease and the terminal stages of arterio-sclerosis.'

Mr Lawrence: 'Is the sole difference between the two cases this, in your opinion, that in the inoperable case the use of drugs would be justified because there was only distress which falls short of severe pain?

'Yes.'

'You are entitled to your opinion but it is the doctor on the spot who has to judge in relation to the patient?'

'I quite agree.'

'Would it be a fair summary of your view that every dose of whatever size or kind had been an attempt to terminate life?'

'I think that is putting it a little bit inaccurately. I agree that every dose was given with a definite intent, but I don't want to

143

give the impression that I thought each dose was expected in itself to kill.'

The Judge: 'What you were inferring was that the Doctor refrained from giving a dose of itself lethal because he thought it was too difficult and might arouse suspicion, and so he had to give a series of doses over a period, the combined effect of which he knew would kill?'

Dr Douthwaite exclaimed from the box:

'That is exactly what I mean! The drugs were given to an individual who was saturated with them. These drugs would accumulate in the body.'

Mr Lawrence: 'Is this based on what is called the theory of accumulation?'

'It is.'

'Is it not a well-known fact that both morphia and heroin are notable for being non-accumulative drugs?'

'In the normal person, yes.'

'They are drugs which are eliminated relatively quickly, are they not?'

'Yes, we believe they are destroyed in the liver.'

'There is no reason at all then to postulate there was any accumulation in the body of this person?'

'Yes, there is every reason.'

'Can you ever say precisely what accumulation of morphia there may be in a body?

'No.'

'It is all speculation?'

'The nearer a patient is to death, the more accumulation will occur – I cannot say more.'

'This woman was in the terminal stages of life in this last fortnight?'

'Yes.'

'Dying, anyhow?'

'Well, she was dying.'

The Judge: 'Do you mean she was dying before November 1st?'

'Yes, My Lord.'

Mr Lawrence returns to the 'first limb' of Dr Douthwaite's theory and asks:

'The Doctor deliberately withdrew morphia on October 31st so that the patient should be rendered most vulnerable?'

'Yes.'

'Do you still adhere to that?'

'Yes.'

'By stopping this morphia over those five days he was removing the shield of protection from the larger doses which she had acquired?'

'Yes, removing that shield.'

'And that was done deliberately?'

The doctor says, 'Yes'.

'With the conscious intention of re-introducing morphia with lethal effect?'

'So it appears.'

With some sarcasm Mr Lawrence asks:

'When did you first think of this theory, Dr Douthwaite?'

'Well, I presume it was when I studied the summary and the medical reports of the case.'

'Before or after you first got into the witness box?'

'I think afterwards.'

'When?' stressed the barrister.

'I cannot remember.'

'Up to that point when My Lord started asking you questions, not a single hint of that theory had emerged from your lips?'

'I accept that.'

'The truth is that all this business is an afterthought on your part?'

'No, that is not true. As I said to My Lord, I have been puzzled by the withdrawal.'

'That, Dr Douthwaite, is part of your evidence which never emerged until My Lord himself asked you questions at the end of hours of examination in chief, of cross-examination and re-examination?'

'True.'

'In any case, the medical theory upon which it is based is absolute rubbish, isn't it?'

Dr Douthwaite smiles but cares not to reply.

Mr Lawrence: 'You know quite well that morphia and heroin are drugs which are both of the same medical and physiological kind?'

'Very similar.'

'Both are derivatives of opium and there is a cross-tolerance between them. Of all the degrees of cross-tolerance the one between morphia and heroin is the highest. Cross-tolerance means this – if you take morphia and acquire a tolerance to it you are also acquiring a tolerance to its chemical ally, heroin?'

'To some degree, yes.'

'To some considerable degree?'

'Yes.'

'And vice versa?'

'Yes.'

'So this was not the case of a man withdrawing a drug to reduce tolerance and the patient not getting a chemically similar drug?'

'No.'

'The whole of this theory of yours is based on the supposition that this withdrawal of morphia would so greatly reduce her tolerance as to render the later doses lethal?'

'The reduction would make the morphia re-introduced more likely to be lethal.'

Mr Lawrence: 'We can see from the nursing reports that over the first three or four days of no morphia there are no withdrawal symptons. Bearing in mind that you would naturally search for some innocent explanation before you went to the other, you cannot say that you were forced inescapably to place a sinister interpretation on this alteration in the drugging, can you?'

'Well, I can only say I see no explanation for it.'

'The truth of this matter is that you first of all gave evidence of one possibility to support the charge of murder and then thought of something else after you had started?'

146

'I was turning it over in my mind and then it crystallised.'

'But that is your personal view. You can conceive it quite possible that a reasonably-minded physician of equal eminence might by no means find it necessary to postulate an intention to terminate life on the same evidence?'

'I have always agreed that there might be contrary medical opinion – I am expecting it.'

'And that would be medical opinion entitled to as much weight as yours?'

'I do not question that.'

'You therefore admit the possibility of a skilled genuine view to the contrary of your position?'

'Yes.'

The Attorney-General stood up and boomed slowly:

'Have you changed your opinion about the intent of which you have spoken?'

'No.'

'Has it altered at all as to the causes of death?'

'No.'

'Are the variations of doses in the last days consistent with an innocent intent?'

'No.'

The Judge: 'I am not quite sure I have understood your last answer to Mr Lawrence, which was that you accepted the possibility of a skilled genuine view contrary to yours?

'I meant by that, My Lord, that doctors frequently disagree. I would in fact be surprised if an eminent doctor disagreed with me on certain points.'

The Judge: 'If another doctor were to say he disagreed entirely with your views on accumulation, would that be a skilled genuine view to the contrary?'

Dr Douthwaite: 'I can only say I really would be astonished if he does.'

'Your inference that there was an intent to kill on the Doctor's part depends upon your attribution to him of the knowledge that a single dose, not dangerous in itself, would be lethal because of the accumulation of drugs in the body?'

'Yes.'

The Judge: 'Before you were driven to that conclusion you had reviewed and excluded error, ignorance and incompetence?'

'Yes.'

'Could a view contrary to yours on the subject be due to error, ignorance or incompetence, but be honestly held?'

'Yes.'

'Then why do you postulate an intent to kill?'

'I cannot conceive a man with the Doctor's special qualifications having ignorance of this sort.'

'You mean that in the case of a GP it might be due to error... but in the case of a GP with an anaesthetist's qualifications it could not be due to this?'

'That is my view.'

'It must follow then that if the Doctor were to go into the witness box and say, "I disagree entirely with this view", he would be guilty of perjury – he would be saying he held a view which he cannot honestly hold?'

Dr Douthwaite: 'You have put me a very difficult point, My Lord. No – the Doctor could not honestly say so.'

'If any other doctor who is qualified goes into the witness box and says that, your answer would be the same – that he honestly cannot say that?

'That would be my answer.'

The Judge: 'You say the treatment could not have been due to error, ignorance or incompetence and must have been due to an intent to kill?'

'That is my view.'

'It must follow that anybody who expresses a view contrary to yours is expressing a view he cannot honestly hold?'

'Yes.'

'It is very important to see how far you go. It would be quite easy for a medical man in your position to say, "I am saying no

148

more about this treatment by the Doctor than that I think it was wrong and dangerous and I think it caused death. But whether it was administered through error, ignorance or incompetence or intent to kill is not for me to say and I am not going to say it". That is evidence you could have given, but you are going further and saying it could not have been due to error, ignorance or incompetence, but it must have been due to an attempt to kill.'

Dr Douthwaite: 'That is so.'

The Judge: 'One more point. You said that it was clear to the Doctor that she was a dying woman on November 1st. Now, this is quite outside your province, but I am telling you so that you follow what is in my mind. The jury may have to consider what motive the Doctor had. One motive that has been suggested is that if she had lived long enough she might have altered her will and deprived him of the benefits he had, or thought he had, under the will. So would you review the position at the end of October, if you can, to help the jury? If a man had that sort of motive, would he have said, "Well, she had only a month to live anyway, or two months or three months"? How far would a doctor, seeing the medical picture as you see it, have felt it worthwhile to shorten her life for a purpose of that sort?'

'From the medical picture I would have expected her to have lived only for a matter of a few weeks and probably no more than two months.'

The Judge: 'It is the Doctor saying to himself, "She can only live for three weeks anyway"? And would he be embarking then on a course that in fact took thirteen days to bring about her death?'

'He might well have.'

Dr Douthwaite steps from the witness box after twelve hours and twenty minutes. Dr Douthwaite had done his best for the Crown's case but most of the press considered his twelve hours and twenty minutes a period of total confusion and of inevitable doubt in the jury's collective mind.

Dr Douthwaite's place is taken by the Crown's second

medical expert, Dr Michael Ashby, a consultant neurologist to six London hospitals, with an address in Harley Street. Together with the Attorney-General he reviews the early illness of Mrs Morrell and the effects, etc. of drugs and when or how she would have died with or without them.

Very little was decided and in cross-examination by Mr Lawrence he agreed with his colleague on some points and not on others. Barrister and doctor debated the possibility of the old lady not being murdered at all, but dying from natural causes, a discussion which some observing lawyers regarded as a red herring but when a man is standing trial for his life even red herrings can have a purpose.

When the defence thought they were gaining ground on the possibility that Mrs Morrell died of a heart attack or something, the Attorney-General asked Dr Ashby:

'Can it be said, in the sense in which the phrase is commonly used and leaving out medical technicalities, that her death was due to natural causes?'

Dr Ashby: 'I do not think she could have survived that dosage of drugs but that dosage might well have killed her by an apparent natural cause, such as thrombosis or terminal pneumonia.'

The Judge: 'So it may be said that death was the result in the end of natural causes but those natural causes were themselves the result of the drugs given by the Doctor?'

Dr Ashby: 'Certainly.'

'And that, looked at in the ordinary common sense way, means that the cause of death was the result of the drugs given by the Doctor?'

'Yes'.

It is now the thirteenth day in a trial of several sensations and Mr Lawrence now provides another one. He wants the trial stopped! The jury is sent out and for two hours he makes a submission that there is broadly no case to answer – that it is a case based on medical evidence alone and without such evidence there would be no case at all. What the 'theatre audience' at the back of the court had heard and seen so far, even without the defence, was that doctors can't always agree. His submission is not accepted by the Judge who at the end of it says succinctly:

'Mr Lawrence, my conclusion is that the two doctors' evidence does give rise to questions which can only be determined by the jury.'

The jury are back and the trial continues with the first witness for the defence, Dr John Harman. But before Dr Harman can issue one word, Mr Lawrence produces yet another sensation, although expected in many quarters, which sent reporters from the room to their hot lines.

*Dr Adams will not be called to give evidence.* No man or woman on a murder charge is forced to say anything. He has been brought to the court by the Crown and it is up to the Crown to prove him guilty. If he wishes to, he may remain silent from the moment of his arrest to the moment of his freedom, or to the moment of his sentence. That is his right.

The court settles down again to listen to Dr Harman, a consultant physician at St Thomas's Hospital, London. Earlier two doctors briefed by the Crown had given their evidence to support the case for the Crown. Now an eminent physician was being called to square up things and try to seek sense in the defence point of view.

The doctor agrees that he has had experience in the treatment of cerebral thrombosis in elderly people and is *au fait* with Mrs Morrell's condition in Cheshire.

Mr Lawrence: 'Are you prepared to condemn or not to condemn the use of morphia during her stay in Cheshire?'

Dr Harman: 'I am certainly not prepared to condemn.'

'And what do you say about the introduction of heroin later by the Doctor?'

'I should say it was unusual, as it is not a drug commonly given.'

'What is the usual reason for it?'

'Pain.'

'And what is the effect?'

'Compared with morphia there is less soporific action.'

'Do you see anything sinister in its introduction?'

'Nothing at all sinister.'

Mr Lawrence: 'Looking at the nursing notes up to the spring of 1950, what do you say is a fair summary of the position?'

'I should say she has recovered from her stroke ... that she has reached a stage at which one might describe her as being partially crippled but there are no signs of anything further about to happen.'

'What do you say about the continued medication at that period of the regular doses, day after day, of a quarter grain morphia and a third of heroin?'

'The clearest thing about that is that by the time it has been going on for a year and some months and it would certainly have to be continued even if it was producing no good. I can see no evidence it was producing any harm.'

'Why do you say it would have to be continued?'

'Because she was by then addicted.'

'In what sense do you mean addicted?

'I mean one would have to continue with what she was having in order to prevent her from getting withdrawal symptons - in other words, a clear-cut illness lasting about ten days which, while not exactly dangerous, would be extremely unpleasant.'

'If that had been envisaged, would she have had to have some substitute drug?'

'Well, I think that sort of patient in that sort of state certainly would. If the Doctor had withdrawn, he would only have done it with a view to starting again later, since he thought morphia and heroin useful drugs for her. I can see the need for withdrawal from a young or middle-aged person with a normal life before them but in this case the patient was crippled and was going to remain crippled.'

Mr Lawrence: 'So far as heroin is concerned, have you ever known of its use in cases other than severe pain?'

'Oh, yes I have used it in such cases.'

'The nurses say that Mrs Morrell was bad-tempered, irritable and given to outbursts?'

'Then I think it extremely likely that these drugs would have been helpful.'

Mr Lawrence: 'Would you expect them to make an existing irritability better or worse?'

'It would be rash to say exactly what any of these drugs would do in a different patient. Ordinarily they are given to reduce irritability and in the majority of cases they succeed.'

Mr Lawrence: 'When the Doctor was away on holiday, his partner stepped up the morphia by the introduction of omnopon. What does that indicate to you?'

'Presumably the patient was getting restless and needed more sedative.'

'Was it or was it not reasonable for the partner to do that?'

'Entirely reasonable.'

Mr Lawrence then referred to the possibility of her suffering a stroke.

Dr Harman: 'There are several points to consider. There was a significant increase in the dosage... she had difficulty in speech... semi-consciousness can equally well be produced by drugs or by a stroke.'

Mr Lawrence: 'Supposing it was a stroke, what would you expect from a patient of that age and history?'

'If it was a stroke, I should expect further trouble leading progressively to deterioration and, unless something else intervened, to natural death from old age.'

It was felt in the press box that the jury must be feeling like a collective Solomon. How, when, and at what point does murder take over from natural causes in this case?

Mr Lawrence turns to November and asks Dr Harman if he can take the view that she was clearly a dying woman by then.

Dr Harman replies: 'I agree roughly. On November 9th it was much more obvious than on November 1st. It is a question of how soon you make your diagnosis. It is clear that at this point the drugs were no longer working. This is one of the disadvantages of morphia, that at some point later on when one really wants to use it, one finds it is no longer working. That is what I think happened here.'

Mr Lawrence: 'And do you or do you not agree with Dr Ashby that after this point of no return the first duty of a doctor is to promote the comfort of a patient?'

The doctor agrees.

'Do you see anything to suggest that these drugs were given with any other object than to promote her comfort?'

'My own conclusion is that they were given to stop her getting excited, to keep her peaceful, and that they were not working very effectively.'

'I want to ask you about the dosage of paraldehyde?'

Dr Harman: 'I should not think of giving as little as 5cc in a case like this - I never give less than 6cc.'

'Is it a safe hypnotic?'

'The safest - even if she had had that other injection of 5cc on top of the earlier 5cc it would still have been within the normal limits. It was not a large dose.'

(Earlier the jury had heard Dr Douthwaite describe the dosage as "colossal".)

Dr Harman then described death from morphia, telling the jury about convulsions, muscles going taut and jerking the patient violently, and as though on stage he suddenly gave a vivid demonstration. For almost a minute he stands before Judge and jury flaying his arms, throwing his head backwards, open-mouthed and gurgling, snapping his body in jerks and banging it against the wood of the witness box. He looks like a demented puppet without strings, giving a frightening pantomime and portrayal of death from the juice of a poppy.

When he settled down the defence doctor said it was not always known for certain why old ladies who had suffered strokes died. They just died, he said, and it was difficult to know for certain why.

Mr Lawrence: 'Is there any necessity then to link that death with any of the drugs that have gone before?'

Dr Harman: 'I see no necessity to link her death with the doses administered.'

His remarks totally disputed Dr Douthwaite's evidence for the Crown.

Mr Lawrence: 'Is it possible it could be so linked?'

'Oh, it is possible, yes.'

'Could you say whether one hypothesis is more likely than another?'

He felt there was rather a large dose of hypnotics which in general was a bad thing but there was no evidence to answer that question one way or the other. He thought too that the amount of dosages given was reasonable.

Mr Lawrence: 'Have you yourself encountered cases where this amount has been given?'

'Oh, yes, I have had comparable cases - I should not have regarded this as anything to talk about to friends when talking medical shop.'

'Would you have expected the doses to have a fatal result on Mrs Morrell?'

'I would not expect anything. I cannot say that death would not occur. It might very well. But what I would not say is that it would have occurred. Morphia and heroin are drugs oustanding in their variability of effect...'

Mr Lawrence: 'Let me ask you if the doses recorded in the nurses' books are of the freak kind or not?'

Said Dr Harman, 'Not freak at all.'

And the court got the impression that they were quite the norm.

And those in the court paying attention continued to recall Dr Douthwaite's evidence.

Mr Lawrence: 'Can anybody say with any degree of accuracy or truth that this or that amount would be fatal to any patient?'

'Not to any degree of accuracy or truth.'

'It has been suggested that the Doctor as an anaesthetist would know more about the long-term effects of morphia and heroin?'

'I can see no importance in that at all. I know a good many anaesthetists who don't.'

It would be difficult to find another medical witness who would so diametrically oppose the evidence of Dr Douthwaite.

Mr Lawrence said that towards the end, the defendant gave his patient paraldehyde, and asked:

'Can you think of anything better or safer that he could have turned to?'

Dr Harman: 'That is exactly what I would have done.'

Dr Harman then opines for a while on the uses of opium and brightly disagrees with more points made so firmly by Dr Douthwaite on the other side. Dr Harman concluded his evidence by disagreeing with more of what Dr Douthwaite had said, offering an alternative opinion and being mildly evasive if he could not nail his quarry to the stake.

Mr Lawrence asked him: 'Do you agree with Dr Douthwaite that to instruct nurses to give heroin s.o.s. (as required) was an astonishing suggestion?'

'I was not astonished at all.'

Nor were some of the spectators who were by now getting very used to doctors disagreeing. Once again it seemed the crux of the case.


It was the Attorney-General's turn to rip apart a few fables which the jury might have conjured up in their minds. He said with his usual gruffness:

'Dr Harman, have you ever practised as a general practitioner?'

And came the reply: 'Only a fortnight.'

'Prior to this case, have you ever had any occasion to make any special study of heroin and morphia?'

'No special study.'

'And is Dr Douthwaite a recognised authority on heroin and morphia?'

'He is.'

The Attorney-General poses the question: 'It is very important you should not shut your eyes to the obvious, or not give certain factors their full weight?'

'It is.'

'Do doctors normally prescribe morphia and heroin without the intention of using them on the patient?'

'I should think not.'

'You have seen the summary of the prescriptions and you have seen that for the last five days the Doctor prescribed forty-one grains of morphia and thirty-nine heroin?'

'Yes.'

'Did you ignore these factors before expressing an opinion?'

'No.'

'Assuming that all those drugs so prescribed were administered to Mrs Morrell during the five days, what in your opinion would the effect have been?'

'I would be very unwilling to suggest what the effect would have been.'

The Attorney-General, sternly: 'I am asking for your opinion.'

'She certainly could have survived those doses.'

'Of that quantity?

'I think it is possible.'

'Do you think it is likely?'

'Yes, I think it is likely.'

'Would you have expected these doses to do her any good?'

'They might have done.'

'Have you ever heard of any doses like that being prescribed to a dying old lady of eighty-one?'

'I have not heard of an exactly comparable dose.'

'You would never prescribe doses of that quantity for a lady of that age?'

'I have never prescribed them.'

'And you would never?'

'I am not prepared to say what I would do.'

'Do you think you would prescribe doses of that magnitude?'

'I do not think I would.'

'Have you ever heard of any doses like that being prescribed for a lady of eighty-one?'

'Yes.'

'A dying lady, not dying of an inoperable disease?'

'This lady I was thinking of was not dying at all.'

'But this lady, according to you, was?'

'Yes.'

'Did you hear Dr Douthwaite's evidence that in his opinion each one of these prescriptions on these days was a lethal dose?'

'I don't agree with that opinion.'

'You disagree with Dr Douthwaite?'

'I do.'

'Dr Harman, most of the views you have expressed here about drugs, were they formed after reading books before the case?'

'Yes - that is one of the usual ways of gaining knowledge.'

'How many drug addicts have you treated?'

'Two or three - one was a heroin addict and the others morphia.'

'One heroin addict is not a very representative experience on which to base a general opinion. How long ago was that?'

'It was before the war.'

Some of those listening thought that one swallow did not a summer make, and in any case the swallow was a long time dead.

The Attorney-General: 'Your answers to my learned friend yesterday possibly conveyed a different impression of the range of your experience? That impression conveyed to his lordship and the jury would be an erroneous impression?'

'I don't think so.'

'Your dramatic acting yesterday afternoon was based, was it not, on what you read of that kind of convulsions?'

'Yes.'

'You have never seen a morphia convulsion?'

'No.'

One sensed that the Attorney-General, at that moment at any rate, thought that the doctor, on leaving the witness box, should apply for a job with Equity. For the next few minutes the barrister and the doctor entered into a dogfight of words over weaning patients off drugs, treating patients after a stroke, the use of drugs and the results of prolonged drugging. Sir Reginald then says:

'I am asking you as a consultant if you were told that a lady in her late seventies had this course of medication over two years, would you have expected that to be good for her general health?'

Dr Harman: 'I should enquire into the circumstances before I expressed an opinion.'

'And having enquired?'

'It would depend on what the circumstances were.'

The Attorney-General puts down his papers and says impatiently:

'If you do not want to answer I will not press you.'

The dogfight continued, with the Attorney-General listening in disbelief to some of the doctor's answers and getting precious little effect for the jury. Soon afterwards he gave up and the court adjourned.

No matter how disgruntled the Attorney-General was with the good Dr Harman, the truth of the matter was that his courtroom examinations and cross-examinations lacked perception. In the two weeks or so of the trial so far, Sir Reginald Manningham-Buller had lost a little of his arrogant confidence. The press were aware of this fact, the jury too, and many members of the public, judging by overheard conversation. The prosecution had lost the initiative to a defence who by sheer surprise tactics had impressed all those in court - not least the jury. There was a sense of anticlimax too, although the case was far from over. Mr Lawrence's decision not to call the accused Doctor to give evidence and more pertinently, thereby removing any possibility of the Attorney-General facing the

Doctor across that well of court in cross-examination, has, for many, taken the guts out of the trial.

As for the prosecution, that decision of Lawrence's was yet another blow. Hallworth and others, including Scotland Yard detectives, were firmly convinced that Manningham-Buller had entertained the belief that he could destroy Adams in the dock. Now this, and the Attorney-General would be denied.

For the press, anticipation of how the devout Doctor would perform in the dock had occupied many an editorial conference, many a boozy night full of speculation in the local 'pub. Now, they too, would be denied.

But Lawrence did take a calculated gamble. Juries do not like accused forfeiting statements of innocence from the dock. The fact of law that establishes the Crown has to prove guilt and that the defence is not obliged to prove innocence, is well-known. But all in all, they too, would prefer to see the red-face accused answering questions from the dock but, they too, were denied.

# Chapter Nine

*'I do not think that I ought to hestitate to tell you
that here the case for the defence seems to me a
manifestly strong one...'*

SIR PATRICK DEVLIN

In terms of theatre, the fifteenth day was the start of the finale.
The stage has been cleared and all the actors who gave their
witness sit in the wings awaiting the dénouement. Alone on
stage now are the prosecutor and the defender. In the stalls the
audience of jurors listen and the judge sits alone and aloof in the
director's box.

Just one line spoken badly, just one wrong innuendo or
misinterpretation could give the audience a mistaken idea of
the plot. They could miss the point completely, or worse,
wonder what the play had all been about, their minds in
confusion. The small simple word is called, doubt.

Mr Lawrence took his place in the spotlight and with a clear
articulation retold the story. Although it was described on the
bill-posters by the Crown as a dark murder plot, he insisted that
it was quite the opposite. Although the described murderer
had never actually been on stage, Mr Lawrence tried to
persuade the audience that he should never have been in the
theatre at all because he didn't like murders and had never
been to such a sensational first night before. It was all a
mistake and a hoax.

Mr Lawrence's speech was coherent and studded with
moments of brilliance.

The Attorney-General, dressed in black, thundered through his lines, full-toned and reaching the very edge of the theatre, describing the dreadful murderous death of the leading lady who like the leading man never appeared on the stage.

To compare the final speeches by the barristers with theatre is not to be frivolous about the future, the freedom and the dignity of the Doctor. In law, both barristers had presented their cases, perhaps the defence with more dexterity. They carried out their individual tasks with the forethought and solemnity needed in such a house of justice, but to many of the press who had seen it so many times before, there was a forgiveable hint of the acting profession, also with the knowledge that their words would meld into eye-catching headlines.

And now for the judge who has sat throughout the hearing alert, all listening, ready to be gently helpful, to offer understanding to a confused witness but eager to prevent any points of evidence swaying away from the target before the jury.

He looks to the jury, places his hands in a prayer-like position and says:

'You are the sole judges of fact, and from your verdict on a matter of fact there is no appeal. My task is to tell you the law. My task in this case is a light one - there is very little question of law that is in dispute. I propose to deal first with the law, then with certain irrelevancies and inessentials in this case, and then go through the events chronologically. There are four matters of law of which I must tell you. The first is what is meant in law by the word, murder. Murder is an act, or a series of acts, which were intended to kill and did in fact kill. It does not matter for this purpose if death was inevitable. If life was cut short by weeks or months it is just as much murder as if it were cut short by years...

'There has been a good deal of discussion about the circumstances in which a doctor might be justified in giving drugs which would shorten life in cases of severe pain. It is my duty to tell you that the law knows no special defence of this character. But that does not mean that a doctor aiding the sick or the dying has to calculate in minutes or hours, or perhaps in days or weeks, the effect on a patient's life of the medicines which he administers. If the first purpose of medicine - the restoration of health - can no longer be achieved, there is still much for the doctor to do and he is entitled to do all that is proper and necessary to relieve pain and suffering, even if the measures he takes may incidentally shorten life... If, for example, a doctor had done something or omitted to do something and death occurs, say on the 11th or 12th or the Monday instead of the Tuesday, no one with common sense would say the doctor caused the death. They would say the cause of death was the injury, or whatever it was, that brought her to hospital. But it remains a fact and remains a law that no doctor has the right to cut off life deliberately...

'What counsel for the defence was saying was that the treatment that was given by the Doctor was designed to promote comfort, and if it was the right and proper treatment of the case, the fact that incidentally it shortened life does not give any grounds for convicting him of murder.

'The second matter of law is that it is for me to say whether there is evidence on any particular point and not allow you to be troubled with the point unless there is some evidence... I do, therefore, direct you as a matter of law that there is no evidence on which you would properly come to the conclusion that any drugs were administered to Mrs Morrell over and above the injections recorded in the nursing notebooks. If the case for the prosecution had rested solely on the prescription list and the suggestion that the quantities shown there had been administered to Mrs Morrell, I should not have allowed the case to go to you at all...

'I should like to say this - and I say it with the approval of the Lord Chief Justice – it is not desirable that on matters of this sort judges should express what are merely their personal views – I think it would have been wiser in this case if the preliminary

163

proceedings before the magistrates had been held in private. Because when you have a case which arouses widespread discussion it is inevitable that reports should appear in the press which are read by the public and consequently by members of the public who might be asked to serve on the jury; and the proceedings before the preliminary magistrates were quite different from the proceedings as they emerged in this court...

'But having said that, members of the jury, I venture to wonder whether, after three weeks of sitting in this court, there is anything left of it that really affects your mind. If you have not learned within those weeks to distinguish between what is solid fact, sifted, gone over again and again, and what is gossip and rumour, then, members of the jury, you will not be the sort of jury that I believe you are and that ordinarily serves in these courts. If you have not learned to distinguish as easily as one can distinguish, if one is an expert, between different textures of stuff – good quality, on the one hand, and shoddy, on the other – between what is evidence and really proves something, and is mere suspicion, gossip, and of no value whatsoever, then, as I say, you would have learned nothing. But I am completely confident that you have, and I entertain no doubt at all that anything that may conceivably have been in your minds at the beginning has sunk to the bottom, as it were, as the dregs which will trouble you not at all in arriving at your verdict...

'It is the duty of the prosecution to satisfy you beyond reasonable doubt before you arrive at a verdict of guilty. The accused, as he sits in the dock, is as innocent as anyone else in the court and will so remain until the jury by their verdict have convicted him. The Doctor sitting there has the right to the advantage of what I may call the initial incredulity that any assertion of that sort, that a doctor has murdered his patient, would give rise to in the minds of ordinary men. And the prosecution must demolish that...

'Reasonable doubt does not mean a feverish or haunting doubt, a doubt which one might wake up with in the middle of the night. It means a cool, sane, reasonable doubt...

'The rule that you must be satisfied beyond all reasonable doubt is a rule which is expressly designed for the benefit of the accused. Satisfaction on the balance of probabilities is not enough. That means, does it not, that persons who may probably be criminals, but cannot be shown to be so beyond a reasonable doubt, go free. You may feel if you started to speculate about it, that that is not a state of affairs that you like to see. You may feel you ought to be allowed to consider all the material that might seem to you to be relevant and not to be restricted to what is put before you in this court. But, members of the jury, whether you like the rules or not, they are the rules which you must accept and must be bound by. Anything outside the evidence is outside your responsibility, and your responsibility, Heaven knows, is great enough.

'It is not your responsibility to wonder what might happen if you allow a man to go free who is probably a criminal. The rule about reasonable doubt is the instrument which is given to you to use and you are not responsible for whether it is the right or wrong instrument, it is the one that you must use...

'These rules are not inventions that have not been found to work. They are rules which have been well settled by generations of experience. They are rules, I think, which accord with our notions of how justice should be administered. They are not lawyers' rules. We pride ourselves, do we not, that a man who is convicted by a jury is undoubtedly guilty. The price of making sure that the innocent are not convicted must be that the guilty sometimes go free. It is to carry out that great principle that the common law has evolved these rules, the rules of evidence and proof, and it is upon those rules that our juries have been instructed for generations...'

The Judge referred to the difficulty faced by the jury when considering the conflicting evidence given by the medical witnesses.

'In most cases medical evidence is only ancillary and plays a minor part, whereas in this case the prosecution has had to rely upon their medical evidence to establish the very fact of murder. And there you have three eminent physicians going into the witness box and disagreeing with each other...

'You have heard the examinations and cross-examinations and got a general impression from them... And fundamentally your task in court is just this – you will have to make up your mind. What impression did the doctors make upon you in the witness box? Which of them inspired the most confidence? You saw them and you listened to them, you heard their qualifications, you heard the answers they gave. You have heard their answers criticised. You have heard Dr Harman criticised by the Attorney-General. You have heard Dr Douthwaite criticised by Mr Lawrence, not on the basis, as I understand it, that he is not a great authority, but much more on the basis that he is a man who jumps to conclusions, who, perhaps naturally without the full material at his disposal, forms an opinion from which he is reluctant to depart. Some people are more opinionated than others. All those things you have to take into account...

'Another unusual feature – I think it is fair to call it unusual – is that the accused himself has not gone into the witness box. I say it is unusual, but then in many respects this is an unusual case... I want to face this frankly with you because it is something that may be troubling your minds. It is perhaps a natural reaction for laymen, and perhaps for lawyers too, to say, "Why hasn't he gone into the witness box if he is an innocent man? He is the doctor who attended the patient. He can tell us more about this than anyone else can. Why has he not gone into the witness box, unless he fears that questions will be put to him that he cannot satisfactorily answer?" You heard Mr Lawrence address you on this point. You heard him tell the reasons, or some of the reasons at any rate, why on his advice – and a client might well be a foolish man if he did not in such a matter follow his lawyer's advice – the Doctor had not gone into the witness box. You may have found those reasons convincing, or you may have not. I am not going to deal with them. What I

166

am going to tell you is simply this – that it does not matter. You have not got to judge whether the reasons are convincing or not. The Doctor has a right not to go in the witness box... I shall elaborate on that at the end, because it is so important... Let me tell you that it would be, in my judgement – and indeed as a matter of law – utterly wrong if you were to regard the Doctor's silence as contributing in any way towards proof of guilt. The prisoner who goes into the witness box goes there for this own benefit and his own defence. It is perfectly true that they sometimes make matters worse for themselves. But the prosecution has no right to rely on that at all. The duty of the prosecution is to prove their case before the question ever arises as to whether the prisoner should be called or not...'

The Judge pointed out to the jury that the Doctor was what might be called a "potential witness for the defence". Any gap which might be left in the evidence by his silence must remain unfilled. They must not speculate on what he might have said.

'Let me illustrate this in relation to some of the issues in this case. You heard the police officers give evidence about statements that have been made by the Doctor. You have also heard it suggested that the Doctor had not said some of the things attributed to him. Now you might have said to yourself, "Well, we see no reason why we shouldn't accept the police evidence provisionally but of course we must keep open minds until we have the Doctor's version". Well, you have not heard it and you will not hear it. You are left to decide that question without the potential evidence of the defence...You are not obliged to think that if the Doctor had gone into the witness box he might have given a convincing answer...'

It was now the afternoon of the sixteenth day and the Judge began to go through the salient dates, from June 25th 1948, when Mrs Morrell had a stroke while staying with her son in Cheshire. She spent nine days in hospital where she was given a quarter grain of morphia per day.

'That has been criticised by Dr Douthwaite but not by the other doctors in the case.'

On Mrs Morrell's return to Eastbourne by ambulance on July 5th the Doctor took charge of her case. On July 9th he prescribed morphia, on July 21st heroin. That was criticised by Dr Douthwaite and by Dr Ashby.

'Dr Harman has defended that treatment but you may think – and it is a matter entirely for you – that he was not altogether enthusiastic about it.'

Nurse Randall came on February 12th 1949 and remained as Mrs Morrell's night nurse until the end.

'In the following April there took place the first of two conversations between the Doctor and Mrs Morrell's solicitor. It is the first suggestion we have that testamentary matters were under discussion, the first suggestion that the Doctor had got this lady under his influence... On August 24th the will was made which tells us precisely what the Doctor got. He knew that Mrs Morrell, who left an estate of £157,000 net, left most of it to her son and left a number of legacies that you were reminded of... So you may think that it was not a very great achievement – an oak chest of silver valued at £276, compared with £300 to the night nurse and £1,000 to the chauffeur...'

From June 1949 when the nursing records began, a quarter grain of morphia and a quarter grain of heroin were given daily, with slight variations, until September 1950. Then the dosage increased so rapidly that Dr Ashby felt it was bound to end in disaster, unless she was weaned.

In September Mrs Morrell executed a codicil cutting the Doctor out of her will but in October she tore up the codicil and the pieces were sent to her solicitor by her son. Whether the Doctor knew he was getting any of these things we do not know.

On October 9th Mrs Morrell had what may have been a second stroke, claimed by the prosecution to be caused by the large amount of drugs prescribed. From October 31st to November 6th morphia was withdrawn, from which Dr Douthwaite inferred an intention to kill. On November 8th hyperduric morphia was given and on the evening of the 9th the Doctor gave instructions for one grain of heroin to be given as required. The following day the instructions were changed to one grain hourly s.o.s. Dr Douthwaite selected that date as marking the complete inevitability of death. On November 12th at about 5 p.m. is the last recorded injection of morphia and heroin. Later in the evening came the first injection of paraldehyde. At 2 a.m. on the 13th she died.

On the following day the Doctor filled in the cremation form, stating that he had no pecuniary interest 'in so far as I am aware'. The cremation took place on the 15th. On February 6th the chest of silver was delivered to the Doctor, and about that time he also received the Rolls-Royce.

'Well, then, members of the jury, there is a long gap of six years and it is right that you should be reminded, as Mr Lawrence reminded you, that at the end there was no suspicion at all about the way in which Mrs Morrell died. The nurses departed and went about their avocations. The estate was cleared up. The relatives dealt with the legacies and other matters and there was no suggestion that anything sinister had occurred. It is not in fact until August or September, the summer of 1956, five and a half years later, that anything is heard of this matter. Then we know that inquiries were made from the nurses by Superintendent Hannam and they made statements upon which, no doubt, these proceedings in due course were founded.

'Those inquiries led to four police interviews with the Doctor in 1956. October 1st was the encounter outside the garage which was a casual encounter... The second took place on November 24th, when the house was searched for dangerous drugs. There was a conversation about drugs, the list was given to the Doctor to consider, he made his remark about very, very seldom using morphia and heroin. He said all the drugs on the list were used and he said, "Poor soul, she was in terrible agony."

'The third of the interviews was on November 26th at the police station, and then it was that the Doctor referred to easing her passing and her being a dying woman. The last was when the

Doctor was arrested on December 19th, and said, "Murder? Can you prove it was murder?" There was also the phrase to the receptionist, "See you in Heaven". There was a lot of cross-examination on that at the time but it has disappeared from the case, and quite rightly so. You have not been reminded of it by either side. You cannot attach weight or importance to words of that sort which were obviously said under great emotional strain.'

After dealing briefly with the police evidence, the Judge continued:

'... Second, what help, if any, can you get from the whole period of this illness before October 31st or November 1st, when as it has been put, the design for murder begins? You have heard the Doctor's treatment criticised and you have heard it defended but how does it help you to answer the real question which in this case you have to answer? As stated by the prosecution – and indeed you may think to some extent on the admitted facts – it is not a very pretty story. Of course I can well understand a legacy being left to a doctor who is an old family friend, or something of the sort, and the last thing I should wish to do would be to try to lay down terms and conditions under which doctors can properly receive legacies. But if you find a patient who is given drugs by a doctor, and a doctor angling for a legacy and expressing excessive anxiety for what he is likely to get under the will, when the doctor goes on holiday and is taken out of the will, and shortly before the patient's death is back in the will again, and then signs a form about cremation – well, there are many members of the medical profession who would tell the executor they could not have anything to do with such a legacy... But there is a very, very big difference between something of that sort and a charge of murder.

'Suppose you are going to come to the conclusion, as the prosecution invites you, that the Doctor was engaged in a sinister scheme. How does it help? In one way it weakens the case for the prosecution. Their case would be stronger if it could be said: there was a doctor who for two years had been treating a patient in a completely model way, doing the right thing at the right time, and then suddenly goes completely off the rails. In that sense it is much weaker if the prosecution say they find a doctor giving wrong treatment right from the beginning at a time when they do not suggest he had murder in his mind...

'Members of the jury, you may well come to the conclusion that the Doctor was a fraudulent rogue – indeed, rogue would be too mild a word – who deliberately tried to get a patient under his influence to get something out of the patient; but all fraudulent rogues are not murderers. Fraud and murder are poles apart... If you think, as you might think, that the truth about the treatment is somewhere between the two, that the Doctor administered drugs not with any sinister purpose in his mind but simply because he found it the easiest way to cope with a very difficult patient – if you thought that, does it help you when you come to the term murder? The prosecution must point to a specific date when they say the design was formed. You have to consider what was done in relation to the condition in which the patient was then, and not mind, it seems to me, one way or the other, how she got there.

'The third matter is – and I leap now to the very end – the doses of paraldehyde. You will remember there was great discussion at one time as to whether Nurse Randall really did give a second injection which is not recorded in the books. Does it help? The fact is, is it not, that on the case for the prosecution the Doctor had made up his mind to murder with the use of morphia and heroin. If that is so, you really don't need to bother about these two injections of paraldehyde. All they could have done at most was to accelerate the death by a few hours. And if the Doctor was not using morphia and heroin to bring about her death, then no one in their senses can suggest that one, or two injections of paraldehyde at the very end themselves constitute murder...

'Now I come to what is the last of what I call the inessentials, and that is the big discrepancy between the amounts of the drugs that were prescribed and the amounts that were administered and which are recorded in the books... The prescriptions, of course, are no direct evidence of what was administered. Some link must be shown between the two, and the Attorney-General has submitted: Why do doctors prescribe drugs unless they intend them to be administered? Well, of course, they do not, and that raises a presumption, no doubt. But that presumption, as it seems to me, is completely rebutted if you get nurses coming and saying, "We have recorded the injections in writing and these books contain all the injections that were given". It rebuts the presumption and makes it mere conjecture, (upon which you can never act in a criminal case of any sort) that any drugs in excess of that were given. There is no direct evidence that the Doctor actually collected or received any of these drugs that are set down in the prescription list... As to the special injections recorded in the books, some of them you will probably think are proved to your satisfaction as relating quite clearly to vitamins and so on. Others the prosecution point to, saying that they must have been morphia and heroin. That is a matter for you. But what seems to me quite clear is that the special injections cannot possibly account for the difference between the amounts prescribed and the amounts that were actually administered.'

Between November 9th and 12th only four special injections were given. The amount of morphia unaccounted for during that time was more than thirty grains and the amount of heroin nearly twenty-two grains.

'... So you may think that those four special injections are quite incapable of accounting for the discrepancy.

'It is of course possible to say that the Doctor, at any time when he was visiting Mrs Morrell and being alone in her room, gave her a large injection. No one can say that is inconceivable. It is possible that he told the nurse that he had given half a grain of morphia or half a grain of heroin, when he had given a much greater dose but it is not that sort of conjecture upon which you can act when there is a charge of murder. You have got the medical history in the nurses' notes. If there had been anything in those notes which pointed to a much larger injection than that which is recorded, the doctors would have called your attention to it but they have not. They are the skilled readers of those notes, not you or I. If the doctors could point to any injection about which they can say, "Well, we cannot understand how she had symptons of that sort if the dose is as small as its recorded here," then you might have a genuine case which you could begin to investigate. But short of that, members of the jury, you have nothing except mere conjecture.

'Moreover, it is no use saying, "Oh, well, if all the difference was not given, then at least something more than was recorded must have been given". It is no use saying that, for this reason : that if that is the position, then there must be some channel existing by which the drugs prescribed were improperly disappearing; and once you accept the existence of such a channel, then there is nothing to show you that it did not account for the whole of the discrepancy.

'Was there in fact such a channel? Members of the jury, I come to a difficult part of the case, but a part you may want to face, and that I must help you to face so far as I can. Let me put it this way. Supposing you were to think – there are no grounds on which you can safely think so – but supposing you were to think that the Doctor had been dishonest about drugs, how much better would it be that you should unjustly suspect him of that sort of thing than that you should unjustly convict him of murder? There must have been, must there not, carelessness or dishonesty somewhere. You may say, if you like, that there must have been some carelessness on the Doctor's part, that he ought to have noticed when these prescriptions were being made that he was prescribing for quantities that were far larger than the quantities which the nurses' books show to have been given. You might think that you ought to go further and that in some way these drugs were disappearing in a way in which they ought not to. One knows that dangerous drugs are things in which there is an illicit traffic and you might think that someone was dealing dishonestly with them and that someone must either have been the Doctor himself or one of the nurses. If you were ever to get so far as to begin to wonder which of those people was most likely, you would in fairness to the Doctor have to bear in mind that two of the nurses have told lies about this matter in the witness box. One of them lied about whether the drugs were kept locked or not – that was Nurse Stronach – one of the others, either Nurse Mason-Ellis or Nurse Randall, lied about the conversation in the train in which Nurse Randall is supposed to have said, "Don't you say that or you will get me into trouble"; either she said that or she did not, they could not both have been telling the truth about that matter.

'I hope most sincerely that no one will think that I am making accusations against anybody... What I am inviting you to do is to disregard the whole matter as mere speculation... As to the rest, the only safe thing to do when you have a charge of murder by the injection of drugs is to have regard only to those injections which have been clearly proved before you...

'Now, members of the jury, I come to what are the essentials in the case. There are three things that have to be proved and the prosecution has to prove every one of them. It has to prove an act or acts of murder. It has to prove that those acts caused the death of Mrs Morrell. It has to prove that at the time when those acts were committed by the Doctor, the Doctor intended to kill. Those are the three essentials.

'Let me begin with the second: whether the act caused death, because, as Mr Lawrence rightly submitted to you, if it did not, that finishes the whole of this inquiry... He submitted that the immediate physical cause of death was not drugs at all. It was some intervening cause, such as another cerebral thrombosis, or just old age, just people dying, (as Dr Harman put it). Well, upon this, as upon so many other points in this case, you depend entirely, do you not, on the medical evidence. Dr Douthwaite's evidence was quite clear and uncompromising – he regarded the overdose of drugs as causing the death. Dr Ashby also, I think it is fair to say from his evidence, regarded that as being the most likely of the causes, but he could not exclude the other possibility beyond any shadow of doubt. Dr Ashby, coming between the extremes of Dr Douthwaite and Dr Harman, is rather the key witness in the case. Even if you think that what he was admitting was only a bare possibility, something that can never be quite ruled out, you have to put that concession of Dr Ashby's side by side with the evidence that you have got from Dr Harman. What Dr Harman said in effect was, "When you get an old lady of over eighty and one who is suffering from cerebral thrombosis, she may die of anything at any time, and no one can say beyond reasonable doubt what it was that she actually died of".

'Members of the jury, I cannot give you any more help than that... It is for you to say whether you are satisfied that this lady did not in the end die by natural causes, and if you are not satisfied about that, the case for the prosecution ends there.

'Now we come to what is perhaps the central part, the most essential of the three essential things – the act or acts of murder. It is a most curious situation, perhaps unique in these courts, that the act of murder has to be proved by expert evidence. Normally it is something that any jury can understand. Here it is the prosecution saying that the act is recorded somewhere in these books but without a doctor to interpret the books they cannot begin to put their finger on what is suggested to be the act of murder... It may be that the prosecution are in a much more difficult position in this case than they are in other cases. It may be that it is very much more difficult for the Crown ever to prove that a doctor murders his patient than it is to prove other acts of murder. It may be so, but that does not, in law, relieve them of the burden of proof that is upon them... The prosecution identify three acts which they submit to you, and about which you must be satisfied that they amount to an act of murder. If you find some break in the policy, some change, something that the medical evidence says is clearly wrong and apparently inexplicable, that is enough for this stage, because you may then say, "There is an act that needs explanation".

175

I am not bothering at the moment, you see, about the intent; that comes at a later stage of the inquiry. At the moment we are simply looking, you and I, for some act that is capable of being described as a murderous act.

'The first is the dropping of the morphia with the intent that it should be re-introduced with fatal effect, which is the theory of Dr Douthwaite. Well, members of the jury, you heard Mr Lawrence on Friday inviting you in effect to ask yourselves whether you could have sufficient confidence to convict on a charge of murder upon a theory which the doctor himself did not think of until his examination in the witness box was virtually completed. I do not think I need say more about it than this – that if you find a theory which the other doctor for the prosecution is not prepared to support and which the doctor for the defence says is wholly wrong – if indeed Dr Ashby did not equally say it was wrong – you might think that it would be far too dangerous to adopt the theory of Dr Douthwaite, whatever his qualifications may be and however impressed you may have been by the way in which he gave evidence...

'If you are of that view, then pass to the alternative acts. The prosecution say that you will find at or about November 8th a sudden change in the treatment for which there is no justifiable medical reason, and if you do find that sudden change then you may fairly say that it gives you an act which is capable of being a murderous act. Can you find it?

'Well, here again Dr Douthwaite's evidence is, I think, quite positive and uncompromising... He was not willing to credit the Doctor even with ignorance or error. He could find no medical explanation other than that he clearly intended to cause death. Well, that is clear enough. It is Dr Ashby's evidence which you have to consider with the utmost care... So I might perhaps just say this: the position of a doctor who gives evidence for the prosecution is obviously one of considerable difficulty. He can be completely positive and that, of course, is what the lawyers want; they want precise evidence. But men of science cannot always give precise, clear, unqualified answers, particularly if they are dealing with an illness which occurred years ago at which they were not present and about which they have not even the clinical reports... You may think that at times what Dr Ashby gave with one hand he took away with the other. That he was manifestly anxious to be fair, manifestly anxious not to go any further than he felt was justified, you can hardly doubt. He wanted to give both sides of the picture... I cannot read through the whole of Dr Ashby's evidence. I doubt if it would help you if I did. You must remember that, as I have said, you are not sitting here as medical men, you are not sitting here even as a body of men who can call for these transcripts, read them over every day down to the sixteenth and then compare one paragraph with another and endeavour to arrive at a conclusion. That is not the way in which in this country we convict of murder. We convict only if the witness can clearly supply from the witness box the evidence to the jury who, as I say, have not got the transcript in front of them. If, therefore, you come to the conclusion that Dr Ashby's evidence on this vital point was borderline evidence and if it does not leave you with the clear impression that this change, which you will remember he described as coming from the "keeping under", was something which was out of the ordinary course of treatment and accelerated death, well, then, you must leave it. Unless you go the whole way with Dr Douthwaite on this point, you must say that Dr Ashby's evidence was borderline. And in the matter of murder you cannot act upon borderline evidence and therefore you would not be safe in convicting. That must be your attitude in the end.'

And the court adjourned.


On the following morning, the seventeenth day, the Judge resumed the summing up:

'You will remember, members of the jury, that we had reached what was the central and at the same time the most difficult part of the case, and that was the act of murder, whether there was something that stood out from the medical

177

history or not. There are two interpretations of the medical history - one, that it was the natural result, the spiral taking its course, the Doctor coping with a situation which, however it had arisen, was in fact there; and the other, that drugs were given in such quantities as, it was said, would show that a doctor of the Doctor's qualifications quite clearly meant death. Dr Ashby said in his examination-in-chief: "...I can see no justification for the doses given after November 8th. Perhaps 'no justification' is too strong. The right course, I think, would have been to carry on with what may have been the necessary doses of the previous week to keep the patient in an hypnotic state...". And in answer to me he said this: "The instruction to keep her under would be almost certain to accelerate death". Then I asked him: "And that is a conclusion a man of the Doctor's qualifications would have reached?", and he said: "Yes, I think an anaesthetist is particularly conversant with the dangers of a patient being unconscious or semi-conscious".

'In cross-examination Dr Ashby gave an answer on which Mr Lawrence strongly relies. Mr Lawrence had been putting to him his alternative interpretation and he said at the end of it: "It may well be that the drugs after November 8th were given with the sole object of promoting her comfort?" Answer: "I think that is a possible interpretation".

'And later on Mr Lawrence was putting the same thing to him in relation to the spiral: "And the Doctor may well have come to the conclusion that there was no more point in a change, in an attempt to wean her, and that he must go on, that death would overtake the spiral?" Answer: "I would accept that". Question: "And then the case goes on and the Doctor is forced into the spiral until he reaches a point of no return?" Answer: "Yes". Question: "And then it is his major preoccupation to promote her comfort and ease distress?" Answer: "Yes". Question: "That is the impasse in which you said yesterday the Doctor and his patient were?" Answer: "Yes". Question: "Dr Ashby, all that I have been putting to you is a possible view of the case, is it not?" Answer: "Yes, I think it is".

'Well, members of the jury, Dr Ashby then accepts that as a possibility, although, of course, he holds to his own view as being the more probable of the two. Well, you can if you like put that view together with the certainty - I do not think it is too high a word - almost certainty, at any rate, of Dr Douthwaite and say the prosecution case is proved. But you must also consider whether you ought not to put Dr Ashby's view together with the evidence of Dr Harman. And Dr Harman is the reverse way round, as it were. He accepts Dr Ashby's view as a possibility but he himself holds another view. At the very end of his evidence I asked him specifically how far he agreed with Dr Ashby about the drugs accelerating death. I asked: "Would you agree or not that the instructions to 'keep under' would accelerate death?" And Dr Harman answered: "No, I do not think that". Question: "Do you attach any significance to these instructions at all?" Answer: "They signify to me that the patient has got now to the stage of delirium in which she would have remained distressed, excited and uncontrollable if she had not been under some influence of drugs..." Question: "Therefore, in your view, they were the right and natural instructions to give?" Answer: "I would go further and say that sort of policy, if it was a policy, is quite common in such cases".

'Then I put to him Dr Ashby's answer: "The instruction to keep her under would be almost certain to accelerate death". I said to him: "With that you disagree?", and he said: "I would put the emphasis the other way round, I would agree that it might have done so but I should say that it would more probably have not".

'Well, there you have, members of the jury, the evidence on what is the essential part of the case, perhaps the crucial part. It was the part upon which Mr Lawrence made a very strong submission to me. The fact that I held that it was a matter for you to determine and not for me, does not mean he was not in a position to make such a strong submission. On the evidence of Dr Ashby, he clearly was, and he has now been able to fortify it by the evidence of Dr Harman. Each link in the prosecution's chain must be strong enough to stand the strain. It does not matter how strong the other links are...

'If, however, you proceed further, if you decide in favour of the prosecution on those points, if you decide that Mrs Morrell was killed by a piece of medically unjustifiable treatment given to her by the Doctor, you will then have to deal with the question of intent, whether it was done with the intention to murder.'

Intention exists in a man's mind and can only be proved by his own evidence or by inferences drawn from his acts.

'And if he goes into the witness box and tells you and you think he is telling the truth, you would have the best evidence available. It is fair to say that when you approach this last part of the case you necessarily lack that...

'In considering this matter, then, of what was in the Doctor's mind, you must look at all the circumstances of the case... Here we are on much easier ground... We are out of the field of conflict which so far has been dominated by the experts, and are dealing with things which you and I can understand and weigh... First, motive. The Crown is never bound to prove motive. But it is one of the things one looks for in connection with intent. I take it from the Attorney-General's opening that the motive was the motive of gain – that he wished to acquire a legacy by the death of Mrs Morrell.

Mr Lawrence said the chest of silver was a paltry reward for murder.

'And you may think it is. But there must be said in fairness to the other side that the Doctor displayed a considerable interest in acquiring some legacy under the will. But even so, you may think that it was a paltry reward to stimulate a doctor into committing murder and, if the prosecution is right, laying long plans in advance... Mr Lawrence's point does not rest there. He says that this is not a case of dealing out death in order to get a legacy from a strong and hearty woman. This was a woman who, admittedly, was dying. On November 1st she had from a few weeks to two months to live. If the Doctor had calculated that, he would have said to himself, would he not, "Well, she may be dead in two or three weeks and then I will get the chest I have been waiting so long for". Is it likely, it may be asked, to adopt a plan which does not even mean an instantaneous dose which kills her off, but involves a rather elaborate system of change in medication which takes thirteen days to dispose of her? If one takes the lowest estimate, it would have meant that he would have had his chest of silver seven days before he would otherwise have had it. (There was at one time, I thought, a suggestion made that she would alter her will but I do not think that has been pursued. And it is difficult to think that she was in any condition in this last time in November to have effectively altered her will.)

'Well, that is the point that Mr Lawrence put before you. He said that the suggestion that the Doctor had anticipated her death by a few days or weeks for the sake of a chest of silver worth £276 was ludicrous. Ludicrous is a strong word. But, members of the jury, it is a strong point. I listened carefully to the Attorney-General's speech to hear what the answer was. I did not hear the answer.'

The next point was the false filling up of the cremation form.

'And I say false advisedly, for though it is a matter for you to decide, it seems to me that it was false.'

Mr Lawrence had said that the important thing was not whether the Doctor was entitled to anything under the will, but whether he thought he was.

'Well, the answer which the Doctor gave to Superintendent Hannam – which is the only evidence we have – makes it plain that he knew, or thought he knew, he was going to get the chest of silver and the car. The Doctor did not say, "I thought I did not get it under the will but by the gift or favour of the relatives". He did not give that as his explanation. He gave the explanation that he wanted to smooth the way for the cremation. That explanation may or may not be satisfactory to you but you have to remember that it is one thing to give it to a police officer and another thing to go into the witness box and say it on oath and subject to cross-examination and testing.

'The Attorney-General has laid stress on the statements the Doctor made to Superintendent Hannam, and some of them are difficult to justify on the evidence as we know it now: that she was in "terrible agony" at the end, for example. We know very clearly now that she was not. Perhaps that was a lapse of memory and quite understandable. But again, you might have liked to have heard his own explanation about it. You might have liked to have heard, too, his own explanation about "easing the passing", a phrase which might be used quite innocently, but, on the other hand, a phrase which might perhaps go further. However, you must take into account not isolated phrases but the trend of his statements on the whole, and it seems to me that the statements as a whole do show from the beginning to the end that it had never crossed his mind that he was faced, or might be faced, with the charge of murdering Mrs Morrell.

'Take the chance interview last October. At the end of it the Superintendent said to him. "I hope I shall finish all these inquiries soon and we will probably have another talk", and the Doctor answered, "Don't hurry; please be thorough; it is in my own interest. Good night and thank you very much for your kindness". If he was the calculating murderer who felt that perhaps his sins were finding him out, one might have expected him to be very wary in the statements he was making. In fact, he gave away a good deal at the particular interview and when he said he knew about the Rolls-Royce and the silver...

'And when he was asked at the time of the search about drugs, there was that key sentence at the end, "I am not dishonest about drugs". It shows, does it not, that what he thought he was being confronted with was some suggestion that he had been engaged in some sort of illicit traffic – prescribing more than he ought to have prescribed, or something of that sort – but not murder. And that last interview at the very end, of which I remind you, at which he was stunned and shocked by the idea of murder...

'I think there is only one other matter to which I need refer you in this part of the argument and that is the point made by the Attorney-General about the nurses' notebooks. He asked: "Where did they come from? Where had they been? In whose interest was it to keep them?" I do not see a mystery there but it is something one would have liked to know about... Mr Lawrence has not anticipated the point and he did not deal with it in his final address to you but if he had he might have asked a rhetorical question too: "What does the prosecution say these books prove – innocence or guilt? If guilt, why did the Doctor preserve them? If they prove innocence, then surely it does not matter where they come from or who has been keeping them?"

'Members of the jury, I can now sum up the whole issue for you and I sum it up for you once again because it is important that you should not think that it is only the last point that I have been talking about that counts.

'There are three points, are there not? The Crown must satisfy you that Mrs Morrell did not die from natural causes. If it fails to satisfy you of that, you acquit. If it satisfies you, you ask the next question. The Crown must satisfy you that there emerges an act of killing, something which is capable of being murderous. Again, if it fails to satisfy you of that, you acquit. If it succeeds, and only if it succeeds, you go on to the third question. The Crown must satisfy you that if there was an act of that sort, it was done with intent to murder. If it does not satisfy you of that, you acquit; and if it does satisfy you, then you convict.

'Mr Lawrence has submitted to you that the whole case against the Doctor, from beginning to end, is merely suspicion. It may be so... It may be that if this inquiry were ever to be completed the Doctor might appear as a man misjudged by those who suspected him – not a man wrongly prosecuted; no one, I think, can say that the Crown was not justified on the material they had at the beginning of this trial in prosecuting the Doctor – but a man who, if all the facts were known, was guilty of folly, perhaps worse than folly, but who never in his mind came within thought of murder. It may be so – who can say? Not you, members of the jury. Not you. It is not your task to say so. You have not heard the man who knows most about his own mind... You do not sit as a court of inquiry to determine just how or why Mrs Morrell died. You sit to answer one limited question: Has the prosecution satisfied you beyond reasonable doubt that the Doctor murdered Mrs Morrell? On that question the Doctor stood on his rights and did not speak. I have made it quite clear that I am not criticising that. I do not criticise it at all. I hope that the day will never come when that right is denied to any Englishman. It is not a refuge of technicality; the law on this matter reflects the natural thought of England. So great is our horror at the idea that a man might be questioned, forced to speak and perhaps to condemn himself out of his own mouth, that we afford to everyone suspected or accused of a crime, at every stage and to the very end, the right to say, "Ask me no questions, I shall answer none. Prove your case."

'And so this long process ends with the question with which it began: "Murder? Can you prove it?".

'I dare say it is the first time that you have sat in that jury box. It is not the first time that I have sat in this chair. And not infrequently I have heard a case presented by the prosecution that seemed to me to be manifestly a strong one, and sometimes I have felt it my duty to tell the jury so. I do not think, therefore, that I ought to hestitate to tell you that here the case for the defence seems to me to be manifestly a strong one... But it is the same question in the end, always the same – is the case for the Crown strong enough to carry conviction to your mind? It is your question. You have to answer it. It lies always with you, the jury. Always with you. And you will now consider what that answer shall be.'


The four hour summing up by Sir Patrick Devlin was finely balanced in law, beautifully phrased, benign in its help to the jury and memorable in its perception. And of no help to the prosecution.

One phrase in particular from that succinct summing up came to mind: "A man who, on the known facts, was guilty of folly and perhaps worse, might never in his own mind have thought of murder".

Rodney Hallworth murmured to himself an addendum: "of Mrs Morrell".

Forty-five minutes later the jury of ten men and two women returned with their verdict of 'Not Guilty'.

Upon being acquitted of murder by Sir Patrick Devlin, Dr Adams looked flushed, he bowed stiffly to the Judge, his facial muscles twitching slightly.

It was April 10th and the trial had lasted 17 days.

# Chapter Ten

## *'I'm sick of the whole affair'*

CHIEF CONSTABLE OF EASTBOURNE

The jury had returned a verdict of 'Not Guilty'. The longest murder trial in English Legal history was over. The tubby Irishman who had not spoken a word at his trial and who, as inmate No. 7889, had knelt in prayer in his cell at Brixton Jail every night of the capital charge was free after 111 days on remand.

The verdict might have surprised many of the world's press, but it did not surprise Adams. Only four days before he had written to a cousin from his cell, 'Do not worry nor be discouraged. All will be well. British justice and the power of prayer will clear me in God's good time.'

To another old friend in Ireland he had written again from his cell, 'God will only try a man as far as he can bear, then He will find a way of escape. I keep my faith in the power of prayer. My conscience is clear.'

To be fair, the passage of letters was not just one-way. During his period of remand Adams received letters from 150 of his patients who, without exception, believed totally in his innocence.

Another charge of murder, that of Mrs Hullett, was expeditiously forgotten by the Crown. Neither Adams nor justice would be served by enduring another murder trial. That was the opinion of the State prosecutors. So he was quickly

187

given bail on dangerous drugs summonses and others which had been left pending, including obstructing the police, and the Doctor was allowed to go downstairs to freedom, two stones lighter in weight and some fifteen thousand pounds lighter in his wallet.

Freedom at first was confined to an *Evening Standard* newspaper van, part of the *Express Group* of newspapers, which whisked him from the court to a secret rendezvous with senior *Daily Express* reporters.

Outside the court hundreds of people waited in vain for a glimpse of him, including some seventy members of the press. The big ballyhoo had had its day and now the extraordinary trial had ended in an exciting fizzle. Adams was taken by the *Daily Express* back home, but not before he was photographed with a smiling Percy Hoskins on the shore by Beachy Head. On paper, and it is only on paper that counts in Fleet Street, the *Daily Express* and Percy Hoskins had secured a first-class scoop.

Despite that moment during Dr Douthwaite's evidence, when Percy Hoskins had declared Adams 'a dead duck', in the final analysis Hoskins and the *Express* came out on top. Despite the fact that most people 'in the trade' - lawyers, solicitors, policemen, editors, reporters - believed Adams a mass-murderer, the good Doctor Adams had not been proven guilty, where it mattered - in a court of law.

Lawyers are understandably wary of the word 'brilliant' in eye-catching but ephemeral headlines, but for Lawrence the trial *had* ended in glory. Till then he was unknown to the public, working as a backroom boy on Treasury frauds. The trial made him one of the best-known lawyers in the land, and may have precipitated his knighthood and upgrading to judge where he continued a successful but less headlined career until his untimely death.

The trial for the Attorney-General, Sir Reginald Manningham-Buller, was a sorry tale. He was blamed for lack of preparation and research in a case thin on evidence, in parts anyway, and indeed observing lawyers said at the time, Adams was guilty, in their view, but that the patina of evidence was too thin in places to survive the doubt inducing surprises that Lawrence presented with such devastating effect.

But lives and careers moved on. The Judge, Sir Patrick Devlin, became Lord Justice of Appeal 1960–1961, and a Lord of Appeal 1961–1964, before retiring to Pewsey in Wiltshire. Sir Reginald Manningham-Buller was created 1st Viscount Dilhorne and served both law and country as Lord High Chancellor for Great Britain from 1962–1964, before retiring peacefully from political life to his home near Market Harborough, although remaining a Lord of Appeal in Ordinary. Lord Dilhorne died in 1981.

Sir Reginald's Junior Counsel in the Adams trial, Mr Melford Stevenson, was knighted in 1957 and appointed a Justice of the High Court and to the Queen's Bench Division 1961–1979. He retired from the Bench in 1979 and a legal career, spiced with outspoken, often critical remarks on the law and other matters.

Geoffrey Lawrence was knighted and became a Judge of the High Court. His early death was a tragic loss, not only to his family but to the law itself.

Lawrence's very able Junior Counsel, Edward Clarke, QC, was elevated in 1964 to the Judicial team at the Old Bailey, thus continuing an association with that court which began with his grandfather, Sir Edward Clarke, who first got to his feet in the Old Bailey in 1864. Later to unsuccessfully defend Oscar Wilde and become Solicitor General.

Judge Clarke retired in 1981 but the Clarke family tradition continues. His son Peter is a regular advocate at the Old Bailey.

Detective Chief Superintendent Herbert Hannum suffered a severe career disappointment as a result of the Adams acquittal but enjoyed a long retirement until his death in 1983.

Detective Sergeant Charlie Hewitt moved on in an illustrious career. Hewitt spent three years, following the 'Eastbourne Job' on a complex fraud case which successfully ended with the arrest and conviction of a JP and a number of prominent businessmen. He retired with the rank of Detective Chief Superintendent.

A dedicated, much respected 'copper' was Charlie Hewitt. Generations of forebears had been 'coppers', his son now the fifth generation Hewitt on the force. A family of service not self. We could do with more Hewitts and men like them.

A little after the trial Detective-Inspector Brynwel Pugh, Head of Eastbourne's CID, died in early middle-age.

Dr Francis Camps, one of the world's most celebrated pathologists, whom Hallworth was proud to know personally, and who entered the witness box momentarily during the trial to discuss the technicalities of death certificates and the need for post-mortems, died of a stomach complaint on July 8, 1972.

The trial and the very name of Bodkin Adams burdened the last years of the career of the Chief Constable of Eastbourne, Mr Richard Walker. In his own words to Hallworth, 'he was sick of the whole affair'. Soon afterwards he tried for a more senior Chief Constableship in the North of England. The local press printed the names of candidates on the short list, together with their photographs. Captions on some of the others told of their successes; under Richard Walker's photograph went something like this: 'He was involved in the murder investigation of Dr John Bodkin Adams, who was found not guilty'. That was more than unfair to an outstanding police officer.

Mr Walker did not get the job and always felt that the 'Eastbourne Job' went against him. Yet Richard Walker remains the calm, courteous man of old. He finally retired to a bungalow with a large lawn overlooking the harbour at Newhaven, Sussex. A police career of thirty-six years, beginning as a beat constable in Salford, Manchester, and culminating as a Chief Constable. Recipient of the Queen's Police Medal, awarded an OBE in 1964, Richard Walker is the epitome of all that is fine about the English policeman.

So was it all a mistake? Had Scotland Yard been biased by the consistent similarities in the demise and last testaments of the

Doctor's departed patients? Was it just the bumbling of an incompetent doctor? Had the Crown prosecutors built a Sussex sandcastle on vague circumstantial evidence? Were the gossips of Eastbourne just a malicious bunch, resentful of the Doctor's wealth and jealous of his success?

As the last trial day ended a file remained in an office at Scotland Yard as thick as the Bible, and for many still containing unresolved material. In its pages were the names of women and men who, for the police, had died too quickly and too suspiciously in the hands of the Doctor and had made him very rich at the same time. That file remains to this day at Scotland Yard. It is still unresolved, and its material reverberates twenty-seven years after Adams' acquittal of the murder of Mrs Morrell. The question of whether Adams is a mass-murderer or not is raised wherever legal luminaries gather; whenever old press colleagues meet to reminisce and inevitably is a sour cause for conversation amongst retired Scotland Yard officers.

There are those who claim the acquittal came about as the result of an inept prosecution by the Attorney-General Sir Reginald Manningham-Buller. How true is that comment? Does it stand up under analysis? Is there any validity to such accusatory statements? An examination of the Attorney-General's performance tends to suggest this is the case. As the careers of the principals concerned in the Adams murder trial took their individual routes, so did the life of John Bodkin Adams. Vastly different than before, true, but still to be continued in Eastbourne.

As for the Attorney-General's performance the rapid oscillations of the scales of justice during the Adams trial have been referred to more than once. Such varied fluctuations first for the prosecution and then the defence were unusual, a gradual tilting towards one side more the norm. But from beginning to end, the Adams trial was anything but normal.

The prosecution's case had been based on four main points. The weapon – morphia and heroin. The method –

massive overdosing. The motive – gain – to get into the sphere of influence to benefit from a rich woman's generosity. And fourthly, incriminating statements by the Doctor to the Police.

During the Attorney-General's opening, much stress was placed upon the alleged fact that the unfortunate Mrs Morrell did not suffer pain as a result of the stroke she had suffered in Cheshire. Indeed, three nurses were called who had attended upon the patient in her last months to corroborate that statement. Additionally, to add further weight – some might say to belabour the point – a highly qualified medical specialist from Harley Street, Dr Douthwaite, who had never attended upon or had even seen the patient, gave evidence that for pain to follow such a stroke would be most unusual.

It was the prosecution's decision to make such determined emphasis on the stroke/pain syndrome, obviously as a gambit leading toward probing the question of prescribing morphia, a pain-killing addictive drug. That surprised those investigative journalists who had dug into the background of all the principal characters and knew Mrs Morrell suffered severe pain *before the stroke* from rheumatoid arthritis. That debilitating form of arthritis which attacks the joints – fingers, wrists, knees, ankles – enlarging, inflaming and finally disfiguring such joints and all accompanied with excruciating pain and this before her stroke which left the poor woman additionally incapacitated.

Would the arthritis miraculously disappear as a result of the stroke? Of course not! If anything, Mrs Morrell's discomfort and pain would increase without occasional movement helpful to ease the affected joints.

If the prosecution's mania for proving the old lady was not in pain surprised the journalists, it positively staggered Geoffrey Lawrence and his team. For such a mania begged certain questions for the defence to ponder. Lawrence could immediately get to his feet, produce medical evidence of arthritis and pain. But wait! If the prosecution were ignoring arthritis that would merely be a short-sighted omission. But supposing they had even more stupidly neglected to research medical matters before the stroke?

Lawrence decided in light of the Attorney-General's ponderous emphasis on alleged lack of pain, that opportunities would occur to negate, or at the very least, cast doubt upon much of the corner-stone of the prosecution's case. He bided his time. And the prosecution duly obliged the defence.

Using the six-and seven-year-old memories of Nurses, understandably nervous at appearing as witnesses in a murder trial at the Old Bailey, Sir Reginald examined the first Nurse in her evidence, raising the layman's impression of an old lady in no pain and in a comatose condition. In cross-examination, that Nurse's memory and evidence were totally destroyed by Lawrence producing the Nurses' record books for the whole period of months they had been on duty.

The shocked effect upon the prosecution was not lost upon the jury or Lawrence, which again led his defence team to surmise a lack of research and endeavour by either the Police or the Attorney-General. Nursing records are common knowledge. He knew no search had been made for such records by the prosecution. What about medical treatment in Cheshire where Mrs Morrell had first been hospitalised? A telephone call by one of his defence team elicited the information that such inquiries had not been made by the prosecution. Lawrence could hardly believe his luck! And again he bided his time.

Again the production of Nurses' record books totally inhibited the Nurses' testimony. The train gossiping of the Nurses which led to newspaper headlines and the Judge's admonishment, had come about simply because a clerk of Eastbourne solicitors used by the defence for local Eastbourne legwork, had contrived to travel with the Nurses. Never, in a month of Sundays, did the defence expect that such a precaution would bear fruit.

The end result was that the third Nurse witness, Sister Mason-Ellis, was so unnerved that even on direct examination by the prosecution she damaged its own case. A careless moment for the prosecution. In light of previous happenings, the least the prosecution should have done, was to invest a few minutes of quiet talk before Sister Mason-Ellis entered the box to determine her then state of mind.

The work of prosecution or defence is not confined to the public hours of trial. Often long midnight hours are required to update or amend trial tactics. It appeared the Attorney-General was not prepared to invest the necessary time to mend his rickety case.

Overall, the testimony of the three Nurses Stronach, Randall and Mason-Ellis did not help the prosecution case one iota. No jury could be impressed by their evidence. Memories were proven unreliable. Perhaps the reverse was in fact the result of their appearances; that they unwittingly aided the defence.

The prosecution mania regarding the alleged lack of pain had led, as Lawrence expected, into the type and amounts of drugs prescribed. The theatrical production of a 'large, unusually large', in his words, syringe by Sir Reginald from which 5cc of paraldehyde was injected into poor Mrs Morrell, was pure theatre, completely unnecessary, and due to the lack of medical research and preparation by the prosecution, was shown up by the defence to be medically unsound.

Asked by the Judge what would be the normal dose of paraldehyde, Nurse Randall replied: 'It depends how you give it, but I think 4cc or 5cc is a very large dose.'

The Judge: 'Two cc would be the normal dose?'.

'It would.'

Mr Lawrence at least had done his homework evidenced by facing the Nurse:

'I must challenge what you said. Do you know what the British Pharmacopoeia dose of paraldehyde is? I must put it to you formally that the British Pharmacopoeia full dose is 120 minims or 8cc. Did you know that?'

Nurse Randall: 'I did not know that.'

This really was a grossly stupid error by Manningham-Buller. It would have been so easy to check recommended dosages.

Later in the trial Dr Harman had been asked by Lawrence about the dosage of paraldehyde. Dr Harman replied:

'I should not think of giving as little as 5cc in a case like this. *I never give less than 6cc.*'

So completely were Sir Reginald's paraldehyde and his 'large, unusually large' syringe destroyed.

As for the other drugs and their quantities. At first the prosecution's case seemed overwhelming. Over a ten and half a month period, almost 4,000 grains of barbiturates, sedomid, morphia and omnopon, and heroin had been administered to a sick woman.

On the face of it, horrendous amounts. In his opening address, Sir Reginald advised that the maximum of heroin which should be prescribed in a period of twenty-four hours was a quarter grain. On a single day, Dr Adams had administered eight grains. Of morphia the maximum dose recommended is a half grain per twenty-four hours. On November 8, Dr Adams prescribed ten grains. On November 9, twelve grains, on November 11 eighteen grains!

The scales could not weigh down more on the side of the prosecution. Yet more was to follow.

In a case where the medical evidence would be of vital import, the Crown's main medical witness was Dr Douthwaite, who, when asked by Sir Reginald:

'Is there, in your opinion, any justification for injecting morphia and heroin immediately after a stroke?', answered unequivocally, 'No justification whatsoever,' and later, Sir Reginald: 'What conclusion do you draw from the dosage administered in the last days...?'

Dr Douthwaite: 'The only conclusion I can come to is that the intention on November 8 was to end her life.'

Terribly damning evidence from an acknowledged medical expert. Yet Lawrence kept his head. After all, he suspected the real lack of research knowledge gained so far by the prosecution. In facing the egocentric Dr Douthwaite – and many experts and specialists are understandably of like character – Lawrence had a trump-card to play.

The defence counsel brought Dr Douthwaite to the first days of Mrs Morrell's illness following her stroke when hospitalised in Cheshire. Mr Lawrence proceeded to advise Dr Douthwaite that Dr Turner in Cheshire had treated Mrs Morrell with morphia to relieve the patient and to enable her to sleep. And continued this treatment during her Cheshire sojourn. It was not Dr Adams, therefore, who had first prescribed morphia but who continued Dr Turner's original treatment.

Such a disclosure affected the issue but not devastatingly so. That complete turn-round of Dr Douthwaite's evidence in the ears and minds of the jury and others came from Dr Douthwaite himself as Lawrence continued his cross-examination.

Mr Lawrence: '... Does the field of condemnation that you are spreading from the witness box include Dr Turner of Cheshire for having given the patient morphia after a stroke?'

Dr Douthwaite: 'If that was the treatment for the stroke – yes!'

An incredible example of egocentric temper, not lost upon Judge or jury.

Dr Douthwaite gave evidence for twelve hours and twenty minutes on direct, cross-examination and re-direct. Evidence at one and the same time of blanket condemnation, including doctors who were not on trial; of opinionated testimony claiming that anyone who did not agree with him was criminally wrong. And ended under Lawrence's skillful decimation contradicting much of what he had said when being examined by the Attorney-General.

The acknowledged lack of firm medical evidence regarding human tolerance levels of drugs, given increasingly over a period of time, cast doubt on all medical evidence heard during the trial.

Two corner-stones of the prosecution's case, that of sinister intent of treatment and massive usage of drugs, had fallen under some degree of doubt, certainly more than reasonable doubt. What was left from the Attorney-General's remaining opening remarks? Just that of the will, wills, bequests or gifts of Mrs Morrell where Dr Adams was concerned. And the suggested incriminating statements of Dr Adams, when faced by Detective Superintendent Hannam in various interviews culminating at his arrest. How did Lawrence treat such accusations of guilt? Firstly, the last will of Mrs Morrell.

All the testimony of Mrs Morrell's solicitor Herbert Sogno, regarding Dr Adams' compulsive interest in her last will was negated on cross-examination by Lawrence.

Mr Sogno was asked how many previous wills Mrs Morrell had made in the months covering her illness, and was told, six. Mr Sogno also gave evidence that at the time Dr Adams went on holiday to Scotland in September 1950, Mrs Morrell, then angry with the Doctor, asked Sogno to prepare a codicil to her last will in order to deny the Doctor any bequests.

Lawrence asked if this codicil was legally executed, and was told, it was. Lawrence then asked what happened to it. Mr Sogno explained that the codicil was torn up by Mrs Morrell.

Lawrence: 'Did her tearing it up put the Doctor back into the will?'

Sogno: 'Oh, no. Tearing up a document is not an effective way of reviving gifts. The codicil cutting him out was never validly revoked before her death.'

As Lawrence summed up: 'So when Mrs Morrell died in November the Doctor was not in any way a beneficiary under her will?'

Sogno: 'That is correct.'

Lawrence: 'For anything at all?'

Sogno: 'For nothing at all!'

In law, and that is what counts here, Dr Adams was entitled to nothing at all under Mrs Morrell's last will. That he received gifts of her Rolls-Royce, an antique cupboard and a chest of silver, was solely at the discretion of Mrs Morrell's son.

In the single matter of the capital charge of murdering Mrs Morrell, the prosecution's inference that gain motivated Dr

Adams' actions was therefore shown to be unfounded. The Doctor was due for nothing. True, the Doctor's name was not enhanced favourably by his interest and activities concerning Mrs Morrell's many wills but that was a long, long way from proof of intent to murder because of what he may have thought he stood to gain. Again too much doubt.

Doubt clearly held by the Judge, for in his summing up to the jury he said:

'... Well, that is the point that Mr Lawrence put before you. He said that the suggestion that the Doctor had anticipated her death by a few days or weeks for the sake of a chest of silver, worth £276, was ludicrous. Ludicrous is a strong word. But, members of the jury, it is a strong point. I listened carefully to the Attorney-General's speech to hear what the answer was. I did not hear the answer...'

So once again, part of the main prosecution argument dissolved in doubt. It cannot be contested that the simple checking of matters of probate seemed beyond the Attorney-General.

In a matter of minutes, the fact that Dr Adams was not entitled under Mrs Morrell's last will, could have been elucidated. Any second-year law student could have obliged. Another of the imponderables regarding the prosecution's performance.

And so what was left of the prosecution's case revolved around statements allegedly made by Dr Adams when interviewed by Superintendent Hannam and others. Statements given without warning as to his rights, save at the last moments prior to his arrest.

Hannam interviewed Adams on four occasions. At the first, one evening early October 1956, Hannam happened to be passing the Doctor's garage in Lismore Road when Adams drove into his garage. A conversation followed in which Hannam referred to the chest of silver left to Adams. The Doctor replied:

Mrs Morrell was a very dear patient. She insisted a long

198

time before she died that I should have it in her memory. I never wanted it. I am a bachelor and I never use it. I knew she was going to leave it to me and her Rolls-Royce. She told me she had left it to me in her will. Oh, yes, and another cabinet.'

Hannam reminded Adams that on the Morrell cremation form he had declared that he was not a beneficiary under her will and the Doctor's answer:

'Oh, that was not done wickedly. God knows it was not.' And explained he did not want the 'dear relatives upset' and that 'he liked cremations to go off smoothly'.

The second interview took place on November 24, 1956, when a warrant was exercised and the Doctor's house searched for dangerous drugs. Hannam showed Adams a list of prescripted drugs for Mrs Morrell, saying: 'There are a lot of dangerous drugs here. Who administered them?'

The Doctor said: 'I did, nearly all. Perhaps the Nurses gave some but mostly me.'

Hannam asked if any drugs were left over when Mrs Morrell died. The Doctor answered: 'No, none. All was given to the patient. Poor soul, she was in terrible agony.'

The third interview two days later on November 26, was at the instigation of Dr Adams and took place at Eastbourne's Central Police Station. Adams said to Mr Hannam:

'You told Mr James, my solicitor, there might be other charges. I am worried. What are they?'

Hannam answered him: 'I am still enquiring into the deaths of some of your patients, Doctor.'

'Which?'

Hannam: 'Mrs Morrell is certainly one.'

Adams said: 'Easing the passing of a dying person is not all that wicked. She wanted to die – that cannot be murder. It is impossible to accuse a doctor.'

The fourth and last interview took place on December 19, 1956, when Hannam formally cautioned Adams and arrested him for the murder of Mrs Morrell, and Adams replied:

'Murder?' and then, 'I do not think you could prove it was murder. She was dying in any event.'

When his receptionist broke down in tears as Adams left with Hannam, the Doctor said: 'I will see you in heaven.'

These were the statements on record and entered as evidence by the prosecution. Only the last comments of Dr Adams had been preceded by the cautionary warning that anything he said may and could be used in evidence against him.

Without the defence calling on Dr Adams for direct examination the prosecution were unable to question the Doctor under oath. And one result of that became obvious when applied to the Doctor's alleged statements prior to his arrest. Sir Reginald made what he could of the Doctor's words once he had been cautioned but it was extremely thin and so thought the Judge who in his summing up said:

'You cannot attach weight or importance to words of that sort which were obviously said under great emotional strain.'

Indeed, the Doctor's words admitted or not, were ambiguous enough. And most people would say for example, that the first interview Hannam had with Adams was noted for the complete honesty of the Doctor's replies. As to the rest, the Judge thought so little of these alleged statements that he drew the jury's attention to their insignificance in his summing up.

The accusation that the Attorney-General conducted a less than prepossessing case is obvious in retrospect. The popular press hailed a brilliant defence. But Lawrence himself played that down, saying he just did his job. He conducted a workmanlike defence. Skilled in application, true, but most noted for the sheer hard work and hours of research into medical matters and the diligent pursuing of the slightest piece of evidence that would help the Doctor. Geoffrey Lawrence was an honourable man. Despite his dislike for the odious Dr Adams, he did his utmost for his client. The defence team of Lawrence, Edward Clarke and John Heritage had more than earned their fees. It had been a formidable, hard-working defence.

The jolts and surprises dealt out by the defence in every instance could and should have been anticipated or avoided altogether by the prosecution. The Nurses' books; the British Pharmacopoeia dosage of paraldehyde; Sister Mason-Ellis' reluctance to give testimony; neglecting to establish probate details of the Morrell will; the gross mistake of failing to check out the Cheshire medical treatment; the inability of controlling their main medical witness, Dr Douthwaite. These matters neglected by the Attorney-General were pounced on and amplified by the defence to produce the inevitable question of reasonable doubt in the minds of the jury.

Most certainly the charge of ineptitude to describe Manningham-Buller's performance is valid. Poorly prepared and poorly researched. Altercations between principals that had been evident in conferences with the DPP's office continued before, during and after the trial. Hannam took an unfair criticism. The overpowering figure of the Attorney-General inhibited an ideal prosecution team. He was too authoritative, did not delegate at all well and believed totally that he would destroy Dr Adams in the witness box. The enormous tactical error in not anticipating even the possibility that Lawrence might not call Adams, was cardinal. Sir Reginald Manningham-Buller was rightly blamed for the prosecution's woeful performance.

Having stated that fact, it is only fair to balance the statement by observing, on the personal note of a well known legal luminary, if the prosecution had conducted an exemplary case, there was still too much medical conflict to avoid a reasonable doubt. It is thought that Adams would have been acquitted anyway. For, in the view of many experts, the wrong case was brought. In that expert opinion considered the case of Mrs 'Bobbie' Hullett was appreciably stronger of a murder charge.

But even that charge was not to be pressed because of the adverse publicity mounted by the vast majority of the British press and not only British, come to that. In Europe and North

America, far from the libel restrictions of the U.K., Adams had and was receiving an awful press.

The trial of John Bodkin Adams at the Old Bailey had made history and provided an historic verdict. His personal trial was not over. There were more legal matters for him to face. He was due to answer those charges at the next Lewes Assizes. In the meantime Adams and his solicitors considered their own legal actions.

The headlines that had accompanied Adams for more than a year still appeared in a succession of lesser matters. If it was not exactly a breathing space for Adams, life did appear fractionally less dramatic.

# Chapter Eleven

*'One can hardly blame Dr Adams for feeling he had already been condemned at the Bar of Public Opinion.'*

NOEL LEIGH TAYLOR, COUNSEL FOR

ADAMS AT BRITISH MEDICAL COUNCIL

DISCIPLINARY HEARING

In the week following Dr Adams' acquittal, questions were asked of the Home Secretary in the House of Commons regarding the role of the press before and during the trial. Members of Parliament were particularly censorious of the American magazine *Newsweek*, the circulation of which in Britain was temporarily banned owing to a most nefarious article about Dr Adams in an issue whilst the trial was still proceeding. In that particular instance, the Solicitor General's Office stepped in with an injunction suspending *Newsweek* circulation for the duration of the trial. The article referred to: 'The Dark Event at Old Bailey' with photographs of the Judge and the defendant.

Accompanying text began:

> Not since the trials of John George Haigh, "The Vampire" (nine victims), and John R.H. Christie, "The Strangler of Notting Hill" (seven women victims), had a criminal trial aroused such avid interest in Britain. With a ritual going back to Norman times, the presiding justice, Sir Patrick Devlin, whose brother is a famous Shakespearan actor, opened the proceedings at the Old Bailey. In the prisoner's box, alternately smiling and shaking his head, sat the classic defendant: mild, Bible-reading Dr John Bodkin (Odd Bodkin) Adams.

The unsubtle linking of Adams with the convicted murderers Haigh and Christie was bad enough. But under a heading 'Bequests' *Newsweek* correspondents had mentioned the Hullett's and of course Adams at that moment was on trial for the murder of Mrs Morrell – *and no other*. That particular article also referred to Eastbourne gossip pushing Dr Adams' alleged victims as high as 400. In the actual *Newsweek* story, copy referred to Dr Adams' big house; his three servants plus chauffeur; of seventeen patients who had bequeathed him $90,000. And quoting that after the first week of his trial Adams was so pleased with his defence team that he was alleged to have thrown a champagne party in his Brixton remand cell.

Apart from inaccuracies in that copy, enough inferences regarding other patients, sufficient to further blacken the character of an accused whilst on trial, led the Solicitor General to the ban.

From the remove of a quarter-of-a-century one wonders what the Solicitor General and MPs were getting so irate about. British newspapers had published even more anti-Adams material for months preceding the trial. Poor *Newsweek*, whose copy was not really so inflammatory, happened to publish during the trial, and so, rather hypocritically evoked the wrath of much of the law. Wrong it was. Heinous it was not.

That was the most blatant misuse of press power. There were other borderline cases, just fudging the law of libel. But it was the Solicitor General's view that prosecution would only fan the flames of anti-Adams publicity. And, apart from the *Newsweek* injunction, no other official action was taken.

Although for the same reason action for damages against the *Daily Mail*, and others originally contemplated by Adams took much heart-searching, they did proceed on advice from the Doctor's legal team together with *Daily Express* advisers who now held the exclusive rights to the Doctor's comments. Subsequently, damages of over four figures were awarded to the Doctor, much to the chagrin of several journalists and their editors.

April ended with the *Daily Express* presenting the Doctor's version of matters medical as appropriate to Eastbourne.

Mostly taking the line of 'we-told-you-so' the *Express* reiterated their view of the innocence, now proved in the case of Mrs Morrell. Dr Adams and Percy Hoskins were pictured together. And in April each year for the rest of his life, Adams would send a thank you message to Hoskins.

On May 21st, Adams appeared in the magistrates court in Eastbourne and was bound over to appear before the Lewes July Assizes. On June 30th, Adams resigned from the National Health Service. On July 1st, a circular letter was sent to his patients by the Eastbourne Executive of the National Health Service notifying them of the withdrawal of Dr John Bodkin Adams from the local medical list and for them to apply to another doctor for inclusion on his lists.

On July 17th, Adams was brought up at Lewes Assizes and pleaded guilty to fourteen charges involving forgery of National Health prescriptions; making false statements on cremation certificates; failing to keep a register of dangerous drugs; obstructing a police officer and attempting to conceal two bottles of hydro-chloride morphine.

On these charges Adams was fined £2,400 and ordered to pay costs. Adams returned to Eastbourne, to his Trinity Trees house and set about disposing of his partners' interest in the practice. And then, when all business had been settled, quietly continued to treat a number of private patients who still believed in him.

The month of August 1957 saw a hectic holiday season for Eastbourne. The *Daily Express* articles by Percy Hoskins had finished and, for the Doctor, August ended without a court or hearing appearance and without press coverage. It was but a summer interlude only, for on September 10th, the Home Secretary had his say.

The *London Gazette* of that date contained a notice signed by the Home Secretary, stating that on September 4th he had withdrawn from Dr John Bodkin Adams, authority to possess or supply dangerous drugs under Regulation 29 of the Dangerous Drugs Regulations 1953. The notice concluded that 'Dr Adams of 6 Trinity Trees, Eastbourne, has been convicted of offences against the Dangerous Drugs Act 1951'.

On November 28th the final *tour de force* enacted against Dr Adams came from his peers-in-medicine. Adams was summoned to appear before the disciplinary committee of the General Medical Council. He took counsel with him in the form of Mr Noel Leigh Taylor. Acting as solicitor for the GMC was Mr G.J.K. Widgery. The Committee met in public under the chairmanship of Sir David Campbell.

Mr Widgery said that Adams had resigned from the National Health Service on June 30th. His authority under the Dangerous Drugs Act was withdrawn by the Home Office on September 4th. Until recently Dr Adams had been the senior partner in a practice of four doctors and had a substantial practice in Eastbourne for thirty-five years.

Adams, recalled Mr Widgery, appeared before the Committee charged with having been convicted at Lewes Assizes on July 17th, on his own confession of fourteen charges. On these charges Dr Adams was fined a total of £2,400 and ordered to pay costs.

Mr Noel Leigh Taylor appeared for Dr Adams and in entering a plea of mitigation, said that Adams had been arrested a little more than a year before on November 26th, 1956 and since then had never been free of trials of one sort or another. On the first days of New Scotland Yard enquiries various matters were brought into the public arena. The *Daily Mail* proclaimed in a headline 'CID Probe Four Women's Deaths' at the time of an inquest on another patient of Dr Adams; the *Daily Telegraph* referred to '400 women' and the *Daily Mail* said, 'The Yard Probes Mass Poisoning'. So it went on right into October, Mr Leigh Taylor continued. On November 26th the police arrested Adams.

The attempt to conceal two bottles of hydrochloride-morphine occurred when Adams' house was being searched.

'It is not unfair to suggest Adams was in a very rattled condition,' said Mr Leigh Taylor.

Dr Adams remained in prison for 111 days on remand until his acquittal on April 10th, of the charge of murdering Mrs Morrell.

'One can hardly blame Dr Adams for feeling at the time he had already been convicted at the Bar of Public Opinion,' said Mr Leigh Taylor, continuing:

'All these events had occurred with an interval between like a ponderous sledge-hammer, blow after blow.'

'Before and after the murder trial, press speculation about what would happen to Dr Adams was a disgrace to the majority of national newspapers. Only the *Daily Express* had not joined in the general condemnation. And that newspaper made an offer to the Doctor which was unusual in two respects: they said they would take full charge of Dr Adams in the immediate days following his release to see the rest of the press did not get to him. And secondly, the *Express* said that they would allow Dr Adams' solicitors to 'vet' everything before publication. It was on my advice Dr Adams accepted this offer. We could not face the idea that Dr Adams should be thrown to the lions of all the other reporters.

'The offences to which the Committee have been referred in the first instance were the results of no other motive than the well-being of Dr Adams' patients. In the second were no more than what the Judge called, "stupid lies" – the third concerning the drugs register and concealing the morphine, a matter of panic.'

There was little else Mr Leigh Taylor could say.

The Committee withdrew to consider their decision. Taking just ten minutes over their deliberations.

Dr Adams took his place standing at the rostrum facing the Chairman. Sir David Campbell barely glanced at Dr Adams before saying:

'I have to announce that by reason of the convictions proved against you, the Committee have directed that the name of John Bodkin Adams be removed from the Register'.

Dr Adams lowered his head, then turned and swiftly walked from the room.

John Bodkin Adams had been adjudged by his peers as an unfit person to be amongst their number. At the age of 58, Adams had been struck off the British Medical Register.

In the months that followed Dr Adams' acquittal on the charge of murder, a number of feelers were sent to the office of the Director of Public Prosecution by Scotland Yard. Finally, the DPP's legal advisers spelt out their message in clear – there would be no further capital charge action against Adams. The file was to be closed. End of the matter.

Hannam was coldly incensed. Both he and Richard Walker, Eastbourne's Chief Constable, were extraordinarily proud men. Hannam felt much of the criticism leveled at the prosecution trial performance reflected upon the police investigative endeavours. A criticism Hannam stoutly refuted. Considering the number of weary hours, the miles of travelling, the eye-straining reading of thousands of documents, his indignation of the police presented in semi-official circles as scapegoats can be sympathetically understood. And for what remained of his outstanding police career, he carried the chip of false blame upon his shoulders.

For Charlie Hewitt it was a different story. For one thing, his career had a long way to go. He had been the junior investigating officer and not least his mercurial spirit sustained a cheerful disposition. And, again under that rather flash exterior, Charlie Hewitt hid a pragmatic streak. 'You win some - you lose some.' And as he had originally told his 'Guv'nor', their trouble in the Adams affair would be proof in a court of law.

What all three police officers held in consensus was their total undoubting belief that Adams was a murderer – maybe not of Mrs Morrell but certainly of others. They saw Adams as a man who had eluded justice. For the DPP to wash his hands of the Adams job was a dereliction of duty. And all three, Walker, Hannam and Hewitt believed firmly in doing their duty.

Another galling experience for the Police was thought the way the legal fraternity closed ranks around the ineptitude of Manningham-Buller. The brotherhood protecting its own. Not one word of public criticism was aired. Although plenty of private clubland comment passed from lip to ear.

As far as the Police were concerned it was Burke's dictum all over again quoted by Sir Melford Stevenson: 'The only thing necessary for the triumph of evil is for good men to do nothing.'

The closed ranks of barrister and bench brought about an opposing clan of Police and journalists. And that in turn was understandable. For the press often work closely with the Police, particularly on murder enquiries – the communication aspect of vital import to the successful apprehending of a suspect. It is a well-recorded matter of press and Police history that witnesses feel freer to talk first with the press before then being persuaded to give their evidence to officers concerned.

Journalists who had been involved with the police team throughout the Adams enquiry, demonstrated their concern, identifying with Hannam and Hewitt, feeling as aggrieved as the Police in the aftermath of first the acquittal – accepting the doubts that had emerged but finding it quite a different matter to accept the DPP's decision to drop all further interest in John Bodkin Adams. Having worked alongside Hannam and Hewitt for so long, the Adams job had occupied a number of journalists for more than a year; for Rodney Hallworth of the *Daily Mail* exactly a year and a day, and a companionable rapport had grown strong between Hannam's team and the press.

It was inevitable, therefore, that the considerable carping that Hannam was receiving brought his press colleagues solidly to his defence. Hannam's character was such that close relationships were impossible, nonetheless, he attracted considerable professional respect. He had always treated his press colleagues with courtesy and co-operation.

With one notable exception, the press were solidly behind Hannam. To such an extent the Yard responded by a heavy-handed internal enquiry to establish if Hannam gave more away to the press than he should, or was indiscreet, or both.

William Hardcastle was Rodney Hallworth's editor on the *Daily Mail* at this time, his secretary phoning Hallworth at home one morning. The message was brief: 'Get into Hardcastle's office *tout de suite*. A Yard Superintendent by the name of Hawkyard wants to see you in an hour's time.'

For Hallworth the name Hawkyard smelled a 'rubber-heel job' as internal enquiries were known. Hallworth thought he knew every Superintendent at the Yard. And Hawkyard was such a pun of a name, if he actually was of New Scotland Yard, Hallworth would have known him. So maybe he was from outside. Hallworth made Hardcastle's office well before the hour.

'Are you up to anything to warrant the Yard sussing something?' was Hardcastle's first question.

Hallworth thought quickly. Like any other London crime reporter his list of contacts could well attract the Yard's interest but which particular job was getting the Yard hot under the collar?

'I don't think so,' Hallworth answered.

'I hope not,' said Hardcastle, 'I don't want my carpet soiled!'

A moment later Hardcastle's secretary ushered in Hawkyard of New Scotland Yard. The police officer went straight into his spiel.

'Last night, you, Hallworth, met Chief Superintendent Hannam in a pub on Orchard Street. I've seen Superintendent Hannam who has made a full and frank statement to me. I would now like your version.'

It was Hardcastle who answered: 'It's part of my reporters' job to meet detectives. What is all this about, Superintendent?'

Hallworth had not uttered one word, nor would he.

'I'm afraid I can't tell you, sir' came Hawkyard's reply to the editor's question.

'In that case I regret there is nothing Hallworth can tell you.'

For a moment the Yard man looked from Hallworth to his editor and then nodded and left the office. For a few moments there was silence until the secretary confirmed that Hawkyard had left the building.

'What was all that about?' demanded Hardcastle.

'I haven't got a clue, Chief!' Hallworth replied.

'Well, you better go and do what you've got to do!'

From a call box in Holborn, Hallworth spoke to the other journalist that had been with him the previous night to warn him Hawkyard would be over to his paper. And then rang Hannam.

'A big soft-shoe has just been over telling my editor you've made a full and frank statement.'

Hannam chuckled: 'See you around,' and the phone went dead.

That was the first and last Hallworth ever heard of Hawkyard. Who he was and from whatever piece of woodwork he had emerged, Hallworth never found out. The police officer was hardly the most experienced in Hallworth's view. To say to a possible witness that a full and frank statement had been made by another was the oldest trick in the business.

In fact, all that had transpired in the pub the previous evening had been some rehashing of the Adams job. But they had been overheard and a telepone call was made to the Yard. Hannam certainly had his enemies but it was a strangely disquieting interlude. Totally unnecessary, perhaps it had been an unsubtle warning. And no more than that.

Hannam appeared not one whit disturbed by the matter and the strange Hawkyard never even cropped up in conversations between Hannam and Hallworth then or later.

The incredulity of Police and press at the DPP's final decision to close the file on Adams has never subsided for those so closely linked with the case. It was felt that the evil Dr Adams had shewn those who man the English legal system, particularly in the DPP's office, to be a bunch of five-star loons.

When Sir Patrick Devlin summed up in the Old Bailey trial he defined the act of murder in law and concluded:

"… It does not matter for this purpose if death was inevitable. If life was cut short by weeks or months it is just as much murder as it were cut short by years… "

There is a sincerely held belief that Adams did cut short the lives of a number of his patients. And equally sincerely held the belief that the Doctor's insatiable greed for money and possessions provided the motive.

The Adams' background from early childhood provides a character profile for analysis. There was something of a flaw, an unstable quirk in the man of medicine.

# Chapter Twelve

*'I can't bear to see my patients in pain'*

DR ADAMS

Guilty or not, Adams was thick-skinned. He knew his colleagues hated him but still he stayed in the lush hunting grounds of Eastbourne. Obviously, he was aware of the avalanche of lay opinion against him. He had been reprimanded very strongly by the Coroner at the Hullett inquest and exposed as a near incompetent doctor. Most other men of medicine would have packed their bags, bowed their heads and quitted for distant parts. But not Adams.

After his Old Bailey trial he still resided in Eastbourne. After his conviction at Lewes Assizes he stayed in Eastbourne. After being struck off the BMC Register he continued to live at the house in Trinity Trees. Despite the heavy legal costs, the fines, his counsel fees, Adams was still a wealthy man and well able to travel the world to hide his past and identity. He chose not to and lived in Eastbourne for the rest of his days.

Adams' long love affair with shooting had led him into being a founder member of the South East region branch of the Clay Pigeon Shooting Association. He would wholeheartedly embrace this hobby, ultimately becoming President of the Association and in time its senior honorary life Vice-President.

In the immediate aftermath of the Old Bailey trial, Dr Adams immersed himself in his main hobby. Always a good shot, he became an expert marksman. And to forestall any possible loneliness first the decrease and finally the end of his practice might engender, shooting friends remained loyal. As did a number of old patients, remember, 150 of such patients wrote to Dr Adams whilst he was on remand in Brixton.

But those first weeks and months following the trial took their toll upon the Doctor, echoing matters still reached his ear. But surely that was inevitable. In Eastbourne opinion was firmly divided. The Doctor was either a saint or a sinner. With the law, however, opinion was mostly one way – and that all bad.

Many lawyers who had listened to the Old Bailey trial together with the Police who had carried out the investigation were convinced that Adams was not just a killer but a mass-murderer. On the eve of the trial Geoffrey Lawrence's wife went for a hairdo in a Knightsbridge salon and was rumoured to have told her hairdresser:

'Adams is as guilty as hell – but my husband will get him off.' A prophetess indeed.

The medical profession is not free of blemishes. Many doctors drink excessively, probably because of the stress and long hours demanded of the job. Who can blame them. It is possibly the result too, of having to eradicate the whinings and whimperings of some of their quite healthy patients who pester them. Some doctors are known to be sexually hungry and although the balance is against them, they are repeatedly appearing before the Medical Council for taking sexual advantage of some of their prettier patients or equally sex-hungry widows. As students, doctors have been known to rip universities apart in their lust for life. And surely if a man's daily dealings are with death, he is entitled to enjoy life a little.

Elsewhere in this volume the poisonous antics of other doctors have been recorded to show some comparison. But Bodkin Adams, guilty or not, beat the lot for a drama-filled life.

Adams was undeniably greedy. He was certainly a religious crank. He was a bachelor and throughout his life had spent more time with the elderly than with the young. Any man who could stock up his cellar with dozens of new car tyres because he thought there might be a war in the morning, is getting to be a little strange.

Loathed by his medical colleagues; the Police officially looking into the background of nearly four hundred of his patients; two of those patients being exhumed; charged with the murder of one and acquitted; two other murder charges laid fallow by the DPP; fined at Lewes for the wrongful use of drugs; his licence to prescribe drugs withdrawn; struck off the Medical Register. What other doctor, murderer or not, can claim the infamy of that list.

How many doctors are chased from a patient's bedside by an old lady with a gold-headed walking stick, or are turned out of solicitors' offices? It can hardly be normal practice for doctors, in charge of elderly and probably dying patients, to go charging into solicitors' offices or banks, getting the patient to change his or her will to make sure the doctor himself is included. To do so surely begs a question of such a doctor's mentality.

Obviously not one in a hundred doctors takes such callously roughshod and indiscreet measures to ensure they finish up good at the end of their patients' life. Many doctors become personal friends of families and, like the vicar, are included in the will, often out of respect and thanks, just as much as the pecuniary advantage.

It is certainly accepted in the medical profession that some elderly patients do not pay their bills as often as they should and leave money in the will as a sort of, 'Well, I wasn't too good to you while I was alive but at least I've looked after you now I've gone!' It was a sweeter way of doing things than giving the doctor the embarrassment of claiming against the estate.

But the question begs repeating, surely it is not the general practice of General Practioners to hang about solicitors' offices, making desperate phone calls about wills with the determination and tenacity of a stoat, knowing that his patient is lying flat on his back with the hour hand of the clock squeezing his time away?

Thank God it is not the general practice for a doctor to influence two old women to let him sell their house, moving them into a flat and refusing to hand over their money from the house sale until receiving a writ so to do, two years after the sale.

One of the most notorious murdering doctors in Britain was Thomas Neil Cream who killed dozens of prostitutes in dim gaslit cities. Each time he killed some poor wisp of a girl, the excitement made him go cross-eyed. Cream got away with murder for years, because nobody was looking to apprehend a murderer. If some poor slut of a lass with a background of dirty taverns and dirty men was found dead, nobody really cared. In Victorian prudity she got what she invited, and from the Police point of view, the sooner she was hurried off to a pauper's grave the better.

Though Adams had better clients, nobody in Eastbourne was looking for murder either. If some old lady turned up for bridge one day and was dead the next, so what? And it has been shown that many of these old ladies had outlived their families and were lonely. Easier, less dramatic and more polite reasons for their demise were found in Eastbourne, than murder.

So, if the Yard were right, Adams almost had a free hand. For years no one had the bad manners to make such lurid suggestions and the police were given little hard evidence within forensic timing to support an enquiry.

There is little doubt that many more nurses would have been called by the prosecution, had their evidence withstood the test of time. But their evidence was inadmissable because their departed patients had been cremated and the police could not string together enough courtroom evidence to provide a charge.

However, it was clear from intensive questioning that many nurses considered Adams incompetent and that at times his clumsy doctoring even killed. And that was as far as they were prepared to go. But then, who were they to turn to in the small society of Eastbourne? Perhaps these nurses felt that one word out of place could get them the sack and the reputation of a witch for the rest of their lives. It just wasn't worth the hassle.

The most daring amongst the nurses risked the Doctor's wrath and suggested to the family that their sick one should be taken away from Eastbourne, and we know that these patients soon recovered.

In the gruesome story of Dr Pritchard, his victim said shortly before her murder:

'I am all right in Edinburgh – but I am ill in Glasgow,' meaning of course that as soon as the wretched woman was under the attention of her doctor in Glasgow she was unwell. The same thing happened to patients of Dr Adams. We know that when Mrs Hullett was away from Eastbourne, though fidgety with her London friends, she was at least brighter and more her old self. But she had to rush back to get her drugs from Adams. Too many women became addicts under the Doctor's attention and beholden to him.

Hannam could never find a case where Adams had earnestly tried to withdraw drugs from a patient.

In the startling example of Mrs Pilling, it seems her life was saved by clearing out of Eastbourne and living in the Home Counties, where, within a week of being 'practically in a coma' she was sufficiently well to attend Ascot races. It was another Pritchard instance of being well in Edinburgh and ill in Glasgow.

What seems to be undeniable is that Adams over-used his syringe and was unquestionably greedy for other people's possessions. In the view of experienced police officers Adams killed for those possessions.

Many observers thought Adams a schizophrenic. He suffered orgies of religious mania and in those moments, believing he was some specially chosen servant of God, ended the lives of his patients. He thought any pecuniary gain was just an acceptable reward which the more earthly man in him recognised.

Adams was obsessed by religion. He could hardly speak without evoking Almighty God into every sentence. He lived as though God was standing beside him, or in the same room. He would pray at the bedside of patients, holding their hands, and with the women he would comb their hair and even caress their breasts. Sometimes he would pray at the door before entering the sickroom, and one maid who had polished the floor that morning vividly remembered the Doctor falling 'arse-over-elbow' on the 'prayer' mat.

Religious belief is a personal thing. As too the accepted degree of dogma. But if there is a God and He made us in His image, then He also made us to get on with life by holding to the dignity of man and by showing concern and love for our family and our fellow beings. If there is an afterlife, a reflection of our conduct on earth bears a relevance. If life has to have any meaning at all, that is.

Any senior Policeman or psychiatrist will tell you that men or women who are overly concerned with religion are usually mentally unbalanced. This is not to refer to truly religious people who employ their beliefs as a standard for living and rational conduct but to those who are over-zealous and mentally ablaze with their overworked doctrine. Such people are rarely moral leaders but immoral cranks.

Police records show indisputable evidence that people who over-mix religion with everyday living often become criminals. They appear high on the list of sexual offences, fraud, theft and even murder.

Scotland Yard believed that Adams murdered nine people and with less certainty think he killed eight others. Sober opinion at the Yard was that in his thirty-five years of medical practice in Eastbourne, Adams' greed and impatience for money may have caused the hurried death of many more. He poisoned them all.

He was Eastbourne's most fashionable doctor. But his prosperity was built on the bequests from his victims. On the surface he was kindly, charitable and charming but behind his bedroom smile was the calculating brain of a killer. It was as he stroked the hands of his rich, elderly woman patients and combed their hair that he planned the moment of murder.

Adams made his victims dependent on his drugs. They craved the stimulation of his pills. They became addicts. He influenced them to change their wills in his favour. Then the Doctor struck. His murder method was not shocking, startling, gory. He eased them gently out of life with an overdose of drugs.

The Yard probe showed that, of every hundred patients for whom Adams signed death certificates, he explained an improbable sixty-eight deaths as being due to either cerebral haemorrhage or cerebral thrombosis. A wag in Eastbourne once said:

'Adams does his rounds with a bottle of morphia in one pocket and a blank will form in the other!'

The jibe was whispered around the town by many. They did not know how near the truth they were...

This was the Doctor who prayed for, and with, his patients. The man of the Devil used God as his gimmick. A phrase frequently on his lips was: 'I can't bear to see my patients in pain.' It was an approach which fooled many people most of the time.

A leading Dutch sociologist and psychotherapist gives this opinion based upon Dr Adams' character profile:

'This is a man who was never allowed to develop his own personality. Overwhelmed by his mother, afraid of his father, warped by a religious fanaticism. The only child until he was four years old. And then he shared his mother's love until his younger brother's death at age 16. His father's death when John Bodkin Adams was only 14, reinforced the dominating role of his mother.

'It was the mother who handled the family finances, the property matters, and watched them grow. It was the mother who provided the basic needs of a growing adolescent. It was the mother who decided on his education, on his profession. The mother who fed him bought him his clothes, who approved or rejected the few friends he had. It was the mother who would later pick the house in Trinity Trees, select the material and style of his suits. Until the day she died in 1943, when John Bodkin Adams was aged 44, his mother ruled his entire life. His very thinking.'

'The only time that dominance appeared threatened was upon the engagement of her son to Miss O'Hara. But the old lady's fierce determination that all things should be given to her son, that he was entitled to all of God's rich blessings – this healing Doctor son of hers, indicated the extent of her hold on him.

'The O'Hara parents had bought a house for the couple. Most would have been gratefully pleased at such generosity. Not the old Mrs Adams. The house had to be completely furnished and decorated to the old lady's wishes. At this the O'Hara's demurred. The old lady's demands were excessive. In turn, she instructed her son to break off the engagement, he did – instantly.

'He never again courted a woman with marriage in mind. His house and his life were managed by his mother and his cousin Florence Henry. He was dominated and ruled by these two women. His own personality never had a chance to develop. From pre-puberty his character training had been moulded by his mother and his parents' religion.

'The teachings of the Plymouth Brethren emphasises the frugal personal life, the Christian family and charity of the soul and the purse for the needy. And there is nothing wrong with that. The Plymouth Brethren are a responsible, totally Christian belief of immense good, a credit to the good way of life in an international society in which Christian belief is under attack on all social and racial sides.

'But the degree of involvement within any defined religious order is a question of personal decision. The Bodkin's and Adams' of County Antrim were of a pious upbringing.

Members of those families embraced their respective beliefs to a greater or lesser degree. For John Bodkin Adams, his parents embraced their church to an unhealthy degree. The lay-preacher father, the mother convinced that God's rich blessings would shower upon those who tread the chosen path.

'And this was John Bodkin Adams' culture. His philosophy – mother – home – blessings of God – security. A personal frugal life and the blessings would accrue.

'But his blessings always depended upon the goodness of his mother. Her choice of his profession – the healing Doctor – put immense pressure upon him. His breakdown in medical school – the cramming to keep up with his fellow students, all this created pressure. His compelling urge, and by now totally committed, desire to please his mother stultified his own personality growth. John Bodkin Adams was a creation of his mother.

'The pressures were there, the subconscious libido, the self, trying to escape. How were those pressures contained. First speed. Motor-cycles, and later by cars. For the first time he was in control. And later his passion for shooting, for guns.

'Here was the power he never had. A gun, the power of life and death. His passion for game hunting cased the pressures. In no other way that he would ever experience he was happy and content. So long as John Bodkin Adams had three things - his mother, his cars and his guns, he was happy.

'Material gain - the security - would come, of this his mother was insistent. The choice of an Eastbourne practice was no whim. A fashionable doctor in such a town just had to succeed.

'When the first large bequest came his way (£3,000, Mrs Whitton - 1936) and the family objected by forcing a high court hearing, it was the old mother that instructed Dr Adams to defend his bequest, in a situation that would lead the majority of us to a settlement. But no. The blessings must shower upon her Doctor son - the healer. Adams won the case and kept the money.

'As the mother convinced him 'You are entitled to God's share of riches. People should look after you. You deserve and should receive the benefits a Christian life (in the Mrs Bodkin Adams' sense) and example will send your way.'

'Of a necessity, in Eastbourne, a mainly retirement town, Dr Adams worked with and was surrounded by those much older than he. Again the subduing of his own personality. But by the time of his mother's death, John Bodkin Adams was aged 44. He would never have a personality of his own.

'At that time he was already the most fashionable doctor in Eastbourne. A respected, if not particularly well-liked, member of Eastbourne society. And yet he was also immature, possibly unstable, religiously over-zealous and stoking up pressures within. Pressures that led to acquisitive tendencies. His love of cars, the first feeling of his own power led to his acquisition of five at one time. The fact that two Rolls-Royce had belonged to former patients and were the result of gifts or bequests, was only a demonstration of God's blessings. They (the cars) were his to enjoy as a result of his caring, healing 'Christian' way of life.

'Adams was by now convinced that the security of his life by material, earthly riches, was his entitlement. The outward demonstration that the 'good' way of life gave benefits that those less 'Christian' could not expect. It was only fair and correct that bequests were made to Dr Adams, to show those who were less 'good', even if that excluded surviving members of a family from the will, that God looks after his devout children.

'The pressures were still there of course. The game shooting alleviated some of that. The handling of guns, the power he felt from the balance of a Purdy shotgun made to suit his broad shoulder, the association of men with a like power. The grouse moors, the pheasant shoots, the power of life and death.

'In his practice he also held the power of life and death. If an old lady, who would die in a few years or months anyway, was given one pill, she would for the moment recover and he would send one bill. If the old lady was kept under his control by more pills, then more medical bills could be extracted. Should he give even more pills, the patient would die but first he should be 'blessed' by a bequest in her last will. The power of life and death.'

This independent opinion by a respected psychotherapist is worthy of attention. At all points, such a character analysis touches upon demonstrative instances during the life and times of Dr John Bodkin Adams. A man not of his own making.

# Chapter Thirteen

*'He turned from the window, pointed the
Winchester right between my eyes and pulled the
trigger!'* MARK WILLIAMS

The Old Bailey trial of Dr Adams had, understandably, been
followed with avid interest in Eastbourne. Shock waves had
been felt throughout Sussex and beyond. His acquittal of the
murder of Mrs Morrell left those who had been convinced of his
guilt, speechless for the first time in years.

There were now as many who proclaimed they had all along
considered the Doctor innocent, as there had been ready to
condemn before the trial. For if ever a town was divided in its
opinions – Eastbourne was a classic example.

But those original shock waves still produced tremors. In
May, following the trial, Adams appeared in the Eastbourne
Magistrates court bound over to appear at Lewes Assizes in
July. On June 30, Adams resigned from the National Health
Service. At the Assizes Adams pleaded guilty to fourteen
charges, was fined £2,400 and ordered to pay costs. The
wagging tongues of Eastbourne began again. 'There's no smoke
without fire', a favourite saying of the time.

The tremors continued and the gossip thrived once
more. In September the Home Secretary withdrew from
Dr Adams authority to possess or supply dangerous drugs.
In November Dr Adams was struck off the British Medical
Register.

Dr Adams lived in Eastbourne in the heart of the town, but for a number of weeks following the BMC's decision, few people saw anything of him. In spite of the hundred-plus days he had spent on remand in Brixton, working in the prison library, despite the nerve-racking seventeen days of the Old Bailey trial, and notwithstanding the ignominy of pleading guilty at Lewes Assizes. It was, at the end, the thought that his fellow doctors did not want him amongst their midst, which penetrated even that thick skin of the Doctor. He had been adjudged not of a fit moral or medically ethical standard to practise his profession.

For the majority of fair-minded Eastbourne folk, John Bodkin Adams had been found guilty in law of a number of offences committed whilst a doctor. The law had imposed a penalty. His profession had had their say. The matter was over. On the question of more serious matters, the wise held a firm silence.

The young, however, have an immature irreverence to authority of any kind. And students of colleges in and around East Sussex were no less immature or irreverent than their fellows throughout the land.

The first Christmas that followed the Adams acquittal found an Eastbourne students dinner supposedly entertained with a rendition of a popular carol *The Twelve Days of Christmas* with a somewhat less than traditional chorus of:

Twelve missing name plates,
Eleven exhumations,
Ten cremated women,
Nine hypodermics,
Eight forged prescriptions,
Seven Rolls-Royces,
Six foolish spinsters,
Five Inspectors Pugh,
Four night nurses,
Three Dectives Seekings,
Two grouse a'hunting,
One Bodkin Adams of Trinity Trees.

The students' high-jinks caused an uproar. 'It was in bad taste!' – 'Slanderous!' – 'Constituted libel!' – 'Should apologise!' – 'Typical student rubbish!'

And most of Eastbourne thoroughly enjoyed the juvenile wickedness!

But Eastbourne was genuinely divided over Adams. One person who still saw Adams regularly was the lady behind the counter in Marsh's sweet shop in Cornfield Road, where he would still buy Swiss handmade chocolates, and her comment:

'What a fine man the Doctor is! Those evil people who have said so many nasty things about him should be punished themselves.'

Pat Foran suffers from bronchial trouble. At one time he had a bad attack, although Adams wasn't his doctor he was the nearest and immediately treated Mr Foran.

'What do I owe you Doctor?'

'Oh – just give me fifty pence!'

Adams could have charged many times that fee.

At times Adams spent hours as an anaesthetist at the local hospital. At times he never charged a fee.

Fred Davis had a painful elbow. Adams was making a call on a patient in an Eastbourne hotel when he saw the trouble Fred Davis was having:

'What's wrong with your arm?'

Fred told him.

'Here, get this – It'll help you.'

And immediately wrote out a prescription – no charge.

To this day Fred Davis thinks of Adams as, 'A very nice chap.'

David Cuthbert saw two sides of the Adams character. His uncle, an old patient of Adams was kept alive for years by the Doctor's care. And yet David himself, for eleven years worked for a specialist house-cleaning firm, operating under the name, 'Modern Ways'. One house that he worked on was that of the Adams property at 6, Trinity Trees. The house was cleaned from top to bottom but getting money from Adams was another matter. David knows of demands for payments being issued but cannot remember if Adams finally paid without the issue of a writ or not.

As Harry Walshaw said: 'Many people wouldn't hear a thing against Dr Adams.'

Walshaw was a Detective Constable with the Eastbourne Police during the Adams investigation. Although he didn't work on the case himself he retired as a Superintendent.


Yes, Eastbourne was certainly divided at the time of the Old Bailey trial. But for John Bodkin Adams, life was markedly different in the town in the years that followed.

The decimation of his practice left a very lonely man. The monetary loss was unimportant, Adams had more than enough to keep him in comfort until the end of his days. But how were those days to be filled?

Adams' love of shooting, of guns, filled to a degree that lonely void. Always a good shot he became an expert. Small game, rough shoots, clay pigeon competition, the activity and the associated companionship helped Adams considerably.

A founder-member of the South East Region of the Clay Pigeon Shooting Association, he became an officer and a member of the National Executive Committee.

At the Bisley shooting ranges, the Clay Pigeon Shooting Association has its own ground at the upper end of the Bisley complex. And here Adams was seen frequently, a bandolier of shotgun cartridges slung over the shoulder of his shooting jacket, traditionally adorned with multi-hued gun-club and European event badges, as colourful as his contemporaries.

Oslo, Monte Carlo, Lisbon; the badges bespoke the sincerity of Adams' membership. Executive Committee member, he progressed to Vice-Presidency of the National Association. At all times and on various Association meetings other members had nothing but praise for Adams' work on behalf of the Association.

And this is totally in keeping with Adams' character profile. Power, making up for the non-development of one's own personality, comes in many individual forms. For the ex-doctor, the power he had over his patients had been taken away from him. The substitute power from his shooting, from his executive position was seized by his ego and eased the personality pressure.

Slowly Adams eased back into a form of public life within Eastbourne. His Rolls-Royce the ex-Hullett Silver Dawn, was loaned on occasion to the Eastbourne Carnival Committee for the transport around the town of its Carnival Queen.

And then on November 22, 1961, four years after being struck off the British Medical Register, John Bodkin Adams was re-admitted. He was licensed to practise medicine once more. Dr John Bodkin Adams was aged 62 at that date.

There were odd paragraphs in most of the national newspapers recording that re-admission but it was a day's news only and cast away with the fish and chip suppers the day following.

For the relatives of those whose deaths had appeared untimely, Dr Adams' reinstatement was difficult to understand. For those whose loved ones had lived, through a speedy remove from the Doctor's care and some miles placed between them and Eastbourne, the matter seemed incredible, for about them daily, was a loved survivor.

In Hannam and Hewitt's original investigation into wills and bequests concerning the Doctor, Hannam's interest in particular was drawn to two out of twenty-four examples of similarity in Adams' alleged operation.

The first concerned Mrs Emily Louse Mortimer, who Hannam believed was influenced to break a long-standing family tradition. The facts were simply that the Mortimer family held strictly to a tenet which was designed to keep the family fortune inside the family.

Whenever a Mortimer died, the greater part of the estate was *always* divided among the surviving members of the family. The man who broke that tradition was Dr Adams.

In the year she died, Mrs Mortimer added a codicil to her will revoking financial shares intended for members of the family, and transferred them to Adams. Their value – £3,000. In her original will her estate had been divided into twenty-one equal parts of which nineteen parts were to go to the Mortimer family and three parts to Dr Adams.

As a result of the further bequest contained in the later codicil, made shortly before she died, Dr Adams received a total of £5,000 and members of the Mortimer family orginally named were cut out altogether.

The codicil revoking two shares had been intended for two nieces. One niece was Mrs Kate Green, then of Greenway Cottage, Wentworth, Surrey. Mrs Green told Rodney Hallworth:

'My aunt and her husband married late in life. When he died he left all his money to her. I heard she had gone to Eastbourne to live and later that she had died there.

I was out of the country at the time and in later discussions with my sister I heard my aunt had changed her will to include a new beneficiary. My sister and I got nothing. It has always been a family tradition with us that when we die we give as much money as possible back to the family. It was started many years ago by my great-grandfather. My aunt was the first to break that rule, we all thought it was odd at the time. She was the only one to do so. Her relatives certainly expected that some of the money would return to them on her death.

*None of us knew the Doctor.'*

Hannam considered that although already named in Mrs Mortimer's will for £2,000, through undue influence upon the old lady, Adams worked his bequest up to £5,000 and in so doing saw two members of the Mortimer family cut out of the will altogether.

Hannam also considered that such a matter illustrated Adams' avarice, his scheming and his total disregard for surviving family.

The second example had a happier end. Mrs Margaret Pilling was originally suffering from nothing more serious than flu when Dr Adams was called to her. Within a fortnight following heavy drugging she was 'practically in a coma'. Nurses told the family she should be taken away from Eastbourne. She was, and within a fortnight was well enough to attend a London wedding.

Mrs Pilling's family were quite convinced that move saved her life. As her daughter, Mrs Irene Richardson, said:

'Had I not taken her away, I am quite satisfied that she would have died. I am perfectly certain that in taking my mother away from Eastbourne, I saved her life!'

Here Hannam had two first-hand examples of Dr Adams' activities where monied old people were concerned.

And now Dr Adams was licensed to practise medicine again. And did so quietly, and presumably efficiently, for no complaints were ever received again by the local police.

With his practice consisting of a small nucleus of private patients, Dr Adams eased quietly into old age.

His love of shooting continued unabated. He became Honorary Medical Officer to the Clay Pigeon Shooting Association, its Senior Honorary Life Vice-President, continued his executive committee work and took on the treasureship of the South East Region.

The Rolls-Royce departed. From, at one time, five cars, Dr Adams relied upon one, more mundane saloon. A black Triumph Dolomite upon which was proudly affixed the metal badges of the British Olympic Association and the 21st Anniversary badge of the Institute of Advanced Motorists.

So the Doctor at the heart of a Scotland Yard murder enquiry, that, for its scope of inquiry, led to a record number of interviews; the accused in what was then the longest murder trial in English legal history, moved into the evening of his own life. An age at which many of his alleged victims died. Did this fact register upon him?

Rodney Hallworth met Dr Adams outside the dull grey stone of his house in Trinity Trees. Adams denied ever having murdered. As he spoke his eyes kept disappearing towards the top of his head, as though he was seeking God's permission to speak. Assuming he received it, he said:

'Of course I was deeply hurt when I was arrested but I knew Almighty God was with me. There were times when I was bombarded by relatives asking me to end the life of a loved one but I always refused I do not believe in euthanasia. I believe you should wait until Almighty God ends your life. All I ever did was to make my patients as comfortable as possible towards the end.'

Hallworth did not believe him.

The life and times of Dr John Bodkin Adams required a permanent record for a number of reasons:

For those who died an untimely death, alone and with few, if any to mourn them; for the police who were convinced that Dr Adams killed many times; for those who practice the law and are pledged to serve and protect the people; and lastly for the press, often criticised for an undue sensationalism, yet the majority of whom apply an ethically responsible view to reporting news.


In his long and honourable legal career Sir Melford Stevenson has made a number of controversial pronouncements. Of the John Bodkin Adams affair one matter concerns him to this day: Of the law that permits an accused to remain silent, Sir Melford has this forthright view:

'I firmly believe justice is not served by the present law. It should be possible for the prosecution to directly examine an accused.'

In this last, Sir Melford has much support over the broad scope of the law and particularly with the police. Although by no means do all his brothers in law concur.

Sir Melford continued:

'We had so much material it was unbelievable. As I recall it there was hard evidence of six cases of murder and sufficient evidential material to frame a murder charge in something like half-a-dozen cases. He was so incredibly lucky to have literally got away with murder.'

Sir Melford, who now lives on the Sussex coast not far away from Eastbourne, has always firmly rejected the criticism that the prosecution made a serious mistake in choosing to charge Bodkin Adams with the murder of Mrs Morrell instead of another case in which they might have stood a better chance of getting a conviction.

'We chose Morrell because it was such a clear and obvious case of murder that I should have thought no jury could have regarded it in any other way,' he said. 'It was also the case in which the Judge was most likely to rule that the defendant had a case to answer.'

The eighty-year-old Sir Melford admits that the prosecution misjudged the way in which the Old Bailey trial would go. They had been counting on winning by introducing some of their mass damning evidence once they began to cross-examine Bodkin Adams in the witness box.

'It was a clear example of the privilege of silence having enabled a guilty man to escape,' he said. 'I was astonished at the bravery of Geoffrey Lawrence in keeping this man out of the witness box. If a judge has ruled that the defendant has a case to answer, particularly in a case of murder, it requires considerable courage on the part of the defence advocate to say that he's not going to call his client to give evidence.'

From his retirement home, appropriately called 'Truncheons', Sir Melford went on: 'We had an absolute mountain of material to cross-examine Adams about. It is always permissible to cross-examine about similar conduct in other cases and on other occasions. If we had been able to pile on some of the mountain of evidence we had, I'm afraid it would have looked pretty grim for old Adams.'

As a retired Superintendent of Eastbourne Police, Harry Walshaw, put the argument:

'At present a Police Constable giving evidence in a case can quote from his notebook an accused's actions and statements.

On that witnessing he can be cross-examined, quite rightly, by the defence and any part of his testimony given under oath, queried and challenged. Yet, unless the accused is called to give testimony by the defence, the prosecution is given no opportunity to question a defendant in turn on those matters under oath. That seems wrong.'

Under the present climate of direct confrontation between an element of the people and the police; where traditional respect for law and order, for so long an essential fabric of our civilised society is threatened, the changing times in which we live seriously question the pure common-sense attitude on which the law should be based, toward an accused.

During the Adams trial, the Judge, Sir Patrick Devlin, very clearly spelled out the accused's rights in these words: '...the Doctor stood on his rights and did not speak. I have made it quite clear I am not criticising that. I do not criticise it at all. I hope that the day will never come when that right is denied to any Englishman. It is not a refuge of technicality; the law on this matter reflects the natural thought of England. So great is our horror at the idea that a man might be questioned, forced to speak and perhaps to condemn himself out of his own mouth, that we afford to everyone suspected or accused of a crime, at every stage, and to the very end, the right to say, "Ask me no questions, I shall answer none. Prove your case" ...'

Those were Judge Devlin's words twenty-seven years ago and emphasis should be placed upon the sentence: *'I hope that the day will never come when that right is denied to any Englishman'*.

*'The day will never come.'* The law cannot be left behind the society it is pledged to serve and protect. In the view of many inside and outside the law, the day that Judge Devlin dreaded has arrived. The daily newspaper headlines, the radio and television news reinforce the strain civil law and order is under.

Yes. Unequivocally, the law should be changed and long overdue. The prosecution should have the right to examine an accused under oath. Sir Melford Stevenson is absolutely right.

A short time before Dr Adams died, Mark Williams spent some days in Eastbourne. On a Saturday morning he climbed six steps to the green-painted double door of 6, Trinity Trees and rang the bell. A white-coated housekeeper came to the door. The conversation and actions that follow are faithfully and truly recorded, bizarre though that conversation was.

M.W.: 'Good morning. My name is Mark Williams, I am a journalist from Holland. Is it possible to see Dr Adams?'

Housekeeper: 'Just a moment. You are a journalist? What do you want to see the Doctor about? He doesn't see anybody about personal matters. Is it about shooting?'

M.W.: 'Yes. About shooting. I would like to ask him some questions about the Clay Pigeon Association.'

Housekeeper: 'Well. Just a moment. I'll see if the Doctor will see you.'

I was kept waiting on the doorstep for only a short while, perhaps two minutes. Long enough to consider my actions. I wanted to actually meet Dr Adams, to see the inside of his house. I had identified myself correctly. But the rules of the interview had been drawn. Dr Adams, if he saw me at all, would do so only to answer questions about his shooting and the Clay Pigeon Association. I would not be permitted, therefore, to ask him questions unrelated to that subject.

Regardless of my personal feelings about the Doctor, and they were strong, I felt I was honour bound to keep to the shooting aspects of his life. That clear in my mind I heard the housekeeper returning. She held open the door.

Housekeeper: 'The doctor will see you. This way, please.'

She showed me along a hall corridor to the second door on the right. It was the Doctor's surgery. He had been sitting behind his desk. He stood up to meet me. I held out my hand, he took it.

M.W.: 'My name is Mark Williams, I'm a journalist from Holland. Thank you for seeing me. I'd like to write an article about clay pigeon shooting. I understand you were once a Vice-President of the Association.'

J.B.A.: 'I am. I'm the Senior Life Vice-President and I'm on the Executive Committee.'

John Bodkin Adams was shorter than I had imagined, very stocky, broad-shouldered, obese. Dressed in an old navy blue suit, a white collared shirt showing above a greenish woolly. An electric blue tie worn over the woolly clashed terribly. I didn't notice his shoes. He was short-necked, because of his weight I thought, and judged him about seventeen stones. Far too much for his height, about five feet five inches. His large square head was almost completely bald, the pinkish skin flecked with ageing liver spots. Round amber spectacles perched upon his nose. His hands drew my attention. The skin puffy, almost swollen, the fingers large, blunt. The hands of a farm labourer, certainly not those imagined for a doctor.

J.B.A.: 'Sit down. You want to know about clay pigeon shooting?'

M.W.: 'Yes. I don't know much about the sport, I'm afraid. It is not so popular in Holland, although small game hunting is. I thought I would write an article about your sport.* I must tell you I know who you are of course.

Dr Adams grew agitated and waved his podgy hands in front of him.

J.B.A.: 'I don't answer questions about my personal life. I don't want any publicity in England. I've had too much of it. God knows I have.

M.W.: 'Yes. I understand that, of course. About your shooting, how long have you been a member of the Clay Pigeon Shooting Association?'

J.B.A.: 'Oh, fifty years now. Yes, fifty years. I was a founder-member of the South East Region.'

M.W.: 'And how many members are there approximately?'

J.B.A.: 'Now, let's see. I would say about ten thousand.'

M.W.:' A popular sport?'

---

*In point of fact Mark Williams wrote such an article to keep that promise.

J.B.A.: 'Yes. Yes, it is. Steadily growing.'

M.W.: 'And do you shoot at Bisley?'

J.B.A.: 'All over the country. The Regions organise their own shoots and competitions. National events are held at Bisley. We have our own club at the upper end of Bisley.'

Dr Adam's Ulster accent was surprisingly clear to identify. He was more relaxed now. Sitting in his high-backed swivel chair. Thick fingers clasped together across his stomach. I remembered Rodney Hallworth's comment about the Doctor's eyes, or rather his irises disappearing into the tops of his eye sockets leaving a blank expanse of whites of the eye. It was very disconcerting.

Dr Adams' old surgery was a large, square room with one window overlooking the back gardens of Trinity Trees into Lismore Road. A black- or blue-marbelled fireplace held a single bar electric fire, all of thirty years old. On the wall above the fireplace hung his old college emblem painted on an oaken shield. I could see no photographs. In the window wall corner across from me a marble washbasin, it appeared to be the same colour as the fireplace – I thought that strange. Above the washbasin and taps was a mirror and glass tray. Two glass tumblers stood upon the tray.

Beneath the window stood an old-fashioned *chaise longue* covered in maroon velvet, with an adjustable headrest. The right-hand wall from the door, held a table of sorts and a huge roll-topped desk full of pigeon-holes. A clutter of papers, pens, small bottles filled these compartments.

This was the surgery where for many years Dr Adams had dispensed his medicine. I noticed the wooden inset wall cupboard. That was where Dr Adams had clumsily attempted to hide two bottles of hydrochloride morphine from Chief Superintendent Hannam and Inspector Pugh. To which he had pleaded guilty at Lewes Assizes.

That was a good memory to hold, for in truth I had a moment of sorrow for an eighty-three year-old doctor, who in the habit of more than fifty years sat behind his surgery desk, although now retired. A lonely old man.

But I also remembered Miss Welch's statement of how she had found Clara Neil-Miller immediately Dr Adams had left the sick woman's bedroom:

"...This was a bitterly cold winter's night, the bedclothes on her bed had been pulled back and thrown over the bedrail at the base. Her nightdress had been folded back across her body up to her neck. All the bedroom windows had been flung open. A cold gush of wind was sweeping through the bedroom. That is how the Doctor had left her..."

Clara Neil-Miller had died the following day.

I made a point of remembering Clara Neil-Miller and the letters that had been intercepted to and from her only last family, a sister-in-law at Bournemouth. Because the day before I had stood at the Langley Cemetery gravestone of Clara and her sister.

M.W.: ' Do you shoot now, Doctor?'

J.B.A.: 'Yes. I still shoot. I'm going tomorrow with some friends for small game.'

His big head nodded for me to look behind me. And there, bookcases I had missed because they were behind the door, and on top a collection of twenty or so assorted-size silver cups.

M.W.: 'Well I'm blessed! May I look at them?'

J.B.A.: 'Go ahead. See that one. I won that last year. A veteran's cup of course. Won it at Battle with the Eastbourne club.'

M.W.: 'What about shotguns? Don't you have a Purdy?'

J.B.A.: 'Yes. I do. But I have a new Winchester over-and-under. I'll get it for you.'

Dr Adams was away for a few moments and during that time I took a good look around that room. My feet were upon a good quality blue-patterned carpet that almost covered the whole floor.

Dr Adams came back into the surgery carrying a shotgun and his shooting jacket. I took the jacket and looked at and admired his badges.

238

M.W.: 'Tell me about the balance of a gun. How is it fitted to you?'

J.B.A.: 'Well, d'you see, I'm broad shouldered so the stock angles out a little.'

He handed me the shotgun which felt surprisingly light. I handed it back.

M.W.: 'And with clay pigeon shooting you have little time to aim?'

J.B.A.: 'Hardly. You just throw the gun into your shoulder and balance does the rest.'

He showed me, standing astride, pointing towards the window, raising and lowering the shotgun to his shoulder. *Suddenly, he turned toward me, pointed the shotgun right between my eyes and slowly, deliberately pulled the trigger.*

This man, of more than fifty years shooting experience, this Senior Life Vice-President of the Clay Pigeon Shooting Association, did something gun clubs teach as a first tenet, *never, ever point a gun, loaded or not, at anyone.*

I knew the shotgun was unloaded, but that is not the point. I remembered, and will always I think, those grey-green eyes behind his spectacles peering down at me behind two vertical oiled-blue barrels. Why? Because I was a journalist?

Dr Adams' character profile examined the power he would feel behind a shotgun, '...Here was the power he never had. A gun, the power of life and death. His passion for game hunting eased the pressures ...'

At the door we shook hands as I said goodbye. He held on to my hand and arm with his other hand, alternately shaking and squeezing my hand and arm.

J.B.A.: 'You will check with the Office before printing anything – gentleman to gentleman.'

M.W.: 'I will. Thank you for seeing me.'

I turned away down the steps and out of his garden, carefully shutting the gate behind me. I didn't look up at him. He was there, I know, staring at me. I got into the car and drove back to the hotel, full of surging thoughts.

I truly believed John Bodkin Adams was capable of murder. I truly believed he had metaphorically shot me. I believed symbolically killing off all journalists, past and present.

Back in my hotel, I immediately telephoned Rodney Hallworth of my meeting with Dr Adams. 'Jesus Christ!' was his eloquent reaction. I suppose, really, there was nothing else to say.

So the long shadow that Dr John Bodkin Adams threw over Eastbourne is at last gone. Not so ephemeral as the racing clouds that alternately clad Beachy Head and then the town in a checkered quilt of shade and sunshine.

The shadow of the Doctor's machinations fell across Eastbourne first in 1936 and did not leave the town until he finally departed on July 4, 1983.

An end to belief, suspicion, rumour and gossip. Doctor John Bodkin Adams is no more.


Charlie Hewitt is one of the few men close to the original investigation, privy to prosecution conferences, present when New Scotland Yard attempted to persuade the DPP's Office to continue to bring Adams to justice following his acquittal on the charge of murder against Mrs Morrell. Hewitt's verdict on Adams is dispassionate but unequivocal.

Hewitt is convinced that Adams was a mass-murderer. And he also suspects that the Doctor killed a vital witness whose evidence would have sent Adams to the gallows.

'He was as guilty as hell and he had the luck of the devil. He deserved to hang twenty times over. But he was allowed to escape the gallows or imprisonment because the law made an ass of itself.

'The whole business was everyting a murder enquiry should not be. In fact, I have often thought that example should have been used in a training manual at Police College. I blame myself for not pushing that idea. In later years I saw the mistakes made on the Adams Job repeated in other cases. The lessons we learned the hard way could have benefited other enquiries.

'The trouble was that so many of Adam's victims were cremated. Of the twenty-five certain cases murder that we all, Hannam, Pugh, Walker and I, thought were stone bonkers, fourteen had been cremated. That's why it was madness for the prosecution to go for one without a body.

'We had so many better cases than Mrs Morrell, and more specific evidence, and what's more important, with bodies. At Adam's murder trial this lack of a body meant we couldn't get the best out of the finest forensic scientist of the day, Dr Francis Camps.

'Bert Hannam and I didn't really care if the Doctor was hanged for murder. Our main objective was to have him put away. He should have been taken out of society for a long time. That was our job as we saw it, and we could have made certain of that by going for manslaughter. We had more than enough evidence for that.'

Beliefs still strongly held by Charlie Hewitt. But the decision by Sir Reginald Manningham-Buller to go for Mrs Morrell many people believe was made because the Attorney-General firmly believed he would break Adams in the dock on direct examination.

Charlie Hewitt continues:

'But that classic courtroom confrontation never arose because the prosecution never considered the possibility that he might not be put in the witness box. And that was the hallmark of the prosecution case. No anticipation and no attention to detail. It was quite the reverse with the defence. Geoffrey Lawrence was meticulous and he saved his body blows for maximum impact at the trial. The prosecution should have anticipated so much but didn't. As a result, they were constantly and devastatingly taken by surprise in court and never recovered.

'Looking back, the blunders that were made were incredible, and so was the Doctor's luck.'

Here Charlie Hewitt shrugged his shoulders, 'but maybe Adams made his own luck.'

'I thought at the time it would be virtually impossible for Adams to have a fair trial. But he did, thanks to his counsel who detested his client.'

Talking of the Police reaction following the Doctor's acquittal Charlie Hewitt said:

'What made us and so many others in the force feel so bitter was that even after the acquittal Adams could still have been prosecuted on other cases.

'The DPP should have gone ahead with the 'Bobbie' Hullett charge and the rest until they had gained a conviction. But they were too embarrassed by the trial fiasco.'

In an interview with *The Mail on Sunday*, Sir Melford Stevenson seems to subscribe this view. Chester Stern of that newspaper claims that Sir Melford Stevenson said: 'If I had been allowed I could have successfully prosecuted Adams on six murder counts.'

Charlie Hewitt makes one last point: 'Of course we were brought in too late. Five-and-a-half years too late. So many witnesses had died. After all, this was an old people's town.'

In 1980 Rodney Hallworth called by appointment on Lord Dilhorne (Sir Reginald Manningham-Buller had been created the 1st Viscount Dilhorne in 1962) at his house in Northamptonshire, and asked about the Adams murder trial. Lord Dilhorne replied:

'I am still a Lord of Appeal, but one day I may write something myself.'

Alas, Lord Dilhorne never had the opportunity. He died a few weeks later.

A short while before he died Dr Adams saw Rodney Hallworth, and the last few lines of that interview are worth repeating. Said the Doctor:

"...I believe you should wait until Almighty God ends your life. All I ever did was to make my patients as comfortable as possible towards the end.'

Hallworth did not believe him.

In the opinion of many experts Adams died an unconvicted mass-murderer.

The teacups were right.

# Index